OpenVPN 2 Cookbook

100 simple and incredibly effective recipes for harnessing the power of the OpenVPN 2 network

D1065607

Jan Just Keijser

[PACKT] open source*
PUBLISHING   community experience distilled

BIRMINGHAM - MUMBAI

OpenVPN 2 Cookbook

First published: February 2011

Production Reference: 1140211

Published by Packt Publishing Ltd.
32 Lincoln Road
Olton
Birmingham, B27 6PA, UK.

ISBN 978-1-849510-10-3

www.packtpub.com

Cover Image by Ed Maclean (edmaclean@gmail.com)

Credits

Author
Jan Just Keijser

Reviewers
David Sommerseth

Krzee King

Ralf Hildebrandt

Acquisition Editor
Eleanor Duffy

Development Editor
Hyacintha D'Souza

Technical Editors
Ajay Shanker

Mohd. Sahil

Indexer
Hemangini Bari

Editorial Team Leader
Aanchal Kumar

Project Team Leader
Lata Basantani

Project Coordinator
Leena Purkait

Proofreader
Aaron Nash

Graphics
Nilesh R. Mohite

Production Coordinator
Aparna Bhagat

Cover Work
Aparna Bhagat

About the Author

Jan Just Keijser is an open source professional from Utrecht, the Netherlands. He has broad experience in IT, ranging from providing user support, system administration, and systems programming to network programming. He has worked for various IT companies since 1989 and has been working mainly on UNIX/Linux platforms since 1995. He was an active USENET contributor in the early 1990s.

Currently, he is employed as a senior scientific programmer in Amsterdam, the Netherlands, at Nikhef, the institute for sub-atomic physics from the Dutch Foundation for Fundamental Research on Matter (FOM). He is working on grid computing and grid application programming, as well as smartcard applications.

His open source interests include all types of Virtual Private Networking, including IPSec, PPTP, and of course, OpenVPN. In 2004 he discovered OpenVPN and has been using it ever since. He has been providing OpenVPN community support since 2004.

The OpenVPN Cookbook is his first book.

He is interested in nature, science, birds, photography, and fantasy and science-fiction literature.

I would like to thank all the people at Packt Publishing for helping me with writing this book. I would especially like to thank my acquisition editor, Eleanor Duffy, who convinced me to write it in the first place.

I also want to thank my employer, Nikhef, for giving me time off to write it. I mustn't forget my colleagues at the Physics Data Processing group, for sharing their thoughts with me about ideas for yet another recipe.

And I would like to thank my wife for volunteering to get a nice tan beside the swimming pool during our vacation, while I sat in the shade working on my book.

About the Reviewers

David Sommerseth, Senior Quality Assurance Engineer at Red Hat, has been working with Linux professionally since 1998. During this time, David has completed a range of tasks, from serving in system and network administration roles to developing personalization systems for payment cards and online payment transaction handling. David currently works with the Red Hat Enterprise MRG product, mostly focusing on the real-time kernel and its related tools.

David, who is originally from Norway and currently lives in the Czech Republic, enjoys hacking on open source software and has recently become more involved in the OpenVPN development. David has big plans for his own pet project, eurephia (`http://www.eurephia.net/`), which is tightly connected to OpenVPN.

I would like to thank the marvelous OpenVPN community members, who continue to give valuable feedback to the project and its developers. I would also like to thank Red Hat, an amazing employer that both sees the value of being involved in open source software and contributes to it. And last but not least, to my wife, for never-ending patience, support, and encouragements.

Krzee King is a self-taught BSD user who has been helping with OpenVPN for more than three years. He wrote one of the most widely used documents on routing lans over OpenVPN, and helps maintain the IRC channel.

I would like to thank Eric Crist for his work on #OpenVPN. To OpenVPN Technologies for joining with the community, which I think we all agree is for the better. To punk for phear and loathing in nl. And, of course, thanks to the Efnet #IRCpimps.

Ralf Hildebrandt is an active and well-known figure in the Postfix community. He's been a systems engineer for T-Systems, a German telecommunications company, and is now employed at Charite, Europe's largest University hospital. He has spoken about Postfix at industry conferences and contributes regularly to a number of open source mailing lists. Together with Patrick Koetter, he has written the Book of Postfix.

www.PacktPub.com

Support files, eBooks, discount offers and more

You might want to visit www.PacktPub.com for support files and downloads related to your book.

Did you know that Packt offers eBook versions of every book published, with PDF and ePub files available? You can upgrade to the eBook version at www.PacktPub.com and as a print book customer, you are entitled to a discount on the eBook copy. Get in touch with us at service@packtpub.com for more details.

At www.PacktPub.com, you can also read a collection of free technical articles, sign up for a range of free newsletters and receive exclusive discounts and offers on Packt books and eBooks.

http://PacktLib.PacktPub.com

Do you need instant solutions to your IT questions? PacktLib is Packt's online digital book library. Here, you can access, read and search across Packt's entire library of books.

Why Subscribe?

- Fully searchable across every book published by Packt
- Copy & paste, print and bookmark content
- On demand and accessible via web browser

Free Access for Packt account holders

If you have an account with Packt at www.PacktPub.com, you can use this to access PacktLib today and view nine entirely free books. Simply use your login credentials for immediate access.

To Vivi: Thanks for putting up with me.

Table of Contents

Preface

OpenVPN is one of the world's most popular packages for setting up a Virtual Private Network (VPN). OpenVPN provides an extensible VPN framework which has been designed to ease site-specific customization, such as providing the capability to distribute a customized installation package to clients, or supporting alternative authentication methods via OpenVPN's plugin module interface. It is widely used by many individuals and companies, and some service providers even offer OpenVPN access as a service to users in remote, unsecured environments.

This book provides you with many different recipes for setting up, monitoring, and troubleshooting an OpenVPN network. The author's experience in troubleshooting OpenVPN and networking configurations enables him to share his insights and solutions to get the most out of your OpenVPN setup.

What this book covers

Chapter 1, Point-to-Point Networks gives an introduction into configuring OpenVPN. The recipes are based on a point-to-point style network, meaning that only a single client can connect at a time.

Chapter 2, Client-server IP-only Networks introduces the reader to the most commonly-used deployment model for OpenVPN: a single server with multiple remote clients capable of routing IP traffic. This chapter provides the foundation for many of the recipes found in the other chapters.

Chapter 3, Client-server Ethernet-style Networks covers another popular deployment model for OpenVPN: a single server with multiple clients, capable of routing Ethernet traffic. This includes non-IP traffic as well as bridging. The reader will also learn about the use of an external DHCP server, and also the use of the OpenVPN status file.

Chapter 4, PKI, Certificates, and OpenSSL introduces the reader to the Public Key Infrastructure (PKI) and X.509 certificates, which are used in OpenVPN. You will learn how to generate, manage, manipulate, and view the certificates, and you will also learn about the interactions between OpenVPN and the OpenSSL libraries that it depends upon.

Chapter 5, Two-factor Authentication with PKCS#11 gives an introduction into the support for two-factor authentication in OpenVPN. Two-factor authentication is based on the idea that in order to use a system, you need to possess a security token, such as a smart card or hardware token, and you need to know a password. OpenVPN supports PKCS#11 authentication, which is an industry standard for setting up a secure authentication and authorization system.

Chapter 6, Scripting and Plugins covers the powerful scripting and plugin capabilities that OpenVPN offers. You will learn to use client-side scripting, which can be used to tail the connection process to the site-specific needs. You will also learn about server-side scripting and the use of OpenVPN plugins.

Chapter 7, Troubleshooting OpenVPN: Configurations is all about troubleshooting OpenVPN misconfigurations. Some of the configuration directives used in this chapter have not been demonstrated before, so even if your setup is functioning properly this chapter will still be insightful.

Chapter 8, Troubleshooting OpenVPN: Routing gives an insight into troubleshooting routing problems when setting up a VPN using OpenVPN. You will learn how to detect, diagnose, and repair common routing issues.

Chapter 9, Performance Tuning explains how you can optimize the performance of your OpenVPN setup. You will learn how to diagnose performance issues, and how to tune OpenVPN's settings to speed up your VPN.

Chapter 10, OS Integration covers the intricacies of integrating OpenVPN with the operating system it is run on. You will learn how to use OpenVPN on the most-used client operating systems: Linux, Mac OS X, and Windows.

Chapter 11, Advanced Configuration goes deeper into the configuration options that OpenVPN has to offer. The recipes will cover both advanced server configuration, such as the use of a dynamic DNS, as well as the advanced client configuration, such as using a proxy server to connect to an OpenVPN server.

Chapter 12, New Features of OpenVPN 2.1 and 2.2 focuses on some of the new features found in OpenVPN 2.1 and the upcoming 2.2 release. You will learn to use inline certificates, connection blocks, and port-sharing.

What you need for this book

In order to get the most from this book, there are some expectations of prior knowledge and experience. It is assumed that the reader has a fair understanding of the system administration, as well as knowledge of TCP/IP networking. Some knowledge on installing OpenVPN is required as well, as can be found in the book "Beginning OpenVPN 2.0.9".

Who this book is for

This book is for anyone who wants to know more about securing network connections using the VPN technology provided by OpenVPN. The recipes in this book are useful for individuals who want to set up a secure network to their home network, as well for business system administrators who need to provide secure remote access to their company's network.

This book assumes some prior knowledge about TCP/IP networking and OpenVPN, which is available either from the official documentation, or other books on this topic.

Conventions

In this book, you will find a number of styles of text that distinguish between different kinds of information. Here are some examples of these styles, and an explanation of their meaning.

Code words in text are shown as follows: "The open ssl req command generates both the private key and the certificates in one go."

A block of code is set as follows:

```
user   nobody
group nobody
persist-tun
persist-key
keepalive 10 60
ping-timer-rem
```

When we wish to draw your attention to a particular part of a code block, the relevant lines or items are set in bold:

```
[Static Encrypt:
CIPHER KEY: 8cf9abdd 371392b1 14b51523 25302c99
```

Any command-line input or output is written as follows:

```
[root@server]# openvpn --genkey --secret secret.key
```

New terms and **important words** are shown in bold. Words that you see on the screen, in menus or dialog boxes for example, appear in the text like this: "Click **Next** on the first screen, and again **Next** on the second screen."

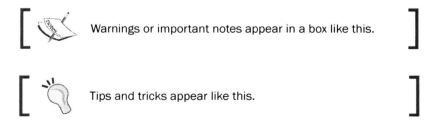

Warnings or important notes appear in a box like this.

Tips and tricks appear like this.

Reader feedback

Feedback from our readers is always welcome. Let us know what you think about this book—what you liked or may have disliked. Reader feedback is important for us to develop titles that you really get the most out of.

To send us general feedback, simply send an e-mail to feedback@packtpub.com, and mention the book title via the subject of your message.

If there is a book that you need and would like to see us publish, please send us a note in the **SUGGEST A TITLE** form on www.packtpub.com or e-mail suggest@packtpub.com.

If there is a topic that you have expertise in and you are interested in either writing or contributing to a book on, see our author guide on www.packtpub.com/authors.

Customer support

Now that you are the proud owner of a Packt book, we have a number of things to help you to get the most from your purchase.

Downloading the example code for the book

You can download the example code files for all Packt books you have purchased from your account at http://www.packtpub.com. If you purchased this book elsewhere, you can visit http://www.packtpub.com/support and register to have the files e-mailed directly to you.

Errata

Although we have taken every care to ensure the accuracy of our content, mistakes do happen. If you find a mistake in one of our books—maybe a mistake in the text or the code—we would be grateful if you would report this to us. By doing so, you can save other readers from frustration and help us improve subsequent versions of this book. If you find any errata, please report them by visiting http://www.packtpub.com/support, selecting your book, clicking on the **errata submission form** link, and entering the details of your errata. Once your errata are verified, your submission will be accepted and the errata will be uploaded on our website, or added to any list of existing errata, under the Errata section of that title. Any existing errata can be viewed by selecting your title from http://www.packtpub.com/support.

Piracy

Piracy of copyright material on the Internet is an ongoing problem across all media. At Packt, we take the protection of our copyright and licenses very seriously. If you come across any illegal copies of our works, in any form, on the Internet, please provide us with the location address or website name immediately so that we can pursue a remedy.

Please contact us at `copyright@packtpub.com` with a link to the suspected pirated material.

We appreciate your help in protecting our authors, and our ability to bring you valuable content.

Questions

You can contact us at `questions@packtpub.com` if you are having a problem with any aspect of the book, and we will do our best to address it.

1
Point-to-Point Networks

In this chapter, we will cover:

- ▸ Shortest setup possible
- ▸ OpenVPN secret keys
- ▸ Multiple secret keys
- ▸ Plaintext tunnel
- ▸ Routing
- ▸ Configuration files versus the command-line
- ▸ IP-less configurations
- ▸ Complete site-to-site setup
- ▸ 3-way routing

Introduction

The recipes in this chapter will provide an introduction into configuring OpenVPN. The recipes are based on a point-to-point style network, meaning that only a single client can connect at a time.

A point-to-point style network is very useful when connecting to a small number of sites or clients. It is easier to set up, as no certificates or Public Key Infrastructure (PKI) is required. Also, routing is slightly easier to configure, as no client-specific configuration files containing `--iroute` statements are required.

The drawbacks of a point-to-point style network are:

► The lack of perfect forward secrecy— a key compromise may result in a total disclosure of previous sessions

► The secret key must exist in plaintext form on each VPN peer

Shortest setup possible

This recipe will explain the shortest setup possible when using OpenVPN. For this setup two computers are used that are connected over a network (LAN or Internet). We will use both a TUN-style network and a TAP-style network and will focus on the differences between them. A TUN device is used mostly for VPN tunnels where only IP-traffic is used. A TAP device allows full Ethernet frames to be passed over the OpenVPN tunnel, hence providing support for non-IP based protocols such as IPX and AppleTalk.

While this may seem useless at first glance, it can be very useful to quickly test whether OpenVPN can connect to a remote system.

Getting ready

Install OpenVPN 2.0 or higher on two computers. Make sure the computers are connected over a network. For this recipe, the server computer was running CentOS 5 Linux and OpenVPN 2.1.1 and the client was running Windows XP SP3 and OpenVPN 2.1.1.

How to do it...

1. We launch the server (listening)-side OpenVPN process for the TUN-style network:

    ```
    [root@server]# openvpn --ifconfig 10.200.0.1 10.200.0.2 \
        --dev tun
    ```

     The above command should be entered as a single line. The character '\' is used to denote the fact that the command continues on the next line.

2. Then we launch the client-side OpenVPN process:

    ```
    [WinClient] C:\>"\Program Files\OpenVPN\bin\openvpn.exe" \
        --ifconfig 10.200.0.2 10.200.0.1 --dev tun \
        --remote openvpnserver.example.com
    ```

The following screenshot shows how a connection is established:

```
[] OpenVPN 2.1.1 F4:EXIT F1:USR1 F2:USR2 F3:HUP                          _ □ ×
C:\Program Files\OpenVPN\bin>openvpn --ifconfig 10.200.0.2 10.200.0.1 --dev tun
                          --remote openvpnserver.example.com
Wed Nov 10 17:47:52 2010 OpenVPN 2.1.1 i686-pc-mingw32 [SSL] [LZO2] [PKCS11] built on Dec 11 2009
Wed Nov 10 17:47:52 2010 IMPORTANT: OpenVPN's default port number is now 1194, based on an official p
ort number assignment by IANA. OpenVPN 2.0-beta16 and earlier used 5000 as the default port.
Wed Nov 10 17:47:52 2010 NOTE: OpenVPN 2.1 requires '--script-security 2' or higher to call user-defi
ned scripts or executables
Wed Nov 10 17:47:52 2010 ******* WARNING *******: all encryption and authentication features disabled
-- all data will be tunnelled as cleartext
Wed Nov 10 17:47:52 2010 TAP-WIN32 device [vpn0] opened: \\.\Global\{178255DB-3DC8-47B1-816B-48A03386
3127}.tap
Wed Nov 10 17:47:52 2010 Notified TAP-Win32 driver to set a DHCP IP/netmask of 10.200.0.2/255.255.255
.252 on interface {178255DB-3DC8-47B1-816B-48A033863127} [DHCP-serv: 10.200.0.1, lease-time: 31536000
]
Wed Nov 10 17:47:52 2010 Successful ARP Flush on interface [2] {178255DB-3DC8-47B1-816B-48A033863127}
Wed Nov 10 17:47:52 2010 UDPv4 link local (bound): [undef]:1194
Wed Nov 10 17:47:52 2010 UDPv4 link remote: 172.30.0.1:1194
Wed Nov 10 17:48:02 2010 Peer Connection Initiated with 172.30.0.1:1194
Wed Nov 10 17:48:08 2010 Initialization Sequence Completed
```

As soon as the connection is established, we can ping the other end of the tunnel.

3. Next, we stop the tunnel by pressing the *F4* function key in the Command window and we restart both ends of the tunnel using the TAP device:

4. We launch the server (listening)-side OpenVPN process for the TAP-style network:

    ```
    [root@server]# openvpn --ifconfig 10.200.0.1 255.255.255.0 \
        --dev tap
    ```

5. Then we launch the client-side OpenVPN process:

    ```
    [WinClient] C:\>"\Program Files\OpenVPN\bin\openvpn.exe" \
        --ifconfig 10.200.0.2 255.255.255.0 --dev tap \
        --remote openvpnserver.example.com
    ```

The connection is established and we can again ping the other end of the tunnel.

How it works...

The server listens on UDP port 1194, which is the OpenVPN default port for incoming connections. The client connects to the server on this port. After the initial handshake, the server configures the first available TUN device with IP address 10.200.0.1 and it expects the remote end (Peer address) to be 10.200.0.2.

The client does the opposite: after the initial handshake, the first TUN or TAP-Win32 device is configured with IP address 10.200.0.2. It expects the remote end (Peer address) to be 10.200.0.1. After this, the VPN is established.

In case of a TAP-style network, the server configures the first available TAP device with the IP address 10.200.0.01 and netmask 255.255.255.0. Similarly, the client is configured with IP address 10.200.0.2 and netmask 255.255.255.0.

Notice the warning:

******* WARNING *******: all encryption and authentication features disabled -- all data will be tunnelled as cleartext

Here, the data is not secure: all the data that is sent over the VPN tunnel can be read!

There's more...

Using the TCP protocol

In the previous example, we chose the UDP protocol. For this example, it would not have made any difference if we had chosen the TCP protocol, provided that we do that on the server side (the side without - -remote):

```
[root@server]# openvpn --ifconfig 10.200.0.1 10.200.0.2 \
    --dev tun --proto tcp-server
```

And also on the client side:

```
[root@server]# openvpn --ifconfig 10.200.0.2 10.200.0.1 \
    --dev tun --proto tcp-client
```

Forwarding non-IP traffic over the tunnel

It is now possible to run non-IP traffic over the tunnel. For example, if AppleTalk is configured correctly on both sides, we can query a remote host using the aecho command:

```
aecho openvpnserver
22 bytes from 65280.1: aep_seq=0. time=26. ms
22 bytes from 65280.1: aep_seq=1. time=26. ms
22 bytes from 65280.1: aep_seq=2. time=27. ms
```

A tcpdump -nnel -i tap0 shows that the type of traffic is indeed non-IP based AppleTalk.

OpenVPN secret keys

This recipe uses OpenVPN secret keys to secure the VPN tunnel. It is very similar to the previous recipe but this time a shared secret key is used to encrypt the traffic between the client and the server.

Getting ready

Install OpenVPN 2.0 or higher on two computers. Make sure the computers are connected over a network. For this recipe, the server computer was running CentOS 5 Linux and OpenVPN 2.1.1 and the client was running Windows XP SP3 and OpenVPN 2.1.1.

How to do it...

1. First, we generate a secret key on the server (listener):

   ```
   [root@server]# openvpn --genkey --secret secret.key
   ```

2. We transfer this key to the client side over a secure channel (for example, using `scp`).

3. Next, we launch the server (listening)-side OpenVPN process:

   ```
   [root@server]# openvpn --ifconfig 10.200.0.1 10.200.0.2 \
       --dev tun --secret secret.key
   ```

4. Then, we launch the client-side OpenVPN process:

   ```
   [WinClient] C:\>"\Program Files\OpenVPN\bin\openvpn.exe" \
       --ifconfig 10.200.0.2 10.200.0.1 \
       --dev tun --secret secret.key \
       --remote openvpnserver.example.com
   ```

   The connection is established:

```
[] OpenVPN 2.1.1 F4:EXIT F1:USR1 F2:USR2 F3:HUP                          _ □ ×
C:\Program Files\OpenVPN\config>..\bin\openvpn --ifconfig 10.200.0.2 10.200.0.1 --dev tun
                          --secret secret.key --remote openvpnserver.example.com
Wed Nov 10 17:56:53 2010 OpenVPN 2.1.1 i686-pc-mingw32 [SSL] [LZO2] [PKCS11] built on Dec 11 2009
Wed Nov 10 17:56:53 2010 IMPORTANT: OpenVPN's default port number is now 1194, based on an official p
ort number assignment by IANA.  OpenVPN 2.0-beta16 and earlier used 5000 as the default port.
Wed Nov 10 17:56:53 2010 NOTE: OpenVPN 2.1 requires '--script-security 2' or higher to call user-defi
ned scripts or executables
Wed Nov 10 17:56:53 2010 TAP-WIN32 device [vpn0] opened: \\.\Global\{178255DB-3DC8-47B1-816B-48A03386
3127}.tap
Wed Nov 10 17:56:53 2010 Notified TAP-Win32 driver to set a DHCP IP/netmask of 10.200.0.2/255.255.255
.252 on interface {178255DB-3DC8-47B1-816B-48A033863127} [DHCP-serv: 10.200.0.1, lease-time: 31536000
]
Wed Nov 10 17:56:53 2010 Successful ARP Flush on interface [2] {178255DB-3DC8-47B1-816B-48A033863127}
Wed Nov 10 17:56:53 2010 UDPv4 link local (bound): [undef]:1194
Wed Nov 10 17:56:53 2010 UDPv4 link remote: 172.30.0.1:1194
Wed Nov 10 17:57:03 2010 Peer Connection Initiated with 172.30.0.1:1194
Wed Nov 10 17:57:09 2010 Initialization Sequence Completed
```

How it works...

This example works exactly as the very first: the server listens to the incoming connections on UDP port 1194. The client connects to the server on this port. After the initial handshake, the server configures the first available TUN device with IP address 10.200.0.1 and it expects the remote end (Peer address) to be 10.200.0.2. The client does the opposite.

There's more...

By default, OpenVPN uses two symmetric keys when setting up a point-to-point connection:

- ▸ A Cipher key to encrypt the contents of the packets being exchanged.
- ▸ An HMAC key to sign packets. When packets arrive that are not signed using the appropriate HMAC key they are dropped immediately. This is the first line of defense against a "Denial of Service" attack.

The same set of keys are used on both ends and both keys are derived from the file specified using the `--secret` parameter.

An OpenVPN secret key file is formatted as follows:

```
#
# 2048 bit OpenVPN static key
#
-----BEGIN OpenVPN Static key V1-----
<16 lines of random bytes>
-----END OpenVPN Static key V1-----
```

From the random bytes, the OpenVPN Cipher and HMAC keys are derived. Note that these keys are the same for each session!

See also

The next recipe, *Multiple secret keys*, will explain in detail about the secret keys.

Multiple secret keys

As stated in the previous recipe, OpenVPN uses two symmetric keys when setting up a point-to-point connection. However, it is also possible to use shared, yet asymmetric keys in point-to-point mode. OpenVPN will use four keys in this case:

- ▸ A Cipher key on the client side
- ▸ An HMAC key on the client side
- ▸ A Cipher key on the server side
- ▸ An HMAC key on the server side

The same keying material is shared by both sides of the point-to-point connection but those keys that are derived for encrypting and signing the data are different for each side. This recipe explains how to set up OpenVPN in this manner and how the keys can be made visible.

Getting ready

For this recipe, we use the `secret.key` file from the previous recipe. Install OpenVPN 2.0 or higher on two computers. Make sure that the computers are connected over a network. For this recipe, the server computer was running CentOS 5 Linux and OpenVPN 2.1.1. The client was running Windows XP SP3 and OpenVPN 2.1.1.

How to do it...

1. We launch the server (listening) side OpenVPN process with an extra option to the `--secret` parameter and with more verbose logging:

   ```
   [root@server]# openvpn \
      --ifconfig 10.200.0.1 10.200.0.2 \
      --dev tun --secret secret.key 0 \
      --verb 7
   ```

2. Then we launch the client-side OpenVPN process:

   ```
   [WinClient] C:\>"\Program Files\OpenVPN\bin\openvpn.exe" \
      --ifconfig 10.200.0.2 10.200.0.1 \
      --dev tun --secret secret.key 1\
      --remote openvpnserver \
      --verb 7
   ```

   The connection will be established with a lot of debugging messages.

3. If we look through the server-side messages (searching for `crypt`), we can find the negotiated keys on the server side. Note that the output has been reformatted for clarity:

   ```
   … Static Encrypt:
   Cipher 'BF-CBC' initialized with 128 bit key
   … Static Encrypt:
   CIPHER KEY: 80797ddc 547fbdef 79eb353f 2a1f3d1f
   … Static Encrypt:
   Using 160 bit message hash 'SHA1' for HMAC authentication
   … Static Encrypt:
   HMAC KEY: c752f254 cc4ac230 83bd8daf 6141e73d 844764d8
   … Static Decrypt:
   Cipher 'BF-CBC' initialized with 128 bit key
   … Static Decrypt:
   CIPHER KEY: 8cf9abdd 371392b1 14b51523 25302c99
   … Static Decrypt:
   Using 160 bit message hash 'SHA1' for HMAC authentication
   … Static Decrypt:
   HMAC KEY: 39e06d8e 20c0d3c6 0f63b3e7 d94f35af bd744b27
   ```

On the client side, we will find the same keys but the 'Encrypt' and 'Decrypt' keys have been reversed:

```
... Static Encrypt:
Cipher 'BF-CBC' initialized with 128 bit key
... Static Encrypt:
CIPHER KEY: 8cf9abdd 371392b1 14b51523 25302c99
... Static Encrypt:
Using 160 bit message hash 'SHA1' for HMAC authentication
... Static Encrypt:
HMAC KEY: 39e06d8e 20c0d3c6 0f63b3e7 d94f35af bd744b27
... Static Decrypt:
Cipher 'BF-CBC' initialized with 128 bit key
... Static Decrypt:
CIPHER KEY: 80797ddc 547fbdef 79eb353f 2a1f3d1f
... Static Decrypt:
Using 160 bit message hash 'SHA1' for HMAC authentication
... Static Decrypt:
HMAC KEY: c752f254 cc4ac230 83bd8daf 6141e73d 844764d8
```

If you look at the keys carefully, you can see that each one of them is mirrored on the client and the server side.

How it works...

OpenVPN derives all keys from the `static.key` file, provided that there is enough entropy (randomness) in the file to reliably generate four keys. All keys generated using the following will have enough entropy:

```
$ openvpn --genkey --secret secret.key
```

An OpenVPN static key file is 2048 bits in size. The Cipher keys are each 128 bits, whereas the HMAC keys are 160 bits each, for a total of 776 bits. This allows OpenVPN to easily generate four random keys from the static key file, even if a cipher is chosen that requires a larger initialization key.

There's more...

The same secret key files are used in a client/server setup when the following parameter is used: `tls-auth ta.key`.

See also

▶   Chapter 2's recipe, *Setting up the public and private keys*, in which the `tls-auth` key is generated in a very similar manner.

Plaintext tunnel

In the very first recipe, we created a tunnel in which the data traffic was not encrypted. To create a completely plain text tunnel, we also disable the HMAC authentication. This can be useful when debugging a bad connection, as all traffic over the tunnel can now easily be monitored. In this recipe, we will look at how to do this. This type of tunnel is also useful when doing performance measurements, as it is the least CPU-intensive tunnel that can be established.

Getting ready

Install OpenVPN 2.0 or higher on two computers. Make sure the computers are connected over a network. For this recipe, the server computer was running CentOS 5 Linux and OpenVPN 2.1.1 and the client was running Fedora 13 Linux and OpenVPN 2.1.1.

As we are not using any encryption, no secret keys are needed.

How to do it...

1. Launch the server (listening)-side OpenVPN process:

   ```
   [root@server]# openvpn \
       --ifconfig 10.200.0.1 10.200.0.2 \
       --dev tun --auth none
   ```

2. Then launch the client-side OpenVPN process:

   ```
   [root@client]# openvpn \
       --ifconfig 10.200.0.2 10.200.0.1 \
       --dev tun --auth none\
       --remote openvpnserver.example.com
   ```

3. The connection is established with two warning messages in the output:

   ... ******* WARNING *******: null cipher specified, no encryption will be used

   ... ******* WARNING *******: null MAC specified, no authentication will be used

How it works...

With this setup, absolutely no encryption is performed. All the traffic that is sent over the tunnel is encapsulated in an OpenVPN packet and then sent "as-is".

There's more...

To actually view the traffic, we can use `tcpdump`:

- ▸ Set up the connection as outlined.

- ▸ Start `tcpdump` and listen on the network interface, **not** the tunnel interface itself:

  ```
  [root]@client]# tcpdump -w -I eth0 -s 0 host openvpnserver \
      | strings
  ```

- ▸ Now, send some text across the tunnel, using something like `nc` (Netcat). First, launch `nc` on the server side:

  ```
  [server]$ nc -l 31000
  ```

- ▸ On the client side, launch `nc` in client mode and type the words `hello` and `goodbye`.

  ```
  [client]$ nc 10.200.0.1 3100
    hello
    goodbye
  ```

- ▸ In the `tcpdump` window, you should now see:

```
Example1-5                                                 _ □ ▨
File  Edit  View  Terminal  Help
[root@server]# tcpdump -l -w - -i eth0 -s 0 host 192.168.4.64 | strings   ▲
tcpdump: listening on eth0, link-type EN10MB (Ethernet), capture size 65535 bytes
hello
goodbye                                                                   ▼
```

Routing

Point-to-point style networks are great if you want to connect two networks together over a static, encrypted tunnel. If you only have a small number of endpoints (fewer than four), then it is far easier than using a client/server setup as described in *Chapter 2, Client-server IP-only Networks*.

Getting ready

For this recipe, we use the following network layout:

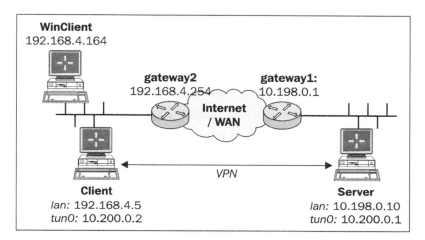

Install OpenVPN 2.0 or higher on two computers. Make sure the computers are connected over a network. For this recipe, the server computer was running CentOS 5 Linux and OpenVPN 2.1.1 and the client was running Fedora 13 Linux and OpenVPN 2.1.1. We'll use the `secret.key` file from the *OpenVPN Secret keys* recipe here.

How to do it...

1. First we establish the connection, but we also make sure OpenVPN daemonized itself:

    ```
    [root@server]# openvpn \
      --ifconfig 10.200.0.1 10.200.0.2 \
      --dev tun --secret secret.key \
      --daemon --log /tmp/openvpnserver.log
    ```

2. Then we launch the client-side OpenVPN process:

    ```
    [client]$ openvpn \
      --ifconfig 10.200.0.2 10.200.0.1 \
      --dev tun --secret secret.key \
      --remote openvpnserver \
      --daemon --log /tmp/openvpnclient.log
    ```

The connection is established:

```
[server]$ tail -1 /tmp/openvpnserver.log
    Initialization Sequence Completed
```

Now we add routing:

1. On the server side, we add a static route:

    ```
    [root@server]# route add -net 192.168.4.0/24 gw 10.200.0.2
    ```

2. On the client side, we need to do two things:

    ❑   Make sure that you have IP traffic forwarding enabled. On Linux this can be achieved using the following:

    ```
    [root@client]# sysctl -w net.ipv4.ip_forward=1
    ```

    Note that this setting does not survive a reboot of the system.

    ❑   Make sure that on the Windows client on the client-side LAN there is a route back to the OpenVPN server:

    ```
    C:> route add 10.200.0.0 mask 255.255.255.0 192.168.4.5
    ```

    Here 192.168.4.5 is the LAN IP address of the OpenVPN client.

3. From the server, we can now ping machines on the client LAN. First we ping the LAN IP of the OpenVPN client:

    ```
    [root@server]# ping -c 2 192.168.4.5
     PING 192.168.4.5 (192.168.4.5) 56(84) bytes of data.
     64 bytes from 192.168.4.5: icmp_seq=0 ttl=64 time=31.7 ms
     64 bytes from 192.168.4.5: icmp_seq=1 ttl=64 time=31.3 ms

    --- 192.168.4.5 ping statistics ---
     2 packets transmitted, 2 received, 0% packet loss, time
     1000ms
     rtt min/avg/max/mdev = 31.359/31.537/31.716/0.251 ms, pipe 2
    ```

4. And next the LAN IP of a machine on the OpenVPN client LAN:

    ```
    [root@server]# ping -c 2 192.168.4.164
        [server]$ ping -c 2 192.168.4.164
     PING 192.168.4.164 (192.168.4.164) 56(84) bytes of data.
     64 bytes from 192.168.4.164: icmp_seq=0 ttl=63 time=31.9 ms
     64 bytes from 192.168.4.164: icmp_seq=1 ttl=63 time=31.4 ms

    --- 192.168.4.164 ping statistics ---
     2 packets transmitted, 2 received, 0% packet loss, time
      1001ms
     rtt min/avg/max/mdev = 31.486/31.737/31.989/0.308 ms, pipe 2
    ```

How it works...

In our network setup, the LAN we want to reach is behind the OpenVPN client, so we have to add a route to the server:

```
[server]$ route add -net 192.168.4.0/24 gw 10.200.0.2
```

On the client side, we need to do two things:

- ▸ Make sure that the routing is enabled. If you want routing to remain enabled after a reboot, edit the file /etc/sysctl.cnf.

  ```
  net.ipv4.ip_forward = 1
  ```

- ▸ We also need to make sure that on the client LAN there is a route back to the OpenVPN server. This can be done by adding a route to the LAN gateway or by adding a static route to each of the machines on the client LAN. In this recipe, we added a route to a Windows client that is in the same LAN as the OpenVPN client:

  ```
  C:> route add 10.200.0.0 mask 255.255.255.0 192.168.4.5
  ```

  where 192.168.4.5 is the LAN IP address of the OpenVPN client.

There's more...

Routing issues

On the openvpn-users mailing list, a large number of the problems reported have to do with routing issues. Most of them have little to do with the OpenVPN itself but more with understanding the routing and the flow of packets over the network. *Chapter 8, Troubleshooting OpenVPN: Routing Issues*, provides some recipes to diagnose and fix the most common routing problems.

Automating the setup

It is also possible to add the appropriate routes when the tunnel first comes up. This can be done using the --route statement:

```
[server]$ openvpn \
    --ifconfig 10.200.0.1 10.200.0.2 \
    --dev tun --secret secret.key \
    --daemon --log /var/log/openvpnserver-1.5.log \
    --route 192.168.4.0 255.255.255.0
```

Note that on the client LAN the route back to the server still has to be set manually.

See also

▶ The last recipe of this chapter, *3-way routing*, in which a more complicated setup using three remote sites is explained.

▶ *Chapter 8, Troubleshooting OpenVPN: Routing Issues*

Configuration files versus the command-line

Most recipes in this book can be carried out without using configuration files. However, in most real-life cases a configuration file is much easier to use than a lengthy command-line. It is important to know that OpenVPN actually treats configuration file entries and command-line parameters identically. The only difference is that all command-line parameters start with a double dash ("--") whereas the configuration file entries do not. This makes it very easy to overrule the configuration file entries using an extra command-line parameter.

Getting ready

Install OpenVPN 2.0 or higher on two computers. Make sure the computers are connected over a network. For this recipe, the server computer was running CentOS 5 Linux and OpenVPN 2.1.1 and the client was running Windows XP SP3 and OpenVPN 2.1.1 In this recipe we'll use the `secret.key` file from the *OpenVPN Secret keys* recipe.

How to do it...

1. Create a configuration file based on an earlier recipe:
   ```
   dev tun
   port 1194
   ifconfig 10.200.0.1 10.200.0.2
   secret secret.key
   remote openvpnserver.example.com
   verb 3
   ```

   Save this file as `example1-6-client.conf`.

2. We launch the server (listening)-side OpenVPN process on a non-standard port:
   ```
   [root@server]# openvpn \
     --ifconfig 10.200.0.1 10.200.0.2 \
     --dev tun --secret secret.key \
     --port 11000
   ```

3. Then we launch the client-side OpenVPN process and add an extra command-line parameter:

    ```
    [WinClient] C:\>"\Program Files\OpenVPN\bin\openvpn.exe" \
        --config client.conf \
        --port 11000
    ```

The connection is established:

```
ev [example1-6-client.conf] OpenVPN 2.1.1 F4:EXIT F1:USR1 F2:USR2 F3:HUP        _ □ x
Wed Nov 10 18:27:09 2010 UDPv4 link local (bound): [undef]:11000
Wed Nov 10 18:27:09 2010 UDPv4 link remote: 172.30.0.1:11000
Wed Nov 10 18:27:19 2010 Peer Connection Initiated with 172.30.0.1:11000
Wed Nov 10 18:27:26 2010 TEST ROUTES: 0/0 succeeded len=-1 ret=1 a=0 u/d=up
Wed Nov 10 18:27:26 2010 Initialization Sequence Completed
```

How it works...

The command-line and the configuration file are read and parsed from left to right. This means that most options that are specified before the configuration file can be overruled by entries in that file. Similarly, options specified after the following directive overrule the entries in that file:

    --config client.conf

Hence, the following option overruled the line 'port 1194' from the configuration file:

    --port 11000

However, some options can be specified multiple times, in which case the first occurrence "wins". In that case, it is also possible to specify the option **before** specifying the --config directive.

There's more...

Here is another example to show the importance of the ordering of the command-line parameters:

```
C:\>"\Program Files\OpenVPN\bin\openvpn.exe" \
    --verb 0 \
    --config client.conf \
    --port 11000
```

This produces the exact same connection log as shown before. The 'verb 3' from the `client.conf` configuration file overruled the `--verb 0` as specified on the command line. However, with the following command line:

```
C:\>"\Program Files\OpenVPN\bin\openvpn.exe" \
    --config client.conf \
    --port 11000 \
    --verb 0
```

Then the connection log shows the following:

… NOTE: OpenVPN 2.1 requires '--script-security 2' or higher to call user-defined scripts or executables

This shows all the other messages that have been muted.

OpenVPN 2.1 specifics

Some of the newer features of OpenVPN 2.1 deviate slightly from this principle, notably the `<connection>` blocks and the inline certificates. See *Chapter 12, OpenVPN 2.1 specifics* for more details.

Complete site-to-site setup

In this recipe, we set up a complete site-to-site network, using most of the built-in security features that OpenVPN offers. It is intended as a "one-stop-shop" example of how to set up a point-to-point network.

Getting ready

We use the following network layout:

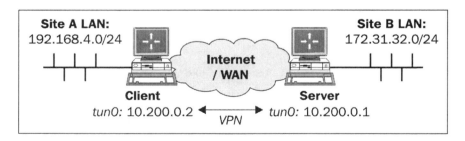

Install OpenVPN 2.0 or higher on two computers. Make sure that the computers are connected over a network. For this recipe, the server computer was running CentOS 5 Linux and OpenVPN 2.1.1 and the client was running Fedora 13 Linux and OpenVPN 2.1.1. We'll use the `secret.key` file from the *OpenVPN Secret keys* recipe here.

Make sure routing (IP forwarding) is configured on both the server and client.

How to do it...

1. Create the server configuration file:

```
dev tun
proto udp
local   openvpnserver.example.com
lport   1194
remote openvpnclient.example.com
rport   1194

secret secret.key 0
ifconfig 10.200.0.1 10.200.0.2
route 192.168.4.0 255.255.255.0

user   nobody
group nobody
persist-tun
persist-key
keepalive 10 60
ping-timer-rem

verb 3
daemon
log-append /tmp/openvpn.log
```

Save it as `example1-7-server.conf`.

2. On the client side, we create the configuration file:

```
dev tun
proto udp
local   openvpnclient.example.com
lport   1194
remote openvpnserver.example.com
rport   1194

secret secret.key 1
ifconfig 10.200.0.2 10.200.0.1
route 172.31.32.0 255.255.255.0
```

```
user   nobody
group  nobody
persist-tun
persist-key
keepalive 10 60
ping-timer-rem

verb 3
daemon
log-append /tmp/openvpn.log
```

Save it as `example1-7-client.conf`.

3. We start the tunnel on both ends:

   [root@server]# openvpn --config example1-7-server.conf

   And:

   [root@client]# openvpn --config client.conf

   Now our site-to-site tunnel is established.

4. Check the log files on both the client and server, to verify that the connection has been established.

   After the connection comes up, the machines on the LANs behind both end points can be reached over the OpenVPN tunnel.

5. For example, when we ping a machine on the client-side LAN from the server, we see the following:

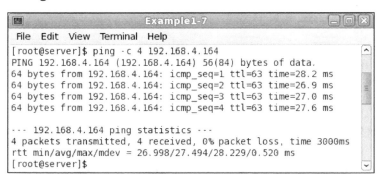

How it works...

The client and server configuration files are very similar:

▶ The server listens only on one interface and one UDP port

▶ The server accepts connections only from a single IP address and port

▶ The client has these options mirrored

Here is the set of configuration options:

```
user    nobody
group nobody
persist-tun
persist-key
keepalive 10 60
ping-timer-rem
```

They are used to make the connection more robust and secure, as follows:

- The OpenVPN process runs as user `nobody`, group `nobody`, after the initial connection is established. Even if somebody is able to take control of the OpenVPN process itself he would still only be user `nobody` and not `root`. Note that on some Linux distributions the group `nogroup` is used instead.

- The `persist-tun` and `persist-key` options are used to ensure that the connection comes back up automatically if the underlying network is disrupted. These options are necessary when using `user  nobody` and `group  nobody` (or `group  nogroup`).

- The `keepalive` and `ping-timer-rem` options cause OpenVPN to send a periodic 'ping' message over the tunnel to ensure that both ends of the tunnel remain up and running.

There's more...

This point-to-point setup can also be used to evade restrictive firewalls. The data stream between the two endpoints is not recognizable and very hard to decipher. When OpenVPN is run in client/server (see *Chapter 2*, Multi-client TUN-style Networks), the traffic is recognizable as OpenVPN traffic due to the initial TLS handshake.

See also

- *Chapter 8, Troubleshooting OpenVPN: Routing Issues*, in which the most common routing issues are explained.

3-way routing

For a small number (less than four) of fixed endpoints, a point-to-point setup is very flexible. In this recipe, we set up three OpenVPN tunnels between three sites, including routing between the endpoints. By setting up three tunnels, we create a redundant routing so that all sites are connected even if one of the tunnels is disrupted.

Getting ready

We use the following network layout:

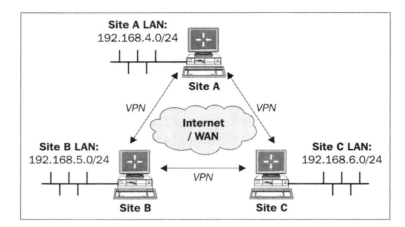

Install OpenVPN 2.0 or higher on two computers. Make sure the computers are connected over a network. In this recipe, the tunnel endpoints were running CentOS 5 Linux or Fedora 13 Linux and OpenVPN 2.1.1. Make sure that the routing (IP forwarding) is configured on all the OpenVPN endpoints.

How to do it...

1. We generate three static keys:

    ```
    [root@siteA]# openvpn --genkey --secret AtoB.key
    [root@siteA]# openvpn --genkey --secret AtoC.key
    [root@siteA]# openvpn --genkey --secret BtoC.key
    ```

    Transfer these keys to all endpoints over a secure channel (for example, using scp).

2. Create the server (listener) configuration file named example1-8-serverBtoA. conf:

    ```
    dev tun
    proto udp
    port  1194

    secret AtoB.key 0
    ifconfig 10.200.0.1 10.200.0.2
    ```

```
route 192.168.4.0 255.255.255.0 vpn_gateway 5
route 192.168.6.0 255.255.255.0 vpn_gateway 10
route-delay

keepalive 10 60
verb 3
Next, create example1-8-serverCtoA.conf:
dev tun
proto udp
port  1195

secret AtoC.key 0
ifconfig 10.200.0.5 10.200.0.6

route 192.168.4.0 255.255.255.0 vpn_gateway 5
route 192.168.5.0 255.255.255.0 vpn_gateway 10
route-delay

keepalive 10 60
verb 3
and example1-8-serverBtoC.conf:
dev tun
proto udp
port  1196

secret BtoC.key 0
ifconfig 10.200.0.9 10.200.0.10

route 192.168.4.0 255.255.255.0 vpn_gateway 10
route 192.168.6.0 255.255.255.0 vpn_gateway 5
route-delay

keepalive 10 60
verb 3
Now, create the client (connector) configuration files example1-8-
clientAtoB.conf:
dev tun
proto udp
remote siteB
port  1194

secret AtoB.key 1
ifconfig 10.200.0.2 10.200.0.1
```

```
route 192.168.5.0 255.255.255.0 vpn_gateway 5
route 192.168.6.0 255.255.255.0 vpn_gateway 10
route-delay

keepalive 10 60
verb 3
Also, create example1-8-clientAtoC.conf file:
dev tun
proto udp
remote siteC
port   1195

secret AtoC.key 1
ifconfig 10.200.0.6 10.200.0.5

route 192.168.5.0 255.255.255.0 vpn_gateway 10
route 192.168.6.0 255.255.255.0 vpn_gateway 5
route-delay

verb 3
and finally the example1-8-clientCtoB.conf:
dev tun
proto udp
remote siteB
port   1196

secret BtoC.key 1
ifconfig 10.200.0.10 10.200.0.9

route 192.168.4.0 255.255.255.0 vpn_gateway 10
route 192.168.5.0 255.255.255.0 vpn_gateway 5
route-delay

keepalive 10 60
verb 3
```

First, we start all the listener tunnels:

```
[root@siteB]# openvpn --config example1-8-serverBtoA.conf
[root@siteB]# openvpn --config example1-8-serverBtoC.conf
[root@siteC]# openvpn --config example1-8-serverCtoA.conf
```

These are followed by the connector tunnels:

```
[root@siteA]# openvpn --config example1-8-clientAtoB.conf
[root@siteA]# openvpn --config example1-8-clientAtoC.conf
[root@siteC]# openvpn --config example1-8-clientCtoB.conf
```

And with that, our three-way site-to-site network is established.

How it works...

It can clearly be seen that the number of configuration files gets out of hand too quickly. In principle, two tunnels would have been sufficient to connect three remote sites, but then there would have been no redundancy.

With the third tunnel and with the configuration options:

```
route 192.168.5.0 255.255.255.0 vpn_gateway 5
route 192.168.6.0 255.255.255.0 vpn_gateway 10
route-delay
keepalive 10 60
```

There are always 2 routes to each remote network.

For example, site A has two routes to site B (LAN 192.168.5.0/24), as seen from the following routing table:

```
[siteA]$ ip route show
[...]
192.168.5.0/24 via 10.200.0.1 dev tun0  metric 5
192.168.5.0/24 via 10.200.0.5 dev tun1  metric 10
[...]
```

A route:

- ▸ Via the "direct" tunnel to site B; this route has the lowest metric
- ▸ Via an indirect tunnel: first to site C and then onward to site B; this route has a higher metric and is not chosen until the first route is down

This setup has the advantage that if one tunnel fails, then after 60 seconds, the connection and its corresponding routes are dropped and are restarted. The backup route to the other network then automatically takes over and all three sites can reach each other again.

When the "direct" tunnel is restored the direct routes are also restored and the network traffic will automatically choose the best path to the remote site.

There's more...

Scalability

In this recipe, we connect three remote sites. This results in six different configuration files that provide the limitations of the point-to-point setup. In general, to connect N possible sites with full redundancy, you will have N * (N − 1) configuration files. This is manageable for up to four sites, but after that, a server/multiple-client setup as described in the next chapters is much easier.

Routing protocols

To increase the availability of the networks, it is better to run a Routing Protocol such as RIPv2 or OSPF. Using a routing protocol, the failing routes are discovered much faster, resulting in less network downtime.

See also

- ► *Chapter 8, Troubleshooting OpenVPN: Routing Issues,* in which the most common routing issues are explained.

2
Client-server IP-only Networks

In this chapter, we will cover:

- ▶ Setting up the public and private keys
- ▶ Simple configuration
- ▶ Server-side routing
- ▶ Using `client-config-dir` files
- ▶ Routing: subnets on both sides
- ▶ Redirecting the default gateway
- ▶ Using an `ifconfig-pool` block
- ▶ Using the status file
- ▶ Management interface
- ▶ Proxy-arp

Introduction

The recipes in this chapter will cover the most commonly used deployment model for OpenVPN: a single server with multiple remote clients capable of routing IP traffic.

We will also look at several common routing configurations in addition to the use of the management interface at both the client and server side.

The last recipe of this chapter will show how it is possible to avoid the use of network bridges for most practical use cases.

As a routed, TUN-style setup is the most commonly used deployment model, some of the sample configuration files presented in this chapter will be reused throughout the rest of the book. In particular, the configuration files such as `basic-udp-server.conf`, `basic-udp-client.conf`, `basic-tcp-server.conf`, and `basic-tcp-client.conf` from the recipe *Server-side routing* will be reused often, as well as the Windows client configuration files `basic-udp-client.ovpn` and `basic-tcp-client.ovpn` from the recipe, *Using an ifconfig-pool block*.

Setting up the public and private keys

Before we can set up a client/server VPN, we need to set up the Public Key Infrastructure (PKI) first. The PKI comprises the Certificate Authority, the private keys, and the certificates (public keys) for both the client and server. We also need to generate a Diffie-Hellman parameter file that is required for perfect forward secrecy.

For setting up the PKI, we make use of the `easy-rsa` scripts supplied by the OpenVPN distribution itself.

Getting ready

The PKI needs to be set up on a trusted computer. This can be the same as the computer on which the OpenVPN server is run, but from a security point of view, it is best if the PKI is kept completely separated from the rest of the OpenVPN services. One option is to keep the PKI Certificate Authority (CA) key located on a separate, external disk, which is attached only when needed. Another option would be to keep the CA private key on a separate computer that is not hooked up to any network at all.

This recipe was done on Linux, but can also be done on a Mac OS machine. On Windows, the commands are very similar as well. The Linux `easy-rsa` scripts are meant to be run from a bash-like shell, so make sure you are not running csh/tcsh (UNIX shells).

How to do it...

1. Create the directories for the PKI and copy over the `easy-rsa` distribution from your OpenVPN installation:

    ```
    $ mkdir -m 700 -p /etc/openvpn/cookbook/keys
    $ cd /etc/openvpn/cookbook
    $ cp -drp /usr/share/openvpn/easy-rsa/2.0/* .
    ```

2. Note that there is no need to run these commands as the `root` user, provided that the user is allowed to create the above directory path.

3. Next, we set up the `vars` file. Create a file containing the following:

```
export EASY_RSA=/etc/openvpn/cookbook
export OPENSSL="openssl"
export KEY_CONFIG=`$EASY_RSA/whichopensslcnf $EASY_RSA`
export KEY_DIR="$EASY_RSA/keys"
export PKCS11_MODULE_PATH="dummy"
export PKCS11_PIN="dummy"
export KEY_SIZE=2048
export CA_EXPIRE=3650
export KEY_EXPIRE=1000
export KEY_COUNTRY="NL"
export KEY_PROVINCE=
export KEY_CITY=
export KEY_ORG="Cookbook"
export KEY_EMAIL="openvpn-ca@cookbook.example.com"
```

Note that the `PKCS11_MODULE_PATH` and `PKCS11_PIN` entries are needed even if you are not using smart cards.

The default KEY_SIZE of 2048 bits is sufficiently secure for the next few years. A larger key size (4096 bits) is possible, but the trade off is a performance penalty. We shall generate a 4096 bit CA private key, as performance is not an issue here.

Adjust the settings (`KEY_ORG`, `KEY_EMAIL`) to reflect your organization. The meaning of these settings is explained in more details later.

4. Source the `vars` file and generate the CA private key and certificate, using a 4096 bit modulus. Choose a strong password for the CA certificate. After that, simply press the *Enter* key every time the script asks for input:

```
$ cd /etc/openvpn/cookbook
$ . ./vars
$ ./clean-all
$ KEY_SIZE=4096 ./build-ca --pass
```

Sample output:

```
Example2-1                                    _ □ ✕
[server]$ clear
[server]$ . ./vars
[server]$ ./clean-all
[server]$ KEY_SIZE=4096 ./build-ca --pass
Generating a 4096 bit RSA private key
...................................................................
......................++
.....................................................................++
writing new private key to 'ca.key'
Enter PEM pass phrase:
Verifying - Enter PEM pass phrase:
-----
You are about to be asked to enter information that will be incorporated
into your certificate request.
What you are about to enter is what is called a Distinguished Name or a DN.
There are quite a few fields but you can leave some blank
For some fields there will be a default value,
If you enter '.', the field will be left blank.
-----
Country Name (2 letter code) [NL]:
State or Province Name (full name) []:
Locality Name (eg, city) []:
Organization Name (eg, company) [Cookbook]:
Organizational Unit Name (eg, section) []:
Common Name (eg, your name or your server's hostname) [Cookbook CA]:
Name []:
Email Address [openvpn-ca@cookbook.example.com]:
[server]$ █
```

5. Next, we build the server certificate. When the script asks for input, press the *Enter* key. When the script asks for the `ca.key` password, enter the password for the CA certificate. Finally, when the script asks for a `[y/n]` answer, type `y`:

    ```
    $ ./build-key-server openvpnserver

        Generating a 1024 bit RSA private key
        .....++++++
        .....................++++++
        writing new private key to 'openvpnserver.key'
        -----
        [...]
        -----
        Country Name (2 letter code) [NL]:
        State or Province Name (full name) []:
        Locality Name (eg, city) []:
        Organization Name (eg, company) [Cookbook]:
        Organizational Unit Name (eg, section) []:
        Common Name (eg, your name or your server's hostname)
        [openvpnserver]:
        Name []:
        Email Address [openvpn-ca@cookbook.example.com]:
    ```

```
Please enter the following 'extra' attributes
to be sent with your certificate request
A challenge password []:
An optional company name []:
Using configuration from /etc/openvpn/cookbook/openssl.cnf
Enter pass phrase for
/etc/openvpn/cookbook/keys/ca.key:[enter CA key password]
Check that the request matches the signature
Signature ok
The Subject's Distinguished Name is as follows
countryName           :PRINTABLE:'NL'
organizationName      :PRINTABLE:'Cookbook'
commonName            :PRINTABLE:'openvpnserver'
emailAddress          :IA5STRING:' openvpn-
                              ca@cookbook.example.com '
Certificate is to be certified until Jan 30 11:59:06 2013 GMT
(1000 days)
Sign the certificate? [y/n]:y


1 out of 1 certificate requests certified, commit? [y/n]y
Write out database with 1 new entries
Data Base Updated
```

6. The first client certificate is generated in a batch. It is a very fast method for generating a client certificate but it is not possible to set a password on the client's private key file:

   ```
   $ ./build-key-server --batch openvpnclient1
   ```

```
[server]$ ./build-key --batch openvpnclient1
Generating a 2048 bit RSA private key
.....+++
................................+++
writing new private key to 'openvpnclient1.key'
-----
Using configuration from /etc/openvpn/cookbook/openssl.cnf
Enter pass phrase for /etc/openvpn/cookbook/keys/ca.key:
Check that the request matches the signature
Signature ok
The Subject's Distinguished Name is as follows
countryName          :PRINTABLE:'NL'
organizationName     :PRINTABLE:'Cookbook'
commonName           :PRINTABLE:'openvpnclient1'
emailAddress         :IA5STRING:'openvpn-ca@cookbook.example.com'
Certificate is to be certified until Aug 14 16:02:47 2013 GMT (1000 days)

Write out database with 1 new entries
Data Base Updated
[server]$
```

7. The second client certificate is generated with a password. Choose a strong password (but different than the CA certificate password!). The output is abbreviated for clarity:

```
$ ./build-key-pass openvpnclient2
Generating a 1024 bit RSA private key
...++++++
..++++++
writing new private key to 'openvpnclient2.key'
Enter PEM pass phrase:[enter private key password]
Verifying - Enter PEM pass phrase: [enter password again]

[...]
Enter pass phrase for
/etc/openvpn/cookbook /keys/ca.key:[enter CA key password]
[...]
Sign the certificate? [y/n]:y

1 out of 1 certificate requests certified, commit? [y/n]y
Write out database with 1 new entries
Data Base Updated
```

8. Next, build the Diffie-Hellman parameter file for the server:

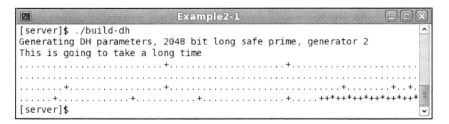

9. And finally, the `tls-auth` key file:

```
$ openvpn --genkey --secret ta.key
```

How it works...

The `easy-rsa` scripts are a handy set of wrapper scripts around some of the `openssl ca` commands. The `openssl ca` commands are commonly used to set up a PKI using X509 certificates. The `build-dh` script is a wrapper for the `openssl dh` command.

There's more...

Using the easy-rsa scripts on Windows

To use the `easy-rsa` scripts on Windows, a command window (`cmd.exe`) is needed and the starting `./` needs to be removed from all the commands, for example:

```
[Win]C:> vars
[Win]C:> clean-all
[Win]C:> build-ca
```

Some notes on the different variables

The following variables are set in the `vars` file:

- `KEY_SIZE=2048`: This is the cipher strength for all private keys. The longer the key size is, the stronger the encryption. Unfortunately, it also makes the encryption process slower.

- `CA_EXPIRE=3650`: This gives the number of days the CA certificate is considered valid, thus translating to a period of 10 years. For a medium-secure setup, this is fine, but if stronger security is required this number needs to be lowered.

- `KEY_EXPIRE=1000`: This gives the number of days for which the client of server certificate is considered valid, thus translating to a period of almost 3 years.

- `KEY_COUNTRY="NL"`, `KEY_PROVINCE=`, `KEY_CITY=`, `KEY_ORG="Cookbook"`, `KEY_EMAIL=openvpn-ca@cookbook.example.com`: These variables are all used to form the certificate Distinguished Name (DN). None of them are required, but both OpenVPN and OpenSSL suggest using at least `KEY_COUNTRY` to indicate where a certificate was issued.

See also

See *Chapter 4, PKI, Certificates, and OpenSSL*, for a lengthier introduction to the `easy-rsa` scripts and the `openssl` commands.

Simple configuration

This recipe will demonstrate how to set up a connection in the client or server mode using certificates.

Getting ready

Install OpenVPN 2.0 or higher on two computers. Make sure the computers are connected over a network. Set up the client and server certificates using the previous recipe. For this recipe, both computers were running Linux and OpenVPN 2.1.1.

How to do it...

1. Create the server configuration file:

   ```
   proto udp
   port 1194
   dev tun
   server 192.168.200.0 255.255.255.0

   ca   /etc/openvpn/cookbook/ca.crt
   cert /etc/openvpn/cookbook/server.crt
   key  /etc/openvpn/cookbook/server.key
   dh   /etc/openvpn/cookbook/dh1024.pem
   ```

   Then save it as example2-2-server.conf.

2. Copy over the public certificates and the server private key from the /etc/openvpn/cookbook/keys directory:

   ```
   [server]$ cd /etc/openvpn/cookbook
   [server]$ cp keys/ca.crt ca.crt
   [server]$ cp keys/openvpnserver.crt server.crt
   [server]$ cp keys/openvpnserver.key server.key
   [server]$ cp keys/dh1024.pem dh1024.pem
   ```

3. Note that there is no need to run the above commands as user 'root', provided that write access to the above directories has been given.

4. Start the server:

   ```
   [root@server]# openvpn --config example2-2-server.conf
   ```

5. Next, create the client configuration file:

```
client
proto udp
remote openvpnserver.example.com
port 1194
dev tun
nobind

ca /etc/openvpn/cookbook/ca.crt
cert /etc/openvpn/cookbook/client1.crt
key /etc/openvpn/cookbook/client1.key
```

Then save it as example2-2-client.conf.

6. Transfer the files such as ca.crt, openvpnclient1.crt, and openvpnclient1.key to the client machine using a secure channel; for example, using the scp command:

```
[client]$ cd /etc/openvpn/cookbook
[client]$ scp openvpnserver.example.com:/etc/openvpn/cookbook/keys/ca.crt ca.crt
ca.crt                                               100% 2179    2.1KB/s   00:00
[client]$ scp openvpnserver.example.com:/etc/openvpn/cookbook/keys/openvpnclient1.crt client1.crt
openvpnclient1.crt                                   100% 6263    6.1KB/s   00:00
[client]$ scp openvpnserver.example.com:/etc/openvpn/cookbook/keys/openvpnclient1.key client1.key
openvpnclient1.key                                   100% 1708    1.7KB/s   00:00
[client]$
```

7. And start the client:

```
[root@client]# openvpn --config example2-2-client.conf
[...]
[openvpnserver] Peer Connection Initiated with openvpnserver:1194
TUN/TAP device tun0 opened
/sbin/ip link set dev tun0 up mtu 1500
/sbin/ip addr add dev tun0 local 192.168.200.6 peer 192.168.200.5
Initialization Sequence Completed
```

After the connection is established, we can verify that it is working by pinging the server (notice the IP address!):

```
[client]$ ping -c 2 192.168.200.1
PING 192.168.200.1 (192.168.200.1) 56(84) bytes of data.
64 bytes from 192.168.200.1: icmp_seq=1 ttl=64 time=30.6 ms
64 bytes from 192.168.200.1: icmp_seq=2 ttl=64 time=30.7 ms
```

How it works...

When the server starts, it configures the first available TUN interface with IP address 192.168.200.1 and with a fake remote address of 192.168.200.2. After that, the server listens on the UDP port 1194 for incoming connections.

The client connects to the server on this port. After the initial TLS handshake, using both the client and server certificates, the client is assigned the IP address 192.168.200.6 (or rather the mini-network 192.168.200.4 - 192.168.200.7). The client configures its first available TUN interface using this information, after which the VPN is established.

There's more...

'net30' addresses

After the connection is established, you can query the tun0 interface like this:

```
[client]$ /sbin/ifconfig tun0 | grep inet
```

Look for the following:

```
      inet addr:192.168.200.6  P-t-P:192.168.200.5
```

The IP address 192.168.200.5 is a placeholder address and can never be reached. With OpenVPN 2.1, it is also possible to assign "linear" addresses to the clients that allow you to have more clients in the same range of IP addresses. This will be explained in the next recipe.

The first address is the VPN client address from a '/30' subnet and the second address is the fake remote endpoint address. Each '/30' subnet has to start at a multiple of four and the VPN client IP address is at the starting address plus two:

- ▶ 192.168.200.[0-3] , VPN IP is 192.168.200.1. This block normally is for the OpenVPN server itself.
- ▶ 192.168.200.[4-7] , client IP is 192.168.200.6. This block normally is for the first client to connect.
- ▶ 192.168.200.[8-11], [12-15], [16-19], and so on, are used for the consecutive clients.

Server-side routing

This recipe will demonstrate how to set up server-side routing in client or server mode. With this setup, the OpenVPN client will be able to reach all the machines behind the OpenVPN server.

Compared to the previous recipe, this recipe contains extra settings that are often used in production environments, as well as OpenVPN 2.1-specific features to make use of `linear` addresses (`topology subnet`).

The configuration files used in this recipe are useful building blocks for other recipes throughout this book, hence, they are named as `basic-udp-server.conf`, `basic-udp-client.conf`, and so on.

Getting ready

We use the following network layout here:

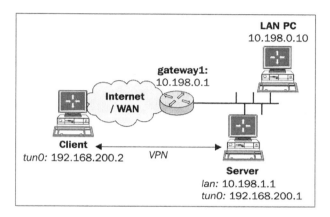

This recipe uses the PKI files created in the first recipe of this chapter. Install OpenVPN 2.1 on two computers. For this recipe, the server computer was running CentOS 5 Linux and OpenVPN 2.1.1 and the client was running Fedora 13 Linux and OpenVPN 2.1.1.

How to do it...

1. Create the server configuration file:

```
proto udp
port 1194
dev tun
server 192.168.200.0 255.255.255.0

ca       /etc/openvpn/cookbook/ca.crt
cert     /etc/openvpn/cookbook/server.crt
key      /etc/openvpn/cookbook/server.key
dh       /etc/openvpn/cookbook/dh1024.pem
tls-auth /etc/openvpn/cookbook/ta.key 0
```

```
persist-key
persist-tun
keepalive 10 60

push "route 10.198.0.0 255.255.0.0"
topology subnet

user  nobody
group nobody

daemon
log-append /var/log/openvpn.log
```

Then save it as `basic-udp-server.conf`. Note that in some Linux distributions, the group `nogroup` is used instead of `nobody`.

2. Copy over the `tls-auth` secret key file from the `/etc/openvpn/cookbook/keys` directory:

   [root@server]# cp keys/ta.key ta.key

3. And start the server:

   root@server]# openvpn --config basic-udp-server.conf

4. Make sure IP-traffic forwarding is enabled on the server:

   [root@server]# sysctl -w net.ipv4.ip_forward=1

5. Next, create the client configuration file:

```
client
proto udp
remote openvpnserver.example.com
port 1194
dev tun
nobind

ca       /etc/openvpn/cookbook/ca.crt
cert     /etc/openvpn/cookbook/client1.crt
key      /etc/openvpn/cookbook/client1.key
tls-auth /etc/openvpn/cookbook/ta.key 1

ns-cert-type server
```

Save it as `basic-udp-client.conf`.

6. Transfer the `tls-auth` secret key file, `ta.key`, to the client machine using a secure channel, such as `scp`:

```
[root@client]# scp \
    openvpnserver:/etc/openvpn/cookbook/keys/ta.key .
```

7. Start the client:

```
[root@client]# openvpn --config basic-udp-client.conf
    OpenVPN 2.1.1 x86_64-redhat-linux-gnu [SSL] [LZO2] [EPOLL]
    [PKCS11] built on Jan  5 2010
    NOTE: OpenVPN 2.1 requires '--script-security 2' or higher to
    call user-defined scripts or executables
    Control Channel Authentication: using '/etc/openvpn/cookbook/
    ta.key' as a OpenVPN static key file
    UDPv4 link local: [undef]
    UDPv4 link remote: 194.171.96.27:1194
    [openvpnserver] Peer Connection Initiated with
    194.171.96.27:1194
```

8. Add a route to the server-side gateway `gateway1` so that all VPN traffic is sent back to the VPN server. In this recipe, we use a router that understands a Linux `ip route` like syntax:

```
[gateway1]> ip route add 192.168.200.0/24 via 10.198.1.1
```

After the VPN is established, verify that we are able to ping a machine on the remote server LAN:

```
[client]$ ping -c 2 10.198.0.10
    PING 10.198.0.10 (10.198.0.10) 56(84) bytes of data.
    64 bytes from 10.198.0.10: icmp_seq=1 ttl=63 time=31.1 ms
    64 bytes from 10.198.0.10: icmp_seq=2 ttl=63 time=30.0 ms
```

How it works...

The server starts and configures the first available TUN interface with IP address 192.168.200.1. With the directive 'topology subnet', the fake remote address is also 192.168.200.1. After that, the server listens on the UDP port 1194 for incoming connections. For security reasons, the OpenVPN process switches to user and group, `nobody`. Even if a remote attacker was able to compromise the OpenVPN process, the security breach would be contained to the user `nobody` instead of the user `root`. When the 'user' and 'group' directives are used, it also wise to add the following as well:

```
persist-key
persist-tun
```

Otherwise, OpenVPN will not be able to restart itself correctly.

Another security measure is the use of the following on the server side (and `ta.key 1` on the client side):

```
tls-auth /etc/openvpn/cookbook/ta.key 0
```

This prevents the server from being overloaded by a so-called **Distributed Denial of Service** (**DDoS**) attack, as OpenVPN will just ignore those packets immediately if the HMAC is not correct.

The following directive sets up a `keepalive` timer on both the client and the server side:

```
keepalive 10 60
```

Every 10 seconds, a packet is sent from the server to the client side and vice-versa, to ensure that the VPN tunnel is still up and running. If no reply is received after 60 seconds on the client side, the VPN connection is automatically restarted. On the server side, the timeout period is multiplied by 2, hence the server will restart the VPN connection if no reply is received after 120 seconds.

Finally, the following directives are very commonly used in a production setup, where the OpenVPN process continues to run in the background (daemonizes itself) after the operator logs out:

```
daemon
log-append /var/log/openvpn.log
```

All output of the OpenVPN process is appended to the log file: `/var/log/openvpn.log`. You can use the `tail -f` command to monitor the output of the OpenVPN process.

The client connects to the server. After the initial TLS handshake, using both the client and server certificates, the client is assigned the IP address 192.168.200.2. The client configures its first available TUN interface using this information and updates its routing table so that traffic for the server-side Site B's LAN is tunneled over the VPN.

There's more...

As the example files used in this recipe are reused later on , it is useful to explain a bit more about the options used.

Linear addresses

After the connection is established, you can query the `tun0` interface like this:

```
[client]$ /sbin/ifconfig tun0 | grep inet
```

Look for the following:

```
inet addr:192.168.200.2  P-t-P:192.168.200.2
```

This is caused by the directive `topology subnet`, which is something new in OpenVPN 2.1. This directive tells OpenVPN to assign only a single IP address to each client. With OpenVPN 2.0, the minimum number of IP addresses per client is four (as we can see in the previous recipe).

Using the TCP protocol

In the previous example, we chose the UDP protocol. The configuration files in this recipe can easily be converted to use TCP protocol by changing the line:

```
proto udp
```

It should be changed to the following:

```
proto tcp
```

This should be done in both the client and server configuration files. Save these files for future use as `basic-tcp-server.conf` and `basic-tcp-client.conf`:

```
$ cd /etc/openvpn/cookbook
$ sed 's/proto udp/proto tcp' basic-udp-server.conf \
    > basic-tcp-server.conf
$ sed 's/proto udp/proto tcp' basic-udp-client.conf \
    > basic-tcp-client.conf
```

Server certificates and ns-cert-type server

On the client side, the directive `ns-cert-type server` is often used in combination with a server certificate that is built using:

```
$ build-key-server
```

This is done in order to prevent Man-in-the-Middle attacks. The idea is that a client will refuse to connect to a server that does not have a special server certificate. By doing this, it is no longer possible for a malicious client to pose as a server. OpenVPN 2.1 also supports the directive:

```
remote-cert-tls server
```

This also supports certificates with explicit key usage and extended key usage based on the RFC 3280 TLS rules.

Masquerading

In this recipe, the gateway on the server-side LAN is configured with an extra route for the VPN traffic. Sometimes, this is not possible, in which case the Linux `iptables` command can be used to set up masquerading:

```
[root@server]# iptables -t nat -I POSTROUTING -o eth0 \
    -s 192.168.200.0/24 -j MASQUERADE
```

This instructs the Linux kernel to rewrite all traffic that is coming from the subnet `192.168.200.0/24` (that is our OpenVPN subnet) and that is leaving the Ethernet interface `eth0`. Each of these packets has its source address rewritten so that it appears as if it's coming from the OpenVPN server itself and not from the OpenVPN client. `iptables` keeps track of these rewritten packets so that when a return packet is received the reverse is done and the packets are forwarded back to the OpenVPN client again. This is an easy method to enable routing to work, but there is a drawback when many clients are used, as it is no longer possible to distinguish traffic on the Site B's LAN if it is coming from the OpenVPN server itself, from client1 via the VPN tunnel, or from clientN via the VPN tunnel.

Using 'client-config-dir' files

In a setup where a single server can handle many clients, it is sometimes necessary to set per-client options that overrule the "global" options. The `client-config-dir` option is very useful for this. It allows the administrator to assign a specific IP address to a client, to push specific options such as compression and DNS server to a client, or to temporarily disable a client altogether.

Getting ready

This recipe is a continuation of the previous one. Install OpenVPN 2.1 on two computers. For this recipe, the server computer was running CentOS 5 Linux and OpenVPN 2.1.1 and the client was running Fedora 13 Linux and OpenVPN 2.1.1. Keep the configuration file, `basic-udp-server.conf`, from the previous recipe at hand, as well as the client configuration file, `basic-udp-client.conf`, at hand.

How to do it...

1. Modify the server configuration file, `basic-udp-server.conf`, by adding a line:

   ```
   client-config-dir /etc/openvpn/cookbook/clients
   ```

   Then save it as `example2-4-server.conf`.

2. Next, create the directory for the `client-config` files and place a file in there with the name of the client certificate:

```
[root@server]# mkdir -m 755 /etc/openvpn/cookbook/clients
[root@server]# cd /etc/openvpn/cookbook/clients
[root@server]# echo "ifconfig-push 192.168.200.7 192.168.200.7" \
  > openvpnclient1
```

3. This name can be retrieved from the client certificate file using:

```
[server]$ openssl x509 -subject -noout -in client1.crt
    subject= /C=NL/O=Cookbook/CN=openvpnclient1/emailAddress=…
```

4. Start the server:

```
[root@server]# openvpn --config example2-4-server.conf
```

5. Start the client using the configuration file from the previous recipe:

```
[root@client]# openvpn --config basic-udp-client.conf
    [...]
    [openvpnserver] Peer Connection Initiated with
    openvpnserver:1194
    TUN/TAP device tun0 opened
    /sbin/ip link set dev tun0 up mtu 1500
    /sbin/ip addr add dev tun0 192.168.200.7/24 broadcast
    192.168.200.255
    Initialization Sequence Completed
```

How it works...

When a client connects to the server with its certificate and with the certificate's common name `openvpnclient1`, the OpenVPN server checks whether there is a corresponding client configuration file (also known as a CCD file) in the `client-config-dir` directory. If it exists, it is read in as an extra set of options for that particular client. In this recipe, we'll use it to assign a specific IP address to a client (although there are more flexible ways to do that). The client is now always assigned the IP address 192.168.200.7.

There's more...

Default configuration file

If the following conditions are met, then the DEFAULT file is read and processed instead:

▸ A `client-config-dir` directive is specified
▸ There is no matching client file for the client's certificate in that directory
▸ A file DEFAULT does exist in that directory

Please note that this name is case sensitive.

Troubleshooting

Troubleshooting configuration problems with CCD files is a recurring topic on the OpenVPN mailing lists. The most common configuration errors are as follows:

- Always specify the full path in the `client-config-dir` directive
- Make sure the directory is accessible and the CCD file is readable to the user which is used to run OpenVPN (`nobody` or `openvpn` in most cases)
- Make sure that the right filename is used for the CCD file, without any extensions

OpenVPN 2.0 'net30' compatibility

OpenVPN 2.0 does not support the directive `topology subnet`. It supports only the `net30` mode, where each client is assigned a '/30' mini subnet containing four IP addresses. The syntax of a CCD file in `net30` mode is slightly different:

```
ifconfig-push 192.168.200.34 192.168.200.33
```

The first address is the client IP address and is at the starting point of the (randomly-chosen) '/30' network 192.168.200.[32-35]. The second address is the address of the fake remote endpoint that is never used.

This also offers a nice way to allow OpenVPN 2.0 clients to connect to a server that is configured to use `topology subnet`. By creating a CCD file containing the following, an OpenVPN 2.0 client can still connect:

```
push "route-gateway 192.168.200.33"
ifconfig-push 192.168.200.34 192.168.200.33
```

Note that the route gateway needs to be pushed explicitly as otherwise an attempt is made to use the VPN server IP 192.168.200.1. Also, note that there is no need to do a `push "topology net30"'` as the OpenVPN 2.0 client does not recognize this directive.

Allowed options in a 'client-config-dir' file

The following configuration options are allowed in a CCD file:

- `push`—for pushing DNS servers, WINS servers, routes, and so on
- `push-reset`—to overrule global `push` options
- `iroute`—for routing client subnets to the server
- `ifconfig-push`—for assigning a specific IP address as done in this recipe
- `disable`—for temporarily disabling a client altogether
- `config`—for including another configuration file

Routing: subnets on both sides

This recipe will demonstrate how to set up server-side and client-side routing in client/server mode. With this setup, the OpenVPN client will be able to reach all machines behind the OpenVPN server and the server will be able to reach all machines behind the client.

Getting ready

We use the following network layout:

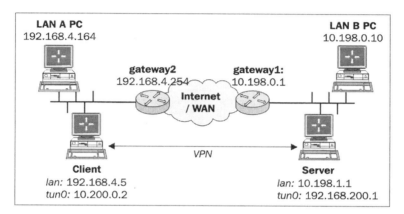

This recipe uses the PKI files created in the first recipe of this chapter. For this recipe, the server computer was running CentOS 5 Linux and OpenVPN 2.1.1 and the client was running Fedora 13 Linux and OpenVPN 2.1.1. Keep the server configuration file, `basic-udp-server.conf`, as well as the client configuration file, `basic-udp-client.conf`, from the recipe *Server-side routing* at hand.

How to do it...

1. Modify the server configuration file, `basic-udp-server.conf`, by adding the lines:

    ```
    client-config-dir /etc/openvpn/cookbook/clients
    route 192.168.4.0 255.255.255.0 192.168.200.1
    ```

    Then save it as `example2-5-server.conf`.

2. Next, create the directory for the client configuration files:

    ```
    [root@server]# mkdir -m 755 /etc/openvpn/cookbook/clients
    ```

3. Place a file in this directory with the name of the client certificate as
   `openvpnclient1` containing:

   ```
   iroute 192.168.4.0 255.255.255.0
   ```

   This name can be retrieved from the client certificate file using:

   ```
   $ openssl x509 -subject -noout -in client1.crt
   subject= /C=NL/O=Cookbook/CN=openvpnclient1/emailAddress=…
   ```

4. Start the server:

   ```
   [root@server]# openvpn --config example2-5-server.conf
   ```

5. Start the client:

   ```
   [root@client]# openvpn --config basic-udp-client.conf
   ```

6. After the VPN is established, we need to set up routing on both sides. Enable the
   IP traffic forwarding on the server:

   ```
   [root@server]# sysctl -w net.ipv4.ip_forward=1
   ```

7. Add a route to the LAN B's Gateway to point to the OpenVPN server itself:

   ```
   [siteB-gw]> ip route add 192.168.4.0/24 via 10.198.1.1
   [siteB-gw]> ip route add 192.168.200.0/24 via 10.198.1.1
   ```

   Here, `10.198.1.1` is the LAN IP address of the OpenVPN server used in this recipe.

8. On the client side:

   ```
   [client]$ sysctl -w net.ipv4.ip_forward=1
   ```

9. And similarly, for the LAN A Gateway:

   ```
   [siteA-gw]> ip route add 10.198.0.0/16 via 192.168.4.5
   [siteA-gw]> ip route add 192.168.200.0/24 via 192.168.4.5
   ```

   Here, `192.168.4.5` is the LAN IP address of the OpenVPN client used in this recipe.

10. Now, we verify that we can ping a machine on the remote server LAN:

    ```
    [client]$ ping -c 2 10.198.0.10
      PING 10.198.0.10 (10.198.0.10) 56(84) bytes of data.
      64 bytes from 10.198.0.10: icmp_seq=1 ttl=63 time=31.1 ms
      64 bytes from 10.198.0.10: icmp_seq=2 ttl=63 time=30.0 ms
    ```

    And vice versa:

    ```
    [server]$ ping -c 2 192.168.4.164
    PING 192.168.4.164 (192.168.4.164) 56(84) bytes of data.
    64 bytes from 192.168.4.164: icmp_seq=1 ttl=64 time=30.2 ms
    64 bytes from 192.168.4.164: icmp_seq=2 ttl=64 time=29.7 ms
    ```

How it works...

When a client connects to the server with its certificate and with the certificate's common name, `openvpnclient1`, the OpenVPN server reads the client configuration file (also known as a CCD file) in the `client-config-dir` directory. The following directive in this file tells the OpenVPN server that the subnet `192.168.4.0/24` is reachable through the client `openvpnclient1`:

```
iroute 192.168.4.0 255.255.255.0
```

This directive has nothing to do with a kernel routing table, and is only used internally by the OpenVPN server process.

The following server directive is used by OpenVPN to configure the routing table of the operating system so that all the traffic intended for the subnet `192.168.4.0/24` is forwarded to the interface with IP address `192.168.200.1`, which is the VPN IP of the server:

```
route 192.168.4.0 255.255.255.0 192.168.200.1
```

With the appropriate routing set up on both ends, site-to-site routing is now possible.

There's more...

Masquerading

We could have used masquerading on both ends as well, but with multiple clients, it becomes very hard to keep track of the network traffic.

Client-to-client subnet routing

If another VPN client needs to reach the subnet `192.168.4.0/24` behind client `openvpnclient1`, the server configuration file needs to extended with the following:

```
push "route 192.168.4.0 255.255.255.0"
```

This instructs all clients that subnet `192.168.4.0/24` is reachable through the VPN tunnel, except for client `openvpnclient1`. The client `openvpnclient1` itself is excluded due to the matching `iroute` entry.

See also

▶   *Chapter 1*'s recipe, *Complete site-to-site setup*, where it is explained how to connect two remote LANs via a VPN tunnel using a point-to-point setup

Redirecting the default gateway

A very common use of a VPN is to route all the traffic over a secure tunnel. This allows one to safely access a network or even the Internet itself from within a "hostile" environment (for example, a poorly protected, but properly trojaned Internet caféteria).

In this recipe, we will set up OpenVPN to do exactly this. This recipe is very similar to the Server-side routing recipe, but there are some pitfalls when redirecting all the traffic over a VPN tunnel.

Getting ready

The network layout used in this recipe is the same as in the recipe *Server-side routing*. This recipe uses the PKI files created in the first recipe of this chapter. For this recipe, the server computer was running CentOS 5 Linux and OpenVPN 2.1.1. The client was running Fedora 13 Linux and OpenVPN 2.1.1. Keep the configuration file, `basic-udp-server.conf`, from the recipe *Server-side routing* at hand, as well as the client configuration file, `basic-udp-client.conf`.

How to do it...

1. Create the server configuration file by adding a line to the `basic-udp-server.conf` file:

    ```
    push "redirect-gateway def1"
    ```

    Save it as `example2-6-server.conf`.

2. Start the server:

    ```
    [root@server]# openvpn --config example2-6-server.conf
    ```

3. In another server terminal, enable IP-traffic forwarding:

    ```
    [root@server]# sysctl -w net.ipv4.ip_forward=1
    ```

4. Start the client:

    ```
    [root@client]# openvpn --config basic-udp-client.conf
    ```

    ```
    Example2-6
    ... ROUTE default_gateway=192.168.4.254
    ... TUN/TAP device tun0 opened
    ... TUN/TAP TX queue length set to 100
    ... /sbin/ip link set dev tun0 up mtu 1500
    ... /sbin/ip addr add dev tun0 192.168.200.2/24 broadcast 192.168.200.255
    ... /sbin/ip route add 10.198.1.1/32 via 192.168.4.254
    ... /sbin/ip route add 0.0.0.0/1 via 192.168.200.1
    ... /sbin/ip route add 128.0.0.0/1 via 192.168.200.1
    ... Initialization Sequence Completed
    ```

5. After the VPN is established, verify that all traffic is going over the tunnel:

```
[client]$ traceroute -n openvpn.net
traceroute to openvpn.net (67.228.116.146), 30 hops max, 60 byte packets
 1   192.168.200.1  1.464 ms  1.807 ms  1.829 ms
 2   10.198.0.1 1.848 ms  1.976 ms  2.078 ms
```

The first address in the `traceroute` output is the address of the OpenVPN server, hence all the traffic is routed over the tunnel.

How it works...

When the client connects to the OpenVPN server, a special route is pushed out by the server to the OpenVPN client:

```
push "redirect-gateway def1"
```

The configuration option `def1` tells the OpenVPN client to add three routes to the client operating system:

```
10.198.1.1 via 192.168.4.254 dev eth0
0.0.0.0/1 via 192.168.200.1 dev tun0
128.0.0.0/1 via 192.168.200.1 dev tun0
```

The first route is an explicit route from the client to the OpenVPN server via the LAN interface. This route is needed as otherwise all the traffic for the OpenVPN server itself would go through the tunnel.

The other two routes are a clever trick to overrule the default route so that all the traffic is sent through the tunnel instead of to the default LAN gateway. The existing default route to the LAN gateway is not deleted due to the `def1` parameter.

There's more...

Redirect-gateway parameters

Originally, OpenVPN supported only the directive:

```
push "redirect-gateway"
```

This is used to delete the original default route and replace it with a route to the OpenVPN server. This may seem like a clean solution, but in some cases, OpenVPN was unable to determine the existing default route. This often happened to clients connecting through UMTS. This also used to create routing lockups, where all traffic was routed through the tunnel, including the packets sent by the OpenVPN client itself.

With OpenVPN, there are several flags for the `redirect-gateway` directive:

- ▶ `local`: It doesn't set a direct route from the client to the server. It is useful only if the client and server are in the same LAN, such as when securing wireless networks.

- ▶ `bypass-dhcp`: It adds a direct route to the local DHCP server. It is picked up automatically by Windows client. On other operating systems, a plugin or script is required.

- ▶ `bypass-dns`: It adds a direct route to the local DNS server. It is also picked up by Windows client automatically and require a plugin or script on other other operating systems.

Split tunneling

In some cases, the `redirect-gateway` parameter is a bit too restrictive. You might want to add a few routes to local networks and route all other traffic over the VPN tunnel. The OpenVPN `route` directive has a few special parameters for this:

- ▶ `net_gateway`: This is a special gateway representing the LAN gateway address that OpenVPN determined when starting. For example, to add a direct route to the LAN 192.168.4.0/24, you would add the following to the client configuration file:
  - ❑ `route 192.168.4.0 255.255.255.0 net_gateway`

- ▶ `vpn_gateway`: This is a special gateway representing the VPN gateway address. If you want to add a route that explicitly sends traffic for a particular subnet over the VPN tunnel, overruling any local routes, you would add:
  - ❑ `route 10.198.0.0 255.255.0.0 vpn_gateway`: This option is used primarily in TAP-style networks where the VPN gateway address is not known in advance

See also

- ▶ The recipe Server-side routing, where the basic setup of setting up server-side routing is explained.

Using an 'ifconfig-pool' block

In this recipe, we will use an `ifconfig-pool` block to separate regular VPN clients from administrative VPN clients. This makes it easier to set up different firewall rules for administrative users.

Getting ready

We use the following network layout:

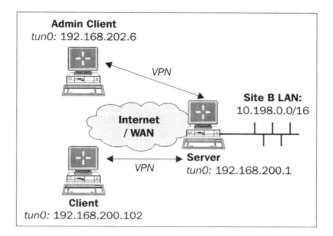

This recipe uses the PKI files created in the first recipe of this chapter. For this recipe, we used the server computer that was running the CentOS 5 Linux and OpenVPN 2.1.1. The VPN client **Client** was running the Windows XP and OpenVPN 2.1.1 and was on the **192.168.200.0** network. The VPN client **Admin Client** was running Fedora 12 Linux and OpenVPN 2.1.1 and was on the 192.168.202.0 network. For the Linux clients, keep the client configuration file `basic-udp-client.conf` from the recipe *Server-side routing* at hand.

How to do it...

1. Create the server configuration file:

```
proto udp
port 1194
dev tun

mode server
ifconfig 192.168.200.1 192.168.200.2
ifconfig-pool 192.168.200.100 192.168.200.120
route 192.168.200.0 255.255.248.0
push "route 192.168.200.1"
push "route 192.168.200.0 255.255.248.0"

ca        /etc/openvpn/cookbook/ca.crt
cert      /etc/openvpn/cookbook/server.crt
```

```
key       /etc/openvpn/cookbook/server.key
dh        /etc/openvpn/cookbook/dh1024.pem
tls-auth /etc/openvpn/cookbook/ta.key 0

persist-key
persist-tun
keepalive 10 60

user   nobody
group nobody

daemon
log-append /var/log/openvpn.log

client-config-dir /etc/openvpn/cookbook/clients
```

Then save it as `example2-7-server.conf`. Note that `topology` `subnet` is not used here.

2. Start the server:

    [root@server]# openvpn --config example2-7-server.conf

3. The administrative VPN client will be assigned a special IP address:

    [root@server]# mkdir -m 755 /etc/openvpn/cookbook/clients

    [root@server]# cd /etc/openvpn/cookbook/clients

    **[root@server]# echo "ifconfig-push 192.168.202.6 192.168.202.5" **

    ** > openvpnclient1**

4. Note that the directory `clients` needs to be world-readable, as the OpenVPN server process will run as user `nobody` after starting up.

5. Next, start the Linux client using the configuration file from the earlier recipe:

    [root@AdminClient]# openvpn --config basic-udp-client.conf

    ```
    [...]
    [openvpnserver] Peer Connection Initiated with
                    openvpnserver:1194
    TUN/TAP device tun0 opened
    /sbin/ip link set dev tun0 up mtu 1500
    /sbin/ip addr add dev tun0 local 192.168.202.6 peer
                    192.168.202.5
    Initialization Sequence Completed
    ```

The IP address that is assigned to the administrative client is highlighted for clarity.

6. Create a configuration file for the Windows client:

```
client
proto udp
remote openvpnserver.example.com
port 1194
dev tun
nobind

ca       "c:/program files/openvpn/config/ca.crt"
cert     "c:/program files/openvpn/config/client2.crt"
key      "c:/program files/openvpn/config/client2.key"
tls-auth "c:/program files/openvpn/config/ta.key" 1

ns-cert-type server
```

Then save it as `basic-udp-client.ovpn`. Note the use of the forward slash ('/'), which is easier to use than the backslash ('\'), as the backslash needs to be repeated twice each time.

7. Transfer the `ca.crt`, `client2.crt`, `client2.key` files, and the `tls-auth` secret key file, `ta.key`, to the Windows machine using a secure channel, such as `winscp` or the PuTTY `pscp` command-line tool.

8. Start the Windows client using the OpenVPN GUI:

Remember that this client's private key file is protected using a password or passphrase. After both the clients are connected, we verify that they can ping each other and the server (assuming that no firewalls are blocking access).

9. On the Admin Client:

[AdminClient]$ ping 192.168.200.1

[AdminClient]$ ping 192.168.200.102

10. And on the "regular" client:

[WinClient]C:> ping 192.168.200.1

[WinClient]C:> ping 192.168.202.6

How it works...

A server configuration file normally uses the following directive to configure the range of IP addresses for the clients:

```
server 192.168.200.0 255.255.255.0
```

This directive is internally expanded to the following:

```
mode server
tls-server

ifconfig 192.168.200.1 192.168.200.2
ifconfig-pool 192.168.200.4 192.168.200.251
route 192.168.200.0 255.255.255.0
push "route 192.168.200.1"
```

So, by not using the `server` directive, but by specifying our own `ifconfig-pool`, we can override this behavior. We then use a CCD file to assign an IP address to the administrative client, which falls outside of the `ifconfig-pool` range. By using the appropriate `route` and `push route` statements, we ensure that all clients can "ping" each other.

There's more...

Configuration files on Windows

The OpenVPN GUI application on Windows always starts in the directory:

```
C:\Program Files\OpenVPN\config
```

Or, `C:\Program Files(x86)\...` on 64-bit versions of Windows. Thus, the directory paths in the `basic-udp-client.ovpn` configuration file can be omitted:

```
ca        ca.crt
cert      client2.crt
key       client2.key
tls-auth ta.key 1
```

Topology subnet

Note that in this recipe we did not make use of the following directive:

```
topology subnet
```

The `subnet` topology is still a new feature in OpenVPN 2.1 and it does not interact very well when using separate `ifconfig-pool` options.

Client-to-client access

With this setup, the VPN clients can connect to each other even though we did not make use of the following directive in the server-side configuration:

```
client-to-client
```

This is possible due to the route and push route statements in the server configuration file. The advantage of not using client-to-client is that it is still possible to filter out unwanted traffic using iptables or another firewalling solution.

If there is no need for the administrative clients to connect to the regular VPN clients (or vice versa), then the netmask can be adjusted to:

```
route 192.168.200.0 255.255.255.0
push "route 192.168.200.0 255.255.255.0"
```

Now, the networks are completely separated.

Using the TCP protocol

In this example, we chose the UDP protocol. The client configuration file in this recipe can easily be converted to use TCP protocol by changing the line:

```
proto udp
```

Change it to the following:

```
proto tcp
```

Save this file for future use as basic-tcp-client.ovpn.

Using the status file

OpenVPN offers several options to monitor the clients connected to a server. The most commonly used method is using a status file. This recipe will show how to use and read the OpenVPN's status file.

Getting ready

We use the following network layout:

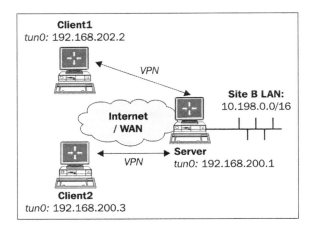

This recipe uses the PKI files created in the first recipe of this chapter. In this recipe, the server computer was running CentOS 5 Linux and OpenVPN 2.1.1. The first client was running Fedora 12 Linux and OpenVPN 2.1.1. The second client was running Windows XP SP3 and OpenVPN 2.1.1. For the Linux server, keep the server configuration file `basic-udp-server.conf` from the recipe *Server-side routing* at hand. For the Linux client, keep the client configuration file `basic-udp-client.conf` from the same recipe at hand. For the Windows client, keep the corresponding client configuration file `basic-udp-client.ovpn` from the previous recipe at hand.

How to do it...

1. Create the server configuration file by adding a line to the `basic-udp-server.conf` file:

    ```
    status /var/log/openvpn.status
    ```

    Save it as `example2-8-server.conf`.

2. Start the server:

    ```
    [root@server]# openvpn --config example2-8-server.conf
    ```

3. First, start the Linux client:

    ```
    [root@client1]# openvpn --config basic-udp-client.conf
    ```

4. After the VPN is established, list the contents of the `openvpn.status` file:

   [root@server]# cat /var/log/openvpn.status

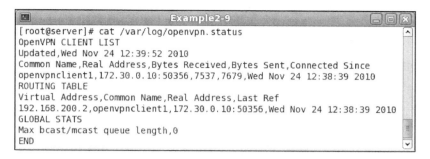

5. Transfer the `ca.crt`, `client2.crt`, `client2.key` files and the `tls-auth` secret key file, `ta.key`, to the Windows machine using a secure channel, such as `winscp` or the PuTTY's `pscp` command-line tool.

6. Start the Windows client on the command-line:

   [WinClient2]C:> cd \program files\openvpn\config

   [WinClient2]C:> ..\bin\openvpn --config basic-udp-client.ovpn

   Remember that this client's private key file is protected using a password or passphrase.

7. List the contents of the status file again on the server:

   [root@server]# cat /var/log/openvpn.status

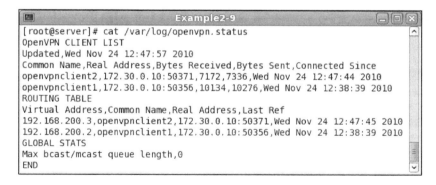

How it works...

Each time a client connects to the OpenVPN server, the status file is updated with the connection information. The **OpenVPN CLIENT LIST** and **ROUTING TABLE** are the most interesting tables, as they show:

- ▸ Which clients are connected
- ▸ From which IP address the clients are connecting
- ▸ The number of bytes each client has received and transferred
- ▸ The time at which the client connected

In addition, the routing table also shows which networks are routed to each client.

Note that the second client is connected to the server using the same Real Address as the first client. This is caused by the fact that the Windows XP client was running as a virtual machine on the Linux client. It also shows that OpenVPN can handle NAT'ted clients quite easily.

There's more...

Status parameters

The status directive takes two parameters:

- ▸ The filename of the status file.
- ▸ Optionally, the refresh frequency for updating the status file. The default value of 60 seconds should suffice for most situations.

Disconnecting clients

Note that when a client disconnects the status file, it is not updated immediately. OpenVPN first tries to reconnect to the client based on the keepalive parameters in the server configuration file. The server configuration file in this recipe uses:

```
keepalive 10 60
```

This tells the server that it will ping the client every 10 seconds. If it does not get response after 60 seconds * 2, the connection is restarted. The OpenVPN server will double the value of the second argument. The server will also tell the client to ping every 10 seconds and to restart the connection after 60 seconds if it does not get any response.

Explicit-exit-notify

One of the lesser-known options of OpenVPN is the following directive:

```
explicit-exit-notify [N]
```

This can be set on the client side so that when the client disconnects it will send an explicit **OCC_EXIT** message to the server (if at all possible). This will speed up the removal of disconnected clients. The optional parameter N indicates the number of times the message will be sent. By default, only a single **OCC_EXIT** message is sent, which can cause problems as the UDP protocol does not guarantee the delivery of packets.

Management interface

This recipe shows how an OpenVPN client is managed using the management interface from the server side.

Getting ready

This recipe uses the PKI files created in the first recipe of this chapter. For this recipe, we used the server computer that runs CentOS 5 Linux and OpenVPN 2.1.1. The client was running Windows XP SP3 and OpenVPN 2.1.1. For the server, one should keep the configuration file `basic-udp-server.conf` from the recipe *Server-side routing* at hand. For the Windows client, keep the configuration file `basic-udp-client.ovpn` from the recipe *Using an 'ifconfig-pool' block* at hand.

How to do it...

1. Start the server using the "default" server configuration file:

   [root@server]# openvpn --config basic-udp-server.conf

2. Create a configuration file for the Windows client by adding a line to the `basic-udp-client.ovpn` file:

   management tunnel 23000 stdin

   Save it as `example2-9.ovpn`.

3. Transfer the `ca.crt`, `client2.crt`, `client2.key` files and the `tls-auth` secret key file `ta.key` to the Windows machine using a secure channel, such as `winscp` or the PuTTY `pscp` command-line tool.

4. Start the Windows client on the command-line:

   [WinClient]C:> cd \program files\openvpn\config

   [WinClient]C:> ..\bin\openvpn --config example2-9.ovpn

   The OpenVPN client will now ask for a password for the management interface. Pick a good password. After that it will ask for the private key passphrase.

5. After the VPN is established, we can connect from the server to the management interface of the OpenVPN client using the 'telnet' program:

[server]$ telnet 192.168.200.3 23000

```
Trying 192.168.200.3...
Connected to 192.168.200.3 (192.168.200.3).
Escape character is '^]'.
ENTER PASSWORD:[enter management password]
SUCCESS: password is correct
>INFO:OpenVPN Management Interface Version 1 -- type 'help' for
    more info
status
OpenVPN STATISTICS
Updated,Mon May 17 16:25:45 2010
TUN/TAP read bytes,5217
TUN/TAP write bytes,1036
TCP/UDP read bytes,9294
TCP/UDP write bytes,13028
Auth read bytes,1084
TAP-WIN32 driver status,"State=AT?c Err=[(null)/0] #O=4
    Tx=[13,0] Rx=[19,0] IrpQ=[1,1,16] PktQ=[0,1,64]
    InjQ=[0,1,16]"
END

signal SIGTERM
```

6. Use *Ctrl+]* or 'quit' to exit the `telnet` program.

How it works...

When the OpenVPN client connects to the server, a special management interface is set up using the directive:

```
management tunnel 23000 stdin
```

It has the following parameters:

▸ `tunnel` to bind the management interface to the VPN tunnel itself. This is useful for testing purposes and some more advanced client setups. On the server side, it is best to always specify `127.0.0.1` for the management IP

▸ The port `23000` on which the management interface will be listening

▸ The last parameter is the password file or the special keyword `stdin` to indicate that the management interface password will be specified when OpenVPN starts up. Note that this password is completely unrelated to the private key passphrases or any other user management passwords that OpenVPN uses.

After the management interface comes up, the server operator can connect to it using **telnet** and can query the client. The client can type the following:

```
signal SIGTERM
```

This effectively shuts itself down as if the user has stopped it! This shows how important it is to protect the management interface and its password.

There's more...

Server-side management interface

The management interface can also be run on the OpenVPN server itself. In that case, it is possible to list the connected clients, disconnect them, or perform a variety of other OpenVPN administrative tasks.

It is expected that the management interface will become more important in future versions of OpenVPN, both on the client and the server side, as the preferred method for programmatically interacting with the OpenVPN software.

See Also

The *Chapter 3* recipe Management Interface in which the use of the server-side management interface is explained in more detail.

Proxy-arp

In this recipe, we will use the `proxy-arp` feature of the Linux kernel to make the VPN clients appear as part of the server-side LAN. This eliminates the need to use bridging, which is desirable in most cases.

Getting ready

We use the following network layout:

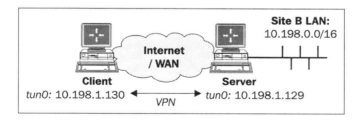

This recipe uses the PKI files created in the first recipe of this chapter. For this recipe, we used the server computer that run CentOS 5 Linux and OpenVPN 2.1.1. The client was running Windows XP SP3 and OpenVPN 2.1.1. For the server, one should keep the configuration file `basic-udp-server.conf` from the recipe *Server-side routing* at hand. For the Windows client, keep the configuration file, `basic-udp-client.ovpn`, from the recipe *Using an ifconfig-pool block* at hand.

How to do it...

1. Create the server config file by adding the following lines to the `basic-udp-server.conf` file:

   ```
   script-security 2
   client-connect    /etc/openvpn/cookbook/proxyarp-connect.sh
   client-disconnect /etc/openvpn/cookbook/proxyarp-disconnect.sh
   ```

   Save it as `example2-10-server.conf`.

2. Create the `proxyarp-connect.sh` script:

   ```
   #!/bin/bash
   /sbin/arp -i eth0  -Ds $ifconfig_pool_remote_ip eth0 pub
   ```

   And the `proxyarp-disconnect.sh` script.

   ```
   #!/bin/bash
   /sbin/arp -i eth0  -d $ifconfig_pool_remote_ip
   ```

3. Make sure that both scripts are executable:

   ```
   [root@server]# cd /etc/openvpn/cookbook

   [root@server]# chmod 755 proxyarp-connect.sh

   [root@server]# chmod 755 proxyarp-disconnect.sh
   ```

4. Start the server:

   ```
   [root@server]# openvpn --config example2-10-server.conf
   ```

5. Then, start the Windows client using the OpenVPN GUI:

After the client has successfully connected, the 'arp' table on the OpenVPN server will have a new entry:

```
10.198.1.130 * * MP eth0
```

From a machine on the server-side LAN, we can now ping the VPN client:

```
[siteBclient]C:> ping 10.198.1.130
```

Note that no special routing is required on the Site B's LAN. The VPN client truly appears as being on the LAN itself.

How it works...

`proxy-arp` is a feature supported by most UNIX and Linux kernels. It is used most often for connecting dial-in clients to a LAN, and nowadays also by ADSL and cable Internet providers. When the OpenVPN client connects, an IP address is borrowed from the Site B's LAN range. This IP address is assigned to the OpenVPN client. At the same time, a special ARP entry is made on the OpenVPN server to tell the rest of the network that the OpenVPN server acts as a proxy for IP `10.198.1.130`. This means that when another machine on the Site B's LAN wants to know where to find the host with IP `10.198.1.130` then the OpenVPN server will respond (with its own MAC address).

There's more...

User 'nobody'

Note that in this example we did not use:

```
user nobody
group nobody
```

as it would have prevented the `proxyarp-*` scripts from working. In order to execute the `/sbin/arp` command, root privileges are required, hence it is not possible to switch to user `nobody` after the OpenVPN server has started. Alternatively, one can configure `sudo` access to the `/sbin/arp` command to circumvent this.

TAP-style networks

`proxy-arp` can also be used in a TAP-style network. In combination with an external DHCP server, this gives almost the same functionality as an Ethernet bridging solution without the drawbacks of Ethernet bridging itself.

Broadcast traffic might not always work

Sending broadcast traffic over a network where `proxy-arp` is used is tricky. For most purposes (for example, Windows Network Neighborhood browsing), `proxy-arp` will work. For some applications that require all clients to be member of a full broadcast domain using `proxy-arp` might not suffice. In that case, Ethernet bridging is a better solution.

See also

▸   Chapter 3's recipe, *Checking broadcast and non-IP traffic*

3
Client-server Ethernet-style Networks

In this chapter, we will cover:

- ▶ Simple configuration—non bridged
- ▶ Enabling client-to-client traffic
- ▶ Bridging—Linux
- ▶ Bridging—Windows
- ▶ Checking broadcast and non-IP traffic
- ▶ External DHCP
- ▶ Using the status file
- ▶ Management interface

Introduction

The recipes in this chapter will cover the deployment model of a single server with multiple remote clients capable of forwarding Ethernet traffic.

We will look at several common configurations, including bridging, the use of an external DHCP server, and also the use of the OpenVPN status file.

Please note that bridging should only be used as a last resort. Most of functionality provided by bridging can be achieved through other methods. Moreover, there are many disadvantages to using bridging, especially in terms of performance and security.

Simple configuration—non-bridged

This recipe will demonstrate how to set up a TAP-based connection in client or server mode using certificates. It also uses masquerading to allow the OpenVPN clients to reach all the machines behind the OpenVPN server. The advantage of masquerading is that no special routes are needed on the server LAN. Masquerading for OpenVPN servers is available only on the Linux and UNIX variants. This recipe is similar to the recipe *Server-side routing* from the previous chapter.

Getting ready

We use the following network layout:

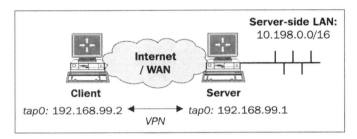

Set up the client and server certificates using the first recipe from *Chapter 2,Client-server IP-only Networks*. For this recipe, the server computer was running CentOS 5 Linux and OpenVPN 2.1.1. The first client was running Fedora 12 Linux and OpenVPN 2.1.1.

How to do it...

1. Create the server configuration file:

```
tls-server
proto udp
port 1194
dev tap

server 192.168.99.0 255.255.255.0

ca      /etc/openvpn/cookbook/ca.crt
cert    /etc/openvpn/cookbook/server.crt
key     /etc/openvpn/cookbook/server.key
```

```
dh       /etc/openvpn/cookbook/dh1024.pem
tls-auth /etc/openvpn/cookbook/ta.key 0

persist-key
persist-tun
keepalive 10 60

push "route 10.198.0.0 255.255.0.0"

user   nobody
group nobody

daemon
log-append /var/log/openvpn.log
```

Save it as example-3-1-server.conf. Note that on some Linux distributions, the group nogroup is used instead of nobody.

2. Start the server:

    [root@server]# openvpn --config example3-1-server.conf

3. Set up IP forwarding and an iptables masquerading rule:

    [root@server]# sysctl -w net.ipv4.ip_forward=1

    **[root@server]# iptables -t nat -I POSTROUTING -i tap+ -o eth0 **
      -s 192.168.99.0/24 -j MASQUERADE

4. Next, create the client configuration file:

    ```
    client
    proto udp
    remote openvpnserver.example.com
    port 1194
    dev tap
    nobind
    ca   /etc/openvpn/cookbook/ca.crt
    cert /etc/openvpn/cookbook/client1.crt
    key  /etc/openvpn/cookbook/client1.key
    tls-auth /etc/openvpn/cookbook/ta.key 1
    ns-cert-type server
    ```

    Save it as example-3-1-client.conf.

5. Start the client:

    ```
    [root@client]# openvpn --config example3-1-client.conf
    ```

```
┌─┬──────────────────────────── Example 3-1 ──────────────────────── _ □ ×─┐
│ File  Edit  View  Terminal  Tabs  Help                                    │
│ [client] # openvpn --config example3-1-client.conf                     ▲ │
│ Fri Jun 11 15:47:12 2010 OpenVPN 2.1.1 x86_64-redhat-linux-gnu [SSL] [LZO2] [EPOLL] [PKCS11]│
│ built on Jan  5 2010                                                       │
│ Fri Jun 11 15:47:12 2010 NOTE: OpenVPN 2.1 requires '--script-security 2' or higher to call u│
│ ser-defined scripts or executables                                        │
│ Fri Jun 11 15:47:12 2010 Control Channel Authentication: using '/etc/openvpn/cookbook/ta.key'│
│  as a OpenVPN static key file                                             │
│ Fri Jun 11 15:47:12 2010 UDPv4 link local: [undef]                        │
│ Fri Jun 11 15:47:12 2010 UDPv4 link remote: 194.171.96.27:1194            │
│ Fri Jun 11 15:47:12 2010 [openvpnserver] Peer Connection Initiated with 194.171.96.27:1194│
│ Fri Jun 11 15:47:14 2010 TUN/TAP device tap0 opened                       │
│ Fri Jun 11 15:47:14 2010 /sbin/ip link set dev tap0 up mtu 1500           │
│ Fri Jun 11 15:47:14 2010 /sbin/ip addr add dev tap0 192.168.99.2/24 broadcast 192.168.99.255│
│ Fri Jun 11 15:47:14 2010 Initialization Sequence Completed             ▼ │
└───────────────────────────────────────────────────────────────────────────┘
```

6. After the connection is established, we can verify that it is working by pinging the server:

    ```
    [client]$ ping -c 2 192.168.99.1
    PING 192.168.99.1 (192.168.99.1) 56(84) bytes of data.
    64 bytes from 192.168.99.1: icmp_seq=1 ttl=64 time=25.3 ms
    64 bytes from 192.168.99.1: icmp_seq=2 ttl=64 time=25.2 ms
    ```

    And that we can ping a host on the server-side LAN:

    ```
    [client]$ ping -c 2 10.198.0.1
    PING 10.198.0.1 (10.198.0.1) 56(84) bytes of data.
    64 bytes from 10.198.0.1: icmp_seq=1 ttl=63 time=29.2 ms
    64 bytes from 10.198.0.1: icmp_seq=2 ttl=63 time=25.3 ms
    ```

How it works...

When the server starts, it configures the first available TAP interface with IP address 192.168.99.1. After that, the server listens on the UDP port 1194 for incoming connections that serves as a OpenVPN default.

The client connects to the server on this port. After the initial TLS handshake using both the client and server certificates, the client is assigned the IP address 192.168.99.2. The client configures its first available TAP interface using this information, after which the VPN is established.

Apart from the OpenVPN configuration, this recipe also uses an `iptables` command to enable the client to reach the Site B's LAN without having to set up additional routes on the Site B's LAN gateway. The following command instructs the Linux kernel to rewrite all the traffic that is coming from the subnet `192.168.99.0/24` (that is our OpenVPN subnet) and that is leaving the Ethernet interface `eth0`:

```
[root@server]# iptables -t nat -I POSTROUTING -i tap+ -o eth0 \
-s 192.168.99.0/24 -j MASQUERADE
```

Each of these packets has its source address rewritten so that it appears as if it is coming from the OpenVPN server itself instead of coming from the OpenVPN client. `iptables` keeps track of these rewritten packets so that when a return packet is received, the reverse is done and the packets are forwarded back to the OpenVPN client again. This is an easy method to enable routing to work, but there is a drawback when many clients are used: it is no longer possible to distinguish traffic on the Site B's LAN if it is coming from the OpenVPN server itself, from client1via the VPN tunnel or from clientN via the VPN tunnel.

There's more...

There are several pitfalls to watch out for when using the 'client-to-client' directive. A few of the most common ones are outlined here.

Differences between TUN and TAP

The differences between this setup and the recipe *Server-side routing* of the previous chapter are minimal. There are a few subtle differences, however, which can lead to unforeseen effects if you are not aware of them:

- ▶ When using a TAP adapter, the full Ethernet frame is encapsulated. This causes a slightly larger overhead.
- ▶ All the machines that are connected to a TAP-style network form a single broadcast domain. The effects of this will become clearer in the next recipe.
- ▶ If bridging is needed, a TAP-style tunnel is required.

Using the TCP protocol

In this example, we chose the UDP protocol. The configuration files in this recipe can easily be converted to use TCP protocol by changing the line:

```
proto udp
```

Change it to:

```
proto tcp
```

Do this in both the client and server configuration files.

The UDP protocol normally gives optimal performance, but some routers and firewalls have problems forwarding UDP traffic. In that case, the TCP protocol often does work.

Making IP fowarding permanent

On most Linux systems, the proper way to permanently set up IP forwarding is:

▸ Add the following line to the `/etc/sysctl.con` file:

```
net.ipv4.ip_forward=1
```

▸ Reload the `sysctl.conf` file using:

```
[root@server]# sysctl -p
```

See also

▸ *Chapter 2*'s recipe, *Server-side routing*, in which a basic TUN-style setup is explained.

Enabling client-to-client traffic

This recipe is a continuation of the previous recipe. It will demonstrate how to set up a TAP-based connection in client or server mode using certificates. By using the `client-to-client` directive, it will also enable different OpenVPN clients to contact each other. For TAP-based networks, this has some important side-effects.

Getting ready

We use the following network layout:

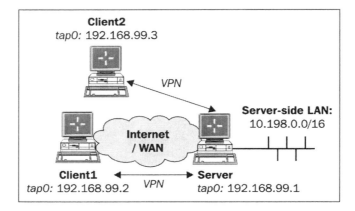

Set up the client and server certificates using the first recipe from *Chapter 2, Client-server IP-only Networks*.

For this recipe, the server was running CentOS 5 Linux and OpenVPN 2.1.1; one client was running Windows 2000 SP4 and OpenVPN 2.1.1, the other client was running Windows XP SP3 and OpenVPN 2.1.1. For the server, keep the configuration file `example3-1-server.conf` from the previous recipe at hand.

How to do it...

1. Create the server configuration file by adding a line to the `example3-1-server.conf` file:

   ```
   client-to-client
   ```

   Save it as `example-3-2-server.conf`.

2. Start the server:

   ```
   [root@server]# openvpn --config example3-2-server.conf
   ```

3. Set up IP forwarding and an `iptables` masquerading rule:

   ```
   [root@server]# sysctl -w net.ipv4.ip_forward=1
   [root@server]# iptables -t nat -I POSTROUTING -i tap+ -o eth0 \
   -s 192.168.99.0/24 -j MASQUERADE
   ```

4. Next, create the client configuration file for the first client:

   ```
   client
   proto udp
   remote openvpnserver.example.com
   port 1194

   dev tap
   nobind

   ca       "c:/program files/openvpn/config/ca.crt"
   cert     "c:/program files/openvpn/config/client1.crt"
   key      "c:/program files/openvpn/config/client1.key"
   tls-auth "c:/program files/openvpn/config/ta.key" 1

   ns-cert-type server

   verb 5
   ```

   Save it as `example-3-2-client1.ovpn`.

5. Similarly, for the second client create the configuration file:

```
client
proto udp
remote openvpnserver.example.com
port 1194

dev tap
nobind

ca       "c:/program files/openvpn/config/ca.crt"
cert     "c:/program files/openvpn/config/client2.crt"
key      "c:/program files/openvpn/config/client2.key"
tls-auth "c:/program files/openvpn/config/ta.key" 1

ns-cert-type server

verb 5
```

And save it as `example-3-2-client2.ovpn`.

6. Start the Windows clients on the command line or from the OpenVPN GUI:

[WinClient1]C:> cd \program files\openvpn\config

[WinClient1]C:> ..\bin\openvpn --config example3-2-client1.ovpn

Client2:

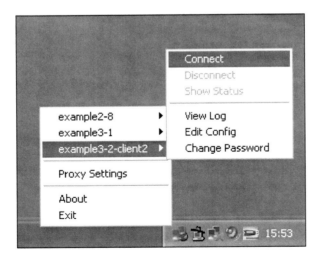

7. After the connection is established, we can verify that it is working by pinging the server:

```
[WinClient1]C:> ping 192.168.99.1

   Pinging 192.168.99.1 with 32 bytes of data:

   Reply from 192.168.99.1: bytes=32 time=24ms TTL=64
   Reply from 192.168.99.1: bytes=32 time=25ms TTL=64
```

And also that we can ping the second client:

```
[WinClient1]C:> ping 192.168.99.3

   Pinging 192.168.99.3 with 32 bytes of data:

   Reply from 192.168.99.3: bytes=32 time=49ms TTL=128
   Reply from 192.168.99.3: bytes=32 time=50ms TTL=128
```

Notice the higher round-trip time.

8. Finally, verify that we can still ping a host on the server-side LAN:

```
[WinClient1]C:\> ping -c 2 10.198.0.9


   Pinging 10.198.0.9 with 32 bytes of data:

   Reply from 10.198.0.9: bytes=32 time=25ms TTL=63
   Reply from 10.198.0.9: bytes=32 time=25ms TTL=63
```

How it works...

Both clients connect to the OpenVPN server in the regular manner. The following directive is all that is needed for the clients to "see" each other:

```
client-to-client
```

Communication between the clients will still pass through the OpenVPN server, which explains the higher round-trip time for the ICMP packets. The flow of an ICMP (ping) echo and reply is:

1. The OpenVPN client encrypts the packet and forwards it to the server over a secure link.

2. The server decrypts the packet and determines that the packet needs to be forwarded to another OpenVPN client. Therefore, the packet is not forwarded to the kernel routing modules but is encrypted again and is forwarded to the second client.

3. The second client receives the packet, decrypts it, and sends a reply back to the server over the secure link.

4. The server decrypts the reply packet and determines that the packet needs to be forwarded to first client. Therefore, the packet is not forwarded to the kernel routing modules but is encrypted again and is forwarded to the original client.

There's more...

Broadcast traffic may affect scalability

All machines that are connected to a TAP-style network form a single broadcast domain. When `client-to-client` is enabled, this means that all the broadcast traffic from all the clients is forwarded to all other clients. Wireshark running on `client2` indeed shows a lot of broadcast packets from `client1`, all of which passed through the OpenVPN server. This can lead to a scalability problem when a large number of clients are connected.

Filtering traffic

In the current version of OpenVPN, it is not possible to filter the traffic between VPN clients when the `client-to-client` directive is used. A future version of OpenVPN will have this functionality. It is also possible to enable client-to-client communications without the `client-to-client` directive, but this requires some `iptables` rules. The advantage is that you can then use the normal `iptables` commands to filter the client-to-client traffic. The downside is that it is less efficient.

TUN-style networks

The `client-to-client` directive can also be used in TUN-style networks. It works in exactly the same manner as in this recipe, except that the OpenVPN clients do not form a single broadcast domain.

Bridging—Linux

This recipe will demonstrate how to set up a bridged OpenVPN server. In this mode, the local network and the VPN network are bridged, which means that all the traffic from one network is forwarded to the other and vice versa.

This setup is often used to securely connect remote clients to a Windows-based LAN, but it is quite hard to get it right. In almost all cases, it suffices to use a TUN-style network with a local WINS server on the OpenVPN server itself. A bridged VPN does have its advantages, however, that will become apparent in the next few recipes.

However, there are also disadvantages to using bridging, especially in terms of performance: the performance of a bridged 100 Mbps Ethernet adapter is about half the performance of a non-bridged adapter.

Getting ready

We use the following network layout:

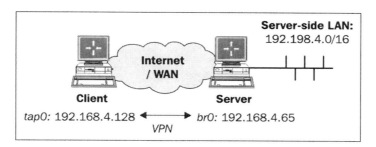

Set up the client and server certificates using the first recipe from *Chapter 2, Client-server IP-only networks*. For this recipe, the server computer was running Fedora 12 Linux and OpenVPN 2.1.1. The client computer was running Windows XP and OpenVPN 2.1.1. For the Windows client, keep the client configuration file `example3-2-client2.ovpn` at hand.

How to do it...

1. Create the server configuration file:

```
proto udp
port 1194
dev tap0 ## the '0' is extremely important

server-bridge 192.168.4.65 255.255.255.0 192.168.4.128
192.168.4.200
push "route 192.168.4.0 255.255.255.0"
ca        /etc/openvpn/cookbook/ca.crt
cert      /etc/openvpn/cookbook/server.crt
key       /etc/openvpn/cookbook/server.key
dh        /etc/openvpn/cookbook/dh1024.pem
tls-auth /etc/openvpn/cookbook/ta.key 0

persist-key
persist-tun
keepalive 10 60

user   nobody
group  nobody

daemon
log-append /var/log/openvpn.log
```

Save it as `example-3-3-server.conf`.

2. Next, create a script to start the network bridge:

```
#!/bin/bash

br="br0"
tap="tap0"

eth="eth0"
eth_ip="192.168.4.65"
eth_netmask="255.255.255.0"
eth_broadcast="192.168.4.255"

openvpn --mktun --dev $tap

brctl addbr $br
brctl addif $br $eth
brctl addif $br $tap
ifconfig $tap 0.0.0.0 promisc up
ifconfig $eth 0.0.0.0 promisc up
ifconfig $br $eth_ip netmask $eth_netmask \
  broadcast $eth_broadcast
```

Save this script as `example3-3-bridge-start` file.

3. And, similarly, use a script for stopping the Ethernet bridge:

```
#!/bin/bash

br="br0"
tap="tap0"

ifconfig $br down
brctl delbr $br
openvpn --rmtun --dev $tap
```

Save this script as `example3-3-bridge-stop` file. These scripts are based on the example `bridge-start` and `bridge-stop` that are part of the OpenVPN distribution.

4. Create the network bridge and verify that it is working:

```
[root@server]# bash example3-3-bridge-start
  TUN/TAP device tap0 opened
  Persist state set to: ON
[root@server]# brctl show
  bridge name bridge id          STP enabled interfaces
  br0         8000.00219bd2d422 no          eth0
              tap0
```

5. Start the OpenVPN server:

```
[root@server]# openvpn --config example3-3-server.conf
```

6. Start the client:

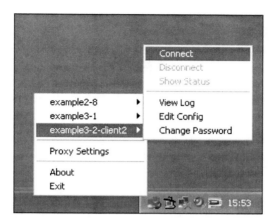

7. Check the assigned VPN address:

```
[WinClient]C:> ipconfig /all
   [...]
   Ethernet adapter tun0:
      Connection-specific DNS Suffix  . :
      Description . . . . . . . . . . . : TAP-Win32 Adapter V9
      Physical Address. . . . . . . . . : 00-FF-17-82-55-DB
      Dhcp Enabled. . . . . . . . . . . : Yes
      Autoconfiguration Enabled . . . . : Yes
      IP Address. . . . . . . . . . . . : 192.168.4.128
      Subnet Mask . . . . . . . . . . . : 255.255.255.0
      Default Gateway . . . . . . . . . :
      DHCP Server . . . . . . . . . . . : 192.168.4.0
```

8. Now, verify that we can ping a machine on the remote server LAN:

```
[WinClient]C:> ping 192.168.4.164
   Pinging 192.168.4.164 with 32 bytes of data:

   Reply from 192.168.4.164: bytes=32 time=3ms TTL=64
   Reply from 192.168.4.164: bytes=32 time=1ms TTL=64
   Reply from 192.168.4.164: bytes=32 time=1ms TTL=64
   Reply from 192.168.4.164: bytes=32 time<1ms TTL=64
```

9. Remember to tear down the network bridge after stopping the OpenVPN server:

```
[root@server]# bash example3-3-bridge-stop
    TUN/TAP device tap0 opened
    Persist state set to: OFF
```

How it works...

The `bridge-start` script forges a bond between two network adapters: on the one side, the LAN adapter `eth0` and on the other side, the VPN adapter `tap0`. The main property of a network bridge is that all the traffic is copied from one side to the other and vice versa. This allows us to set up a VPN where the client almost truly becomes a part of the server-side LAN.

The downside of a bridged network is the increased overhead and the performance penalty on the OpenVPN server itself: if there is a lot of broadcast traffic from many clients on either side, the bridge can become overloaded.

There's more...

Fixed addresses & the default gateway

In this recipe, the OpenVPN server is assigned a fixed address on the server LAN, as is done most often for a bridged interface. The difficulty with assigning a dynamic address to a network bridge is that it is not clear from which network the dynamic address should be chosen. This also enables us to specify a fixed server-bridge address in the server configuration file.

When using bridges, it is also important to check that the default route is available after the bridge is started. In most setups, `eth0` is assigned a dynamic address, including a default gateway. When the `bridge-start` script is executed, `br0` is assigned a fixed address, but as a side affect, the default gateway is often lost.

Name resolution

One of the difficulties in setting up a bridged network in the proper fashion is related to name resolution. OpenVPN only does Ethernet (Layer2) or IP-based routing. Setting up a proper name resolution system (for example, a Domain Controller and/or a WINS server in a Windows network) can also be tricky in a bridged environment.

See also

The next recipe in this chapter, in which bridging on a Windows server is explained.

Bridging—Windows

This recipe will demonstrate how to set up a bridged OpenVPN server on Windows. Bridging on Windows is slightly different from Linux or UNIX, but the concept is the same.

This recipe is very similar to the previous recipe, apart from the different methods used to set up bridging.

Getting ready

We use the following network layout:

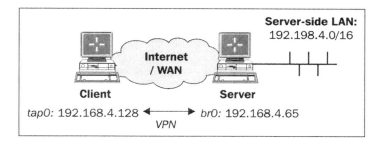

Set up the client and server certificates using the first recipe from *Chapter 2, Client-server IP-only networks*.

For this recipe, the server computer was running Windows XP and OpenVPN 2.1.1. The client computer was running Fedora 12 Linux and OpenVPN 2.1.1. For the Linux client, keep the client configuration file example3-1-client.conf at hand.

How to do it...

1. Create the server configuration file:

    ```
    proto udp
    port 1194
    dev tap
    dev-node tap-bridge

    server-bridge 172.30.0.50 255.255.255.0 172.30.0.80 170.32.0.250
    ```

```
ca        "c:/program files/openvpn/config/ca.crt"
cert      "c:/program files/openvpn/config/server.crt"
key       "c:/program files/openvpn/config/server.key"
dh        "c:/program files/openvpn/config/dh1024.pem"
tls-auth "c:/program files/openvpn/config/ta.key" 0
push "route 172.30.0.0 255.255.255.0"

persist-key
persist-tun
keepalive 10 60
```

Save it as `example-3-4-server.conf`.

2. Next, create the network bridge:

   ❑ Each TAP-Win32 adapter on Windows is assigned a name like **Local Area Connection 2**. Go to the **Network Connections** control panel and rename it to **tap-bridge**.

   ❑ Next, select **tap-bridge** and your Ethernet adapter with the mouse, right click, and then select **Bridge Connections**:

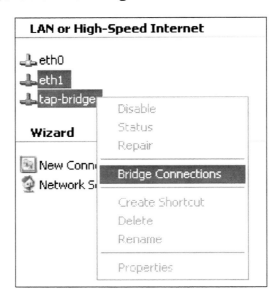

This will create a new bridge adapter icon in the control panel, usually named **Network Bridge (...)**.

3. The network bridge is now ready to be configured:

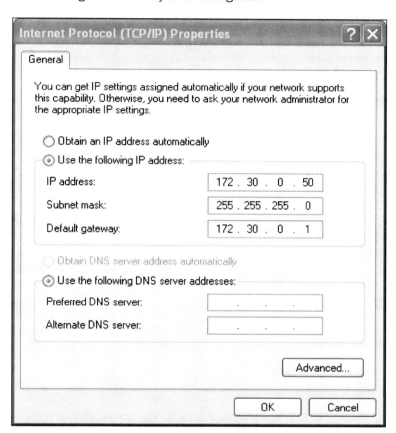

4. In a command window, verify that the bridge is configured correctly:

```
[winserver]C:> netsh interface ip show address "Network Bridge"

    Configuration for interface "Network Bridge"
    DHCP enabled:                 No
    IP Address:                   172.30.0.50
    SubnetMask:                   255.255.255.128
    Default Gateway:              172.30.0.1
    GatewayMetric:                5
    InterfaceMetric:              0
```

5. Start the OpenVPN server:

```
[winserver]C:> cd \program files\openvpn\config
[winserver]C:> ..\bin\openvpn --config example3-4-server.ovpn
```

6. Start the client:

```
[root@client]# openvpn --config example3-1-client.conf
```

7. Now, check the assigned VPN address and verify that we can ping a machine on the remote server LAN:

```
[client]$ /sbin/ifconfig tap1

    tap1   Link encap:Ethernet   HWaddr A2:F4:D4:E7:99:CF
           inet addr:172.30.0.80   Bcast:172.30.0.255
           Mask:255.255.255.0
    [...]
[client]$ ping -c 2 172.30.0.12

    PING 172.30.0.12 (172.30.0.12) 56(84) bytes of data.
    64 bytes from 172.30.0.12: icmp_seq=1 ttl=128 time=24.0 ms
    64 bytes from 172.30.0.12: icmp_seq=2 ttl=128 time=26.0 ms
```

How it works...

Apart from the way the bridge is created and configured, this recipe is very similar to the previous one. The one thing to keep in mind is how the adapter is selected in the server configuration file:

```
dev tap
dev-node tap-bridge
```

On Linux and other UNIX variants, this could be achieved using a single line:

```
dev tap0
```

But the naming scheme for the TAP adapters on Windows is different. To overcome this, the dev-node directive needs to be added.

See also

The previous recipe, where bridging on Linux is explained.

Checking broadcast and non-IP traffic

The main reason for a bridged setup is to create a single broadcast domain for all clients connected, both via the VPN and via a regular network connection.

Another reason is the ability to route or forward non-IP based traffic, such as the older Novell IPX and Appletalk protocols.

This recipe focuses on the use of tools such as tcpdump and wireshark to detect whether the broadcast domain is functioning and if non-IP traffic is flowing in the correct manner.

Getting ready

For this recipe, we use the setup from the recipe *Bridging—Linux* of this chapter. We use the following network layout:

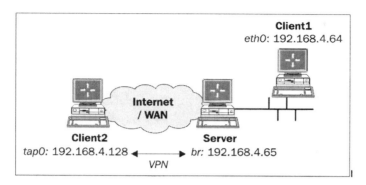

For this recipe, the server computer was running Fedora 12 Linux and OpenVPN 2.1.1. For the server, keep the server configuration file `example3-3-server.conf` from the recipe *Bridging—Linux* ready. The first client computer was running Windows 2000 and was in the same LAN segment as the OpenVPN server. The second client was running Windows XP and OpenVPN 2.1.1. For this client, keep the client configuration file `example3-2-client2.ovpn` from the recipe *Enabling client-to-client traffic* at hand.

Make sure that the Appletalk and IPX protocols are installed on both Windows machines. Bind the protocols to the Local Area Network adapters (this is the default setting).

How to do it...

1. Create the network bridge and verify that it is working:

    [root@server]# bash example3-3-bridge-start

    ```
    TUN/TAP device tap0 opened
    Persist state set to: ON
    ```
    [root@server]# brctl show

    ```
    bridge name bridge id           STP enabled interfaces
    br0         8000.00219bd2d422 no            eth0
                                                tap0
    ```

2. Start the OpenVPN server:

```
[root@server]# openvpn --config example3-3-server.conf
```

3. Start the OpenVPN clients:

```
[WinClient1]C:> cd \program files\openvpn\config
[WinClient1]C:> ..\bin\openvpn --config example3-2-client2.ovpn
```

Client 2:

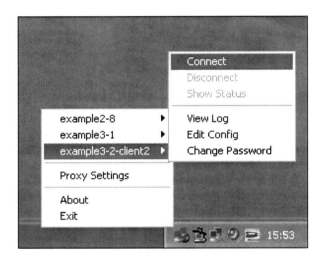

In this recipe, the Windows 2000 client was assigned **192.168.4.64**. The Windows XP client was assigned **192.168.4.128**.

4. After the client has successfully connected, we first check for ARP messages. On the server, run `tcpdump` and listen for traffic on the bridge interface `br0`:

```
[server]# tcpdump -nnel -i br0 arp
listening on br0, link-type EN10MB (Ethernet), capture size 65535 bytes
[...] ARP, Request who-has 192.168.4.64 tell 192.168.4.254,
[...] ARP, Request who-has 192.168.4.1 tell 192.168.4.254,
[...] ARP, Request who-has 192.168.4.65 tell 192.168.4.254,
[...] ARP, Reply 192.168.4.65 is-at 00:21:9b:d2:d4:22,
[...] ARP, Request who-has 192.168.4.128 tell 192.168.4.254,
[...] ARP, Reply 192.168.4.128 is-at 00:ff:17:82:55:db,
[server]#
```

In this output, **192.168.4.254** is the address of the server-side gateway. So, the gateway is asking for ARP information and the ARP replies are coming from both the OpenVPN server and the OpenVPN client itself. This can only happen if the ARP request is forwarded over the bridge to the OpenVPN client.

5. Next, on the Windows 2000 client, check for the broadcast traffic coming from the Windows XP client. For this, we use Wireshark. Wireshark is available for both Linux and Windows. Configure Wireshark to capture all the traffic from the Ethernet adapter.

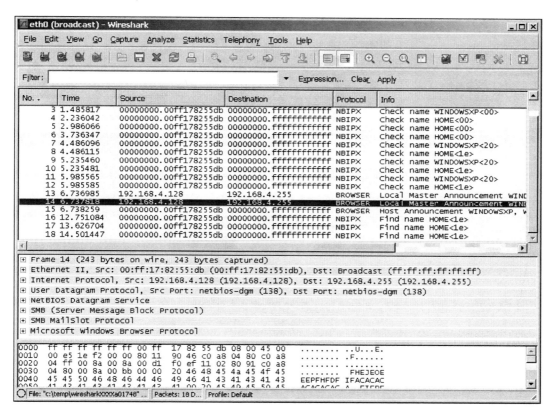

In this output, we see a lot of Netbios broadcast traffic when the OpenVPN client first connects to the network.

6. As a final example, we look for IPX traffic:

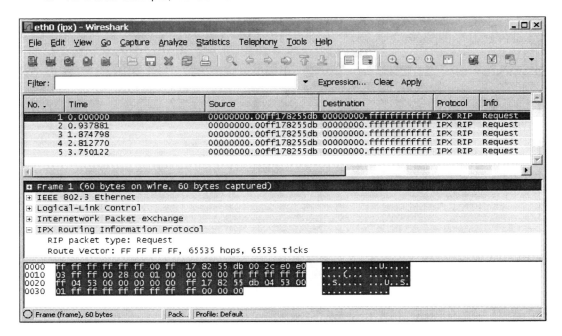

This shows that non-IP traffic is also forwarded over the bridge.

How it works...

All traffic that is forwarded over the bridge is intercepted by programs like Wireshark. By filtering for certain types of traffic, it is easy to show that in a bridged setup traffic from the OpenVPN clients is indeed flowing over the server-side LAN. This is very important when troubleshooting an "almost-working" setup.

External DHCP server

In this recipe, we will configure a bridged OpenVPN server so that it uses an external DHCP server to assign addresses to the OpenVPN clients to further increase the integration of remote clients with the clients already present on the server-side LAN.

Getting ready

We use the following network layout:

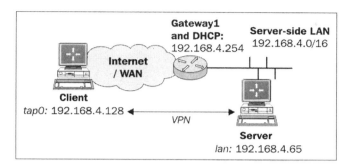

Set up the client and server certificates using the first recipe from *Chapter 2, Client-server IP-only Networks*.

For this recipe, the server computer was running Fedora 12 Linux and OpenVPN 2.1.1. The client was running Windows XP SP3 and OpenVPN 2.1.1. For this client, keep the client configuration file, example3-2-client2.ovpn, from the recipe *Enabling client-to-client traffic* at hand.

How to do it...

1. Create the server configuration file:

    ```
    proto udp
    port 1194
    dev tap0

    server-bridge
    push "route 0.0.0.0 255.255.255.255 net_gateway"

    ca        /etc/openvpn/cookbook/ca.crt
    cert      /etc/openvpn/cookbook/server.crt
    key       /etc/openvpn/cookbook/server.key
    dh        /etc/openvpn/cookbook/dh1024.pem
    tls-auth  /etc/openvpn/cookbook/ta.key 0

    persist-key
    persist-tun
    ```

```
keepalive 10 60

user  nobody
group nobody

daemon
log-append /var/log/openvpn.log
```

and save it as `example3-6-server.conf`.

2. Start the server:

    [root@server]# openvpn --config example3-6-server.conf

3. Start the Windows client:

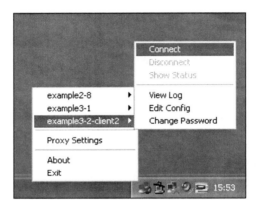

4. After the VPN connection is established, verify the IP address and the routing tables:

    [WinClient] C:> ipconfig /all

    ```
    [...]
    Ethernet adapter tapwin32-0
       Connection-specific DNS Suffix  . : lan
       Description . . . . . . . . . . . : TAP-Win32 Adapter V9
       Physical Address. . . . . . . . . : 00-FF-17-82-55-DB
       Dhcp Enabled. . . . . . . . . . . : Yes
       Autoconfiguration Enabled . . . . : Yes
       IP Address. . . . . . . . . . . . : 192.168.4.66
       Subnet Mask . . . . . . . . . . . : 255.255.255.0
       Default Gateway . . . . . . . . . : 192.168.4.254
       DHCP Server . . . . . . . . . . . : 192.168.4.254
       DNS Servers . . . . . . . . . . . : 192.168.4.254
    [...]
    ```

```
[WinClient]C:> netstat -rn
   [...]
   0.0.0.0   0.0.0.0         172.30.1.2    172.30.1.131  10
   0.0.0.0   255.255.255.255 172.30.1.2    172.30.1.131   1
   0.0.0.0   0.0.0.0         192.168.4.254 192.168.4.66   1
   Default Gateway:         172.30.1.2
   [...]
```

5. And finally, we check that we can reach other hosts in the server-side LAN:

    ```
    [WinClient]C:> ping 192.168.4.64
        Pinging 192.168.4.64 with 32 bytes of data:

        Reply from 192.168.4.64: bytes=32 time=3ms TTL=64
        Reply from 192.168.4.64: bytes=32 time=1ms TTL=64
        Reply from 192.168.4.64: bytes=32 time=1ms TTL=64
        Reply from 192.168.4.64: bytes=32 time<1ms TTL=64
    ```

How it works...

The server directive:

```
server-bridge
```

Without any parameters this instructs OpenVPN to not allocate a pool of IP addresses for the clients. So, all the incoming DHCP requests from the clients are forwarded out over the bridge. The DHCP server on the server-side LAN then replies with an IP address.

The tricky part here is that the DHCP server almost always also returns a default gateway, which will be the LAN gateway. If a remote client sets its default gateway to the gateway of the LAN, funny things will happen, as in most cases, the direct route to the OpenVPN server is lost.

The following directive instructs the OpenVPN client to add an explicit "default" route via the net_gateway, which is always the LAN gateway at the client side:

```
push "route 0.0.0.0 255.255.255.255 net_gateway"
```

For Windows clients, this trick works and the default gateway remains intact.

For Linux clients, it is easier to tweak the dhclient and network-scripts settings. However, this is distribution dependent.

With the default gateway intact, the OpenVPN client is properly assigned an address from the DHCP server on the server side.

There's more...

DHCP server configuration

The proper solution is to configure the DHCP server such that DHCP requests from the VPN clients do not get a default gateway assigned. This adds a burden to the administration of the server-side DHCP server.

In this case, it also makes sense to explicitly set a unique MAC address in each client configuration file using, for example:

```
lladdr CA:C6:F8:FB:EB:3B
```

On Linux, the MAC address is computed randomly when the TAP interface comes up, so each time the OpenVPN client is stopped and started, a new IP address is allocated. It is also possible to create a permanently-fixed MAC address by bringing up the TAP device using the system configuration scripts before OpenVPN starts.

Windows TAP devices also have a randomized initial MAC address, but this can only be changed using a Windows registry editor.

DHCP relay

It is also possible to use an external DHCP server without using bridging. If the TAP adapter is configured before OpenVPN is started and the server configuration file from this recipe is used then an external DHCP server can be used using the Linux `dhrelay` command:

[root@server]# dhrelay -i tap0 -i eth0

Make sure to list both the TAP adapter and the Ethernet adapter to which the external DHCP server is connected. By combining this with a `proxy-arp` script (see *Chapter 2*'s recipe, *Proxy ARP*), it eliminates the need to use bridging in most cases.

Tweaking the /etc/sysconfig/network-scripts

On RedHat, Fedora, and OpenSuSE-based systems, the TAP adapter is brought up using a script `/etc/sysconfig/network-scripts/ifup-tap0` and the command:

[root@client]# /sbin/ifup tap0

By adding the line to the `/etc/sysconfig/network-scripts/ifup-tap0` file, the `dhclient` script ignores the gateway that is assigned from the DHCP server:

```
GATEWAYDEV=eth0
```

A similar hack can be developed for Debian/Ubuntu-based systems.

Using the status file

OpenVPN offers several options to monitor the clients connected to a server. The most commonly-used method is using a status file. This recipe will show how to use and read the OpenVPN status file. We will also focus on some subtleties of the status file in a TAP-style setup.

Getting ready

Set up the client and server certificates using the first recipe from *Chapter 2, Client-server IP-only Networks*. For this recipe the server computer was running CentOS 5 Linux and OpenVPN 2.1.1. The first client was running Fedora 12 Linux and OpenVPN 2.1.1 . The second client was running Windows XP and OpenVPN 2.1.1. For the Linux client, keep the client configuration file example3-1-client.conf at hand. For the Windows client, keep the client configuration file example3-2-client2.ovpn at hand.

How to do it...

1. Create the server configuration file by adding a line to the example3-1-server. conf. file:

    ```
    status /var/log/openvpn.status
    ```

    Save it as example3-7-server.conf.

2. Start the server:

    ```
    [root@server]# openvpn --config example3-7-server.conf
    ```

3. First, start the Linux client using the configuration file from the earlier recipe and ping a host on the remote network:

    ```
    [root@client1]# openvpn --config example3-1-client.conf
    [root@client1]# ping 10.198.0.1
    ```

4. After the VPN is established, list the contents of the openvpn.status file (as user root):

    ```
    [root@server]# cat /var/log/openvpn.status
    OpenVPN CLIENT LIST
    Updated,Fri Jun  4 13:34:39 2010
    Common Name,Real Address,Bytes Received,Bytes Sent,Connected
    Since
    openvpnclient1,192.168.4.65:50183,10024,10159,Fri Jun  4
    13:26:48 2010
    ROUTING TABLE
    ```

```
Virtual Address,Common Name,Real Address,Last Ref
5e:52:73:5c:6a:ce,openvpnclient1,192.168.4.65:50183,Fri Jun  4
13:27:06 2010
GLOBAL STATS
Max bcast/mcast queue length,1
END
```

5. Start the Windows client:

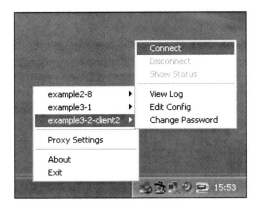

6. Ping a host on the remote network:

   [WinClient2]C:> ping 10.198.0.1

7. List the contents of the status file again on the server:

   [root@server]# cat /var/log/openvpn.status

```
OpenVPN CLIENT LIST
Updated,Fri Jun  4 13:34:39 2010
Common Name,Real Address,Bytes Received,Bytes Sent,Connected
Since
openvpnclient1,192.168.4.65:50183,10024,10159,Fri Jun  4
13:27:08 2010
openvpnclient2,192.168.4.64:50186,18055,9726,Fri Jun  4 13:26:48
2010
ROUTING TABLE
Virtual Address,Common Name,Real Address,Last Ref
5e:52:73:5c:6a:ce,openvpnclient1,192.168.4.65:50183,Fri Jun  4
13:27:06 2010
00:ff:17:82:55:db,openvpnclient2,192.168.4.64:50186,Fri Jun  4
13:27:16 2010
GLOBAL STATS
Max bcast/mcast queue length,1
END
```

How it works...

Each time a client connects to the OpenVPN server, the status file is updated with the connection information. The **OPENVPN CLIENT LIST** and **ROUTING TABLE** are the most interesting tables, as they show:

- ▶ Which clients are connected
- ▶ From which IP address the clients are connecting
- ▶ The number of bytes each client has received and transferred
- ▶ The time at which the client connected

The routing table also shows which networks are routed to each client. This routing table is filled when clients start sending traffic that needs to be routed. The `ping` commands in the recipe were used to trigger the routing table entries.

There's more...

Difference with TUN-style networks

The major difference in the status file when using a 'tap'-style network compared to a 'tun'-style network (see the *Chapter 2* recipe, *Using the status file*) is in the **ROUTING TABLE**. The recipe from the previous chapter shows:

```
192.168.200.2,openvpnclient1,192.168.4.65:56764,<Date>
```

Whereas in this recipe, we see:

```
5e:52:73:5c:6a:ce,openvpnclient1,192.168.4.65:50183,<Date>
```

The address `5e:52:73:5c:6a:ce` is the randomly-chosen MAC address of the 'tap' adapter on the `openvpnclient1` machine.

Disconnecting clients

Note that when a client disconnects, the status file is not updated immediately. OpenVPN first tries to reconnect to the client based on the `keepalive` parameters in the server configuration file. The server configuration file in this recipe uses:

```
keepalive 10 60
```

This tells the server that it will ping the client every 10th second. The OpenVPN server will double the second argument: if it does not get response after 2 * 60 seconds, the connection is restarted. The server will also tell the client to ping the server every 10 seconds and to restart the connection after 60 seconds if it does not get any response.

If the client explicitly closes the connection using the directive `explicit-exit-notify` or when a TCP-based setup is used, the server does not wait for ping responses from the client.

See also

Chapter 2's recipe, *Using the status file*, which explains how the status file can be configured and used for IP-only style networks.

Management interface

This recipe shows how OpenVPN can be managed using the management interface on the server.

Getting ready

We use the following network layout:

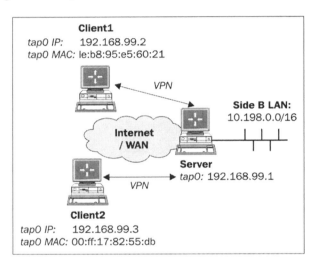

Set up the client and server certificates using the first recipe from *Chapter 2, Client-server IP-only Networks*. For this recipe, the server computer was running CentOS 5 Linux and OpenVPN 2.1.1. For the server, keep the configuration file `example3-1-server.conf` from the first recipe of this chapter at hand. The first client was running Fedora 12 Linux and OpenVPN 2.1.1. The second client was running Windows XP and OpenVPN 2.1.1. For the Linux client, keep the client configuration file `example3-1-client.conf` from the first recipe of this chapter at hand. For the Windows client, keep the client configuration file `example3-2-client2.ovpn` from the recipe *Enabling client-to-client traffic* at hand.

How to do it...

1. Create the server configuration file by adding a line to the `example3-1-server.conf` file:

    ```
    management tunnel 23000 stdin
    ```

    And save it as `example3-8-server.conf`.

2. Start the server:

    ```
    [root@server]# openvpn --config example3-8-server.conf
    ```

    The OpenVPN server will now first ask for a password for the management interface.

3. Start the clients using the configuration files from the earlier recipe:

    ```
    [root@client1]# openvpn --config example3-1-client.conf
    ```

    And the Windows client:

    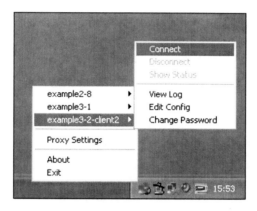

4. After the VPN is established, we can connect from the server to the management interface of the OpenVPN client using the `telnet` program:

    ```
    [server]$ telnet 127.0.0.1 23000
    ```

    ```
    Trying 127.0.0.1...
    Connected to localhost.localdomain (127.0.0.1).
    Escape character is '^]'.
    ENTER PASSWORD:cookbook
    SUCCESS: password is correct
    >INFO:OpenVPN Management Interface Version 1 -- type 'help' for
    more info
    ```

    ```
    status
    OpenVPN CLIENT LIST
    ```

```
Updated,Fri Jun  4 13:57:07 2010
Common Name,Real Address,Bytes Received,Bytes Sent,Connected Since
openvpnclient1,192.168.4.64:50209,7851,8095,Fri Jun  4 13:56:08
2010
openvpnclient2,192.168.4.5:50212,11696,7447,Fri Jun  4 13:56:45
2010
ROUTING TABLE
Virtual Address,Common Name,Real Address,Last Ref
00:ff:17:82:55:db,openvpnclient2,192.168.4.5:50212,Fri Jun  4
13:56:49 2010
1e:b8:95:e5:60:21,openvpnclient1,192.168.4.64:50209,Fri Jun  4
13:56:53 2010
GLOBAL STATS
Max bcast/mcast queue length,1
END
```

Note that it looks exactly like the status file from the previous recipe.

5. It is also possible to disconnect a client:

   kill openvpnclient2
   ```
   SUCCESS: common name 'openvpnclient2' found, 1 client(s) killed
   ```

   status
   ```
   OpenVPN CLIENT LIST
   Updated,Fri Jun  4 13:58:51 2010
   Common Name,Real Address,Bytes Received,Bytes Sent,Connected Since
   openvpnclient1,192.168.4.64:50209,8381,8625,Fri Jun  4 13:56:08
   2010
   ROUTING TABLE
   Virtual Address,Common Name,Real Address,Last Ref
   1e:b8:95:e5:60:21,openvpnclient1,192.168.4.64:50209,Fri Jun  4
   13:56:53 2010
   GLOBAL STATS
   Max bcast/mcast queue length,1
   END
   ```

6. Use Ctrl+] or "exit" to exit the 'telnet' program.

How it works...

When the OpenVPN server starts a special management interface is set up using
the directive:

```
management 127.0.0.1 23000 stdin
```

And with these parameters:

- ▸ `127.0.0.1` to bind the management interface to localhost only.
- ▸ The port `23000` on which the management interface will be listening.
- ▸ The last parameter is the password file or the special keyword `stdin` to indicate that the management interface password will be specified when OpenVPN starts up. Note that this password is completely unrelated to the private key passphrases or any other user management passwords that OpenVPN uses.

After the management interface comes up, the server operator can connect to it using `telnet` and can query the server. By typing the following the operator can disconnect a client:

```
kill <clientcommonname>
```

Note that if the OpenVPN client is configured to automatically reconnect, it will do so after a few minutes.

When comparing the output of the management interface `status` command to the status file output shown in the *Chapter 2* recipe, *Using the status file*, the major difference is the fact that here the clients MAC addresses are listed instead of the VPN IP addresses. The OpenVPN does not even need to know the clients' IP addresses, as they can be assigned by an external DHCP server.

There's more...

Client side management interface

The management interface can also be run on the OpenVPN clients. See Management interface in *Chapter 2, Client-server IP-only Networks*.

It is expected that the management interface will become more important in future versions of OpenVPN both on the client and the server side as the preferred method for programmatically interacting with the OpenVPN software.

See also

- ▸ *Chapter 2*'s recipe, *Management interface*, in which the client-side management interface is explained
- ▸ *Chapter 2*'s recipe, *Using the status file*, where the details of the status file for a TUN-style network are explained.

4

PKI, Certificates, and OpenSSL

In this chapter, we will cover:

- ▶ Certificate generation
- ▶ xCA: a GUI for managing a PKI (Part 1)
- ▶ xCA: a GUI for managing a PKI (Part 2)
- ▶ OpenSSL tricks: x509, pkcs12, verify output
- ▶ Revoking certificates
- ▶ The use of CRLs
- ▶ Checking expired/revoked certificates
- ▶ Intermediary CAs
- ▶ Multiple CAs: stacking, using --capath

Introduction

This chapter is a small detour into the Public Key Infrastructures (PKIs), certificates, and `openssl` commands. The primary purpose of the recipes in this chapter is to show how the certificates, which are used in OpenVPN, can be generated, managed, viewed, and what kind of interactions exist between OpenSSL and OpenVPN.

Certificate generation

This recipe will demonstrate how to create and sign a certificate request using plain `openssl` commands. This is slightly different from using the `easy-rsa` scripts, but very instructive.

Getting ready

Set up the `easy-rsa` certificate environment using the first recipe from *Chapter 2, Client-server IP-only Networks*, by sourcing the `vars` file. This recipe was performed on a computer running Fedora 12 Linux but it can easily be run on Windows or MacOS.

How to do it...

Before we can use plain `openssl` commands to generate and sign a request, there are a few environment variables that need to be set. These variables are not set in the `vars` file by default.

1. Add the missing environment variables:

   ```
   $ cd /etc/openvpn/cookbook
   $ . ./vars
   $ export KEY_CN=dummy
   $ export KEY_OU=dummy
   $ export KEY_NAME=dummy
   $ export OPENSSL_CONF=/etc/openvpn/cookbook/openssl.cnf
   ```

   Note that the `openssl.cnf` file is part of the easy-rsa distribution and should already be present in the directory `/etc/openvpn/cookbook`.

2. Next, we generate the certificate request without a password. This is achieved by adding the option `-nodes` to the `openssl req` command:

   ```
   $ openssl req -nodes -newkey rsa:1024 -new -out client.req \
     -subj "/C=NL/O=Cookbook/CN=MyClient"
   Generating a 1024 bit RSA private key
   .....................................++++++
   ............++++++
   writing new private key to 'privkey.pem'
   -----
   ```

3. Finally, we sign the certificate request using the Certificate Authority private key:

```
$ openssl ca -in client.req -out client.crt
    Using configuration from /etc/openvpn/cookbook/openssl.cnf
    Enter pass phrase for /etc/openvpn/cookbook/keys/ca.key:
    [enter CA key password]
    Check that the request matches the signature
    Signature ok
    The Subject's Distinguished Name is as follows
    countryName           :PRINTABLE:'NL'
    organizationName      :PRINTABLE:'Cookbook'
    commonName            :PRINTABLE:'MyClient'
    Certificate is to be certified until Jun 15 13:46:40 2020 GMT
    (3650 days)
    Sign the certificate? [y/n]:y
    1 out of 1 certificate requests certified, commit? [y/n]y
    Write out database with 1 new entries
    Data Base Updated
```

How it works...

The first step is always to generate a private key. In this recipe, we generate a private key without a password which is not really secure. A certificate request is signed using the private key to prove that the certificate request and the private key belong together. The `openssl req` command generates both the private key and the certificate requests in one go.

The second step is to sign the certificate request using the private key of the Certificate Authority (CA). This results in an X.509 certificate file, which can be used in OpenVPN.

A copy of the (public) X.509 certificate is also stored in the `/etc/openvpn/cookbook/keys` directory. This copy is important if the certificate needs to be revoked later on, so do not remove it from that directory.

There's more...

It is also possible to generate a private key protected by a password ("pass phrase" in OpenSSL terms). In order to generate such a private key, simply remove the `-nodes` command line parameter:

```
$ openssl req -newkey rsa:1024 -new -out client.req \
    -subj "/C=NL/O=Cookbook/CN=MyClient"
```

The OpenSSL command will now ask for a passphrase:

```
    Enter PEM pass phrase:
    Verifying - Enter PEM pass phrase:
```

See also

Chapter 2, Setting up the Public and Private Keys, where the initial setup of the PKI using the `easy-rsa` scripts is explained.

xCA: a GUI for managing a PKI (Part 1)

In this recipe, we will demonstrate the use of xCA, a graphical tool for managing a public key infrastructure (PKI). xCA—available for Linux, Windows, and Mac OS—is open source software and can be downloaded from `http://xca.sourceforge.net`. In this recipe, we use the Windows version of xCA. This recipe is the first of two parts: in this recipe, we create the xCA database and import the CA certificate and private key. In the next recipe, we create a new certificate using the xCA GUI.

Getting ready

Download and install `setupj_xca-0.8.1.exe` from `http://xca.sourceforge.net`. This recipe was tested on a PC running Windows XP SP3.

Copy the files `ca.key` and `ca.crt` from the `easy-rsa` certificate environment of the first recipe from *Chapter 2, Client-server IP-only Networks*, to the Windows PC.

How to do it...

1. Start **xCA** and create a new database using **File | New Database**. Choose a path for the new xCA database file and click on the **OK** button.

2. Next, choose a password for the database:

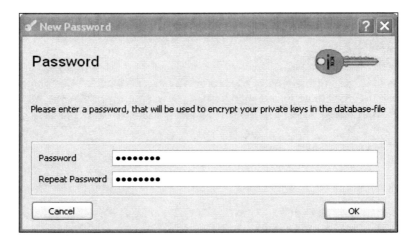

3. In the tab, **Private key**, click on **Import** to import the `ca.key` file. You will be asked to type in the password that was used to encrypt the CA private key:

4. Click on the tab **Certificates** and click on **Import** again. Now, import the `ca.crt` file. After the `ca.crt` file has been properly installed, right-click on it and select **Trust**:

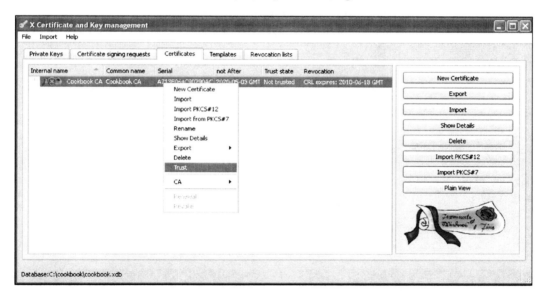

5. In the next dialog, click on **Always trust this certificate** and then on **OK**:

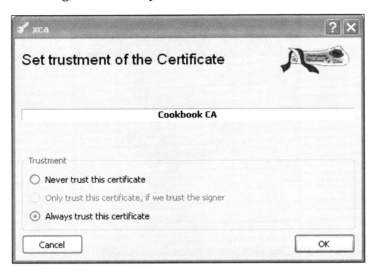

By trusting the CA certificate, it will allow us to generate and sign new certificates.

How it works...

xCA stores all the public and private keys in a database. This database must be protected using a strong password, as it can be used to sign and revoke all the certificates that we want to use in our OpenVPN setups.

There's more...

For this recipe, we choose xCA as the PKI solution. There are many PKI solutions available, both open source and commercial. For example:

▶ tinyCA: http://tinyca.sm-zone.net/

▶ OpenCA: http://www.openca.org

xCA: a GUI for managing a PKI (Part 2)

This recipe is the second part explaining how to use xCA, a graphical tool for managing a public key infrastructure (PKI). In this recipe, we create a new certificate using the xCA GUI.

Getting ready

First, read the previous recipe and follow the instructions.

How to do it...

1. Start **xCA** and open our database using **File | Open Database**. Click on the tab **Certificates** and then right-click on our CA certificate. Choose the option **New certificate**. A dialog box will appear. Click on the tab **Source** and fill in the details **Internal name**, **Country Code**, **Organisation**, **Common name**, and **Email Address**:

2. Do not press **OK**; press **Generate a new key** first:

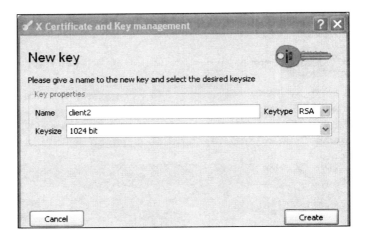

Select the **Keysize** as **1024 bit** (or higher, if desired) and click on the **Create** button.

3. Next, fill in the tab **Extensions** as follows:

- ❏ Select for **Type**, **End Entity**.
- ❏ Mark the checkbox **Subject Key Identifer** as enabled.
- ❏ Mark the checkbox **Authority Key Identifer** as enabled.

4. Finally, go to the tab **Key Usage** and do as follows:

- ❏ In the column **Key Usage**, select **Digital Signature**.
- ❏ In the column **Extended Key Usage**, select **TLS Web Client Authentication** for an OpenVPN client certificate. For an OpenVPN server certificate, choose **TLS Web Server Authentication**. Never choose both for the same certificate! Press **OK** to generate the certificate.

❏ As a last step, we export the certificate for use with OpenVPN. In the tab **Certificates**, select the **client2** certificate and press **Export**:

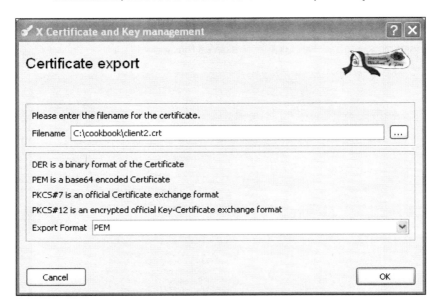

Choose the name as client2.crt and click on **OK**. Go the **Private Keys** tab and do the same for the **client2** private key. Choose the name client2.key.

How it works...

By selecting our CA certificate and choosing the **New certificate**, xCA generates a new certificate that is signed by this CA. Before a certificate can be signed, all appropriate X.509 fields such as **Key usage** and **Extended Key usage** need to be filled in. This recipe also demonstrates that even with a GUI it is still not trivial to manage a proper Public Key Infrastructure (PKI).

There's more...

The xCA GUI has many more features for the generation of certificates, Certificate Revocation Lists (CRLs), and other PKI-related subjects, but that is outside the scope of this book.

OpenSSL tricks: x509, pkcs12, verify output

The OpenSSL commands may seem daunting at first, but there are a lot of useful commands in the OpenSSL toolbox for viewing and managing X.509 certificates and private keys. This recipe will show how to use a few of those commands.

Getting ready

Set up the `easy-rsa` certificate environment using the first recipe from *Chapter 2* by sourcing the `vars` file. This recipe was performed on a computer running Fedora 12 Linux but it can easily be run on Windows or MacOS.

How to do it...

1. To view the subject and expiry date of a given certificate, type:

   ```
   $ cd /etc/openvpn/cookbook/keys
   $ openssl x509 -subject -enddate -noout -in openvpnclient1.crt
       subject= /C=NL/O=Cookbook/CN=openvpnclient1/emailAddress=[...]
           notAfter=Jan 30 12:00:09 2013 GMT
   ```

2. To export a certificate and private key in PKCS12 format:

   ```
   $ openssl pkcs12 -export -in openvpnclient1.crt \
     -inkey openvpnclient1.key -out openvpnclient1.p12
       Enter Export Password:[Choose a strong password]
       Verifying - Enter Export Password:[Type the password again]
   $ chmod 600 openvpnclient1.p12
   ```

   Note that the `chmod 600` ensures that the PKCS12 file is readable only by the user.

3. Verify the purpose of a given certificate:

   ```
   $ openssl verify -purpose sslclient -CAfile ca.crt \
     openvpnclient1.crt
     openvpnclient1.crt: OK
   ```

4. Notice the error if we select the wrong purpose (`sslclient` versus `sslserver`):

   ```
   $ openssl verify -purpose sslclient -CAfile ca.crt \
     openvpnserver.crt
     openvpnserver.crt: C = NL, O = Cookbook, CN = openvpnserver,
     emailAddress = openvpn-ca@cookbook.example.com
     error 26 at 0 depth lookup:unsupported certificate purpose
     OK
   ```

5. Change the password (passphrase) of a certificate:

   ```
   $ openssl rsa -in openvpnclient2.key -aes256 -out newclient.key
     Enter pass phrase for keys/openvpnclient2.key:[old password]
     writing RSA key
     Enter PEM pass phrase:[new password]
     Verifying - Enter PEM pass phrase:[new password]
   ```

How it works...

The OpenSSL toolkit consists of a wide range of commands to generate, manipulate, and view X.509 certificates and their corresponding private keys. The commands in this chapter are but a small subset of the available commands. On Linux and UNIX systems, you can use openssl -h and the manual pages for x509, pkcs12, and req for more details. The manual pages are also available online at:

http://www.openssl.org/docs/apps/openssl.html

Click on the OpenSSL commands lower down in the list of all commands for direct pointers.

Revoking certificates

A common task when managing a PKI is to revoke certificates that are no longer needed or that have been compromised. This recipe demonstrates how certificates can be revoked using the easy-rsa script and how OpenVPN can be configured to make use of a Certificate Revocation List (CRL).

Getting ready

Set up the client and server certificates using the first recipe from *Chapter 2*. This recipe was performed on a computer running CentOS 5 Linux, but it can easily be run on Windows or Mac OS.

How to do it...

1. First, we generate a certificate:

```
$ cd /etc/openvpn/cookbook
$ . ./vars
$ ./build-key client4
[...]
```

2. Then, we immediately revoke it:

```
$ ./revoke-full client4
Using configuration from /etc/openvpn/cookbook/openssl.cnf
Revoking Certificate 08.
Data Base Updated
Using configuration from /etc/openvpn/cookbook/openssl.cnf
client4.crt: /C=NL/O=Cookbook/CN=client4/emailAddress=[...]
error 23 at 0 depth lookup:certificate revoked
```

3. This will also update the CRL list. The CRL can be viewed using the command:

```
$ openssl crl -text -noout -in crl.pem
```

```
[openvpnserver]# openssl crl -text -noout -in crl.pem  | head -15
Certificate Revocation List (CRL):
        Version 1 (0x0)
        Signature Algorithm: md5WithRSAEncryption
        Issuer: /C=NL/O=Cookbook/CN=Cookbook CA/emailAddress=janjust@nikhef.nl
        Last Update: Jun 21 14:20:33 2010 GMT
        Next Update: Jul 21 14:20:33 2010 GMT
Revoked Certificates:
    Serial Number: 05
        Revocation Date: Jun 21 14:12:17 2010 GMT
    Serial Number: 08
        Revocation Date: Jun 21 14:20:33 2010 GMT
    Signature Algorithm: md5WithRSAEncryption
        97:3e:ff:50:21:dc:41:60:44:0c:20:2c:34:84:36:de:50:0f:
        2e:8d:aa:f2:0e:ea:a9:15:b5:f3:e2:52:8d:84:79:56:8e:41:
        f5:a4:f6:af:62:31:61:e9:af:b4:f0:a2:da:d5:c6:73:41:9f:
[openvpnserver]#
```

How it works...

A CRL contains a list of certificate serial numbers that have been revoked. Each serial number can be handed out by a CA only once, so this serial number is unique to this particular CA. The CRL is signed using the CA's private key, ensuring that the CRL is indeed issued by the appropriate party.

There's more...

The question "what exactly is needed to revoke a certificate" is often asked, so the following section goes a bit deeper into this.

What is needed to revoke a certificate

In order to revoke a certificate, the certificate subject ("DN") is required as well as the certificate serial number. If a certificate is lost, then it is simply not possible to revoke it. This shows how important it is to do proper PKI management, including backing up the certificates that have been handed out to users.

See also

▸ The next recipe, *The Use of CRLs*

▸ The last recipe in this chapter, *Multiple CA's: stacking, using –capath*

The use of CRLs

This recipe shows how to configure OpenVPN to use a Certificate Revocation List (CRL). It uses the CRL created in the previous recipe. This recipe is an extension of the recipe *Routing: Masquerading* in *Chapter 2* in the sense that the server and client configuration files are almost identical.

Getting ready

Set up the client and server certificates using the first recipe from *Chapter 2, Client-server IP-only Networks*. Generate the CRL using the previous recipe. For this recipe, the server computer was running CentOS 5 Linux and OpenVPN 2.1.1. The client was running Fedora 12 Linux and OpenVPN 2.1.1. Keep the server configuration file basic-udp-server.conf from the *Chapter 2*'s recipe *Server-side routing* at hand.

How to do it...

1. Copy the generated CRL to a more public directory:

   ```
   [root@server]# cd /etc/openvpn/cookbook
   [root@server]# cp keys/crl.pem .
   ```

2. Modify the server config file basic-udp-server.conf by adding the lines:

   ```
   crl-verify /etc/openvpn/cookbook/crl.pem
   ```

   Save it as example4-6-server.conf.

3. Start the server:

   ```
   [root@server]# openvpn --config example4-6-server.conf
   ```

4. Next, create the client configuration file:

   ```
   client
   proto udp
   remote openvpnserver.example.com
   port 1194
   dev tun
   nobind

   ca       /etc/openvpn/cookbook/ca.crt
   cert     /etc/openvpn/cookbook/client4.crt
   key      /etc/openvpn/cookbook/client4.key
   tls-auth /etc/openvpn/cookbook/ta.key 1

   ns-cert-type server
   ```

   and save it as example4-6-client.conf.

5. Finally, start the client:

```
[root@client]# openvpn --config example4-6-client.conf
```

The client will not be able to connect but instead the server log file shows:

```
Example 4.6

File  Edit  View  Terminal  Tabs  Help
OpenVPN 2.1.1 x86_64-unknown-linux-gnu [SSL] [LZO2] [EPOLL] built on Mar  9 2010
NOTE: OpenVPN 2.1 requires '--script-security 2' or higher to call user-defined scripts or executabl
es
Control Channel Authentication: using '/etc/openvpn/cookbook/ta.key' as a OpenVPN static key file
TUN/TAP device tun0 opened
/sbin/ifconfig tun0 192.168.200.1 pointopoint 192.168.200.2 mtu 1500
GID set to nobody
UID set to nobody
UDPv4 link local (bound): [undef]:1194
UDPv4 link remote: [undef]
Initialization Sequence Completed
192.16.186.197:39057 Re-using SSL/TLS context
192.16.186.197:39057 TLS_ERROR: BIO read tls_read_plaintext error: error:140890B2:SSL routines:SSL3_
GET_CLIENT_CERTIFICATE:no certificate returned
192.16.186.197:39057 TLS Error: TLS object -> incoming plaintext read error
192.16.186.197:39057 TLS Error: TLS handshake failed
```

This rather cryptic message proves that the client is not allowed to connect because the certificate is not valid.

How it works...

Each time a client connects to the OpenVPN server, the Certificate Revocation List (CRL) is checked to see whether the client certificate is listed. If it is, the OpenVPN server simply refuses to accept the client certificate and the connection will not be established.

There's more...

Generating a CRL is one thing and keeping it up-to-date is another. It is very important to ensure that the CRL is kept up-to-date. For this purpose, it is best to set up a cron job that updates the server CRL file overnight. There is an outstanding bug in OpenVPN related to CRL updates: each time a client connects, the OpenVPN server tries to access the CRL file. If the file is not present or not accessible, then the OpenVPN server process aborts with an error. The proper behavior would be to temporarily refuse access to the clients but unfortunately this is not the case.

See also

The last recipe in this chapter, *Multiple CAs: stacking, using –capath*, in which a more advanced use of CA and CRL is explained.

Checking expired/revoked certificates

The goal of this recipe is to give an insight into some of the internals of the OpenSSL CA commands. We will show how a certificate's status is changed from "Valid" to "Revoked", or "Expired".

Getting ready

Set up the client and server certificates using the first recipe from *Chapter 2*. This recipe was performed on a computer running CentOS 5 Linux but it can easily be run on Windows or Mac OS.

How to do it...

1. Before we can use plain `openssl` commands, there are a few environment variables that need to be set. These variables are not set in the `vars` file by default:

   ```
   $ cd /etc/openvpn/cookbook
   $ . ./vars
   $ export KEY_CN=dummy
   $ export KEY_OU=dummy
   $ export KEY_NAME=dummy
   $ export OPENSSL_CONF=/etc/openvpn/cookbook/openssl.cnf
   ```

2. Now, we can query the status of a certificate using its serial number:

   ```
   $ cd keys
   $ openssl x509 -serial -noout -in openvpnserver.crt
   serial=01
   openssl ca -status 01
   Using configuration from /etc/openvpn/cookbook/openssl.cnf

   01=Valid (V)
   ```

   This shows that our OpenVPN server certificate is still valid.

3. The certificate we revoked in the recipe *Revoking certificates* shows the following:

   ```
   $ openssl x509 -serial -noout -in client4.crt
   serial=08
   $ openssl ca -status 08
   Using configuration from /etc/openvpn/cookbook/openssl.cnf
   08=Revoked (R)
   ```

4. If we look at the file `index.txt` in the `/etc/openvpn/cookbook/keys` directory, we see:

```
V   130130115906Z                 01 unknown .../CN=openvpnserver
R   130317141936Z    100621142033Z 08 unknown .../CN=client4
```

5. Next, we modify this file using a normal text editor and replace the `R` with an `E` and we blank out the third field `100621142033Z` with spaces. This field is the timestamp when the certificate was revoked. The second line now becomes:

```
E   130317141936Z                 08 unknown .../CN=client4
```

6. Now, if we check the status again we get:

```
$ openssl ca -status 08
```

```
Using configuration from /etc/openvpn/cookbook/openssl.cnf
08=Expired (E)
```

If we generate the CRL again, we see that the certificate has been "un-revoked":

```
[server]# openssl crl -text -noout -in crl.pem  | head -15
Certificate Revocation List (CRL):
        Version 1 (0x0)
        Signature Algorithm: md5WithRSAEncryption
        Issuer: /C=NL/O=Cookbook/CN=Cookbook CA/email [...]
        Last Update: Jun 21 15:03:10 2010 GMT
        Next Update: Jul 21 15:03:10 2010 GMT
Revoked Certificates:
    Serial Number: 05
        Revocation Date: Jun 21 14:12:17 2010 GMT
        Signature Algorithm: md5WithRSAEncryption
        87:12:da:a1:d7:da:61:55:06:46:57:9e:e3:2c:1c:04:58:31:
        b2:51:fd:0e:a0:66:43:b1:db:f4:53:b9:88:68:17:24:dd:02:
```

How it works...

The OpenSSL `ca` command generates its CRL by looking at the `index.txt` file. Each line that starts with an 'R' is added to the CRL, after which the CRL is cryptographically signed using the CA private key.

By changing the status of a revoked certificate to `E` or even `V` we can `unrevoke` a certificate.

There's more...

In this recipe, we have changed a certificate from `Revoked` to `Expired`. This would allow the client from the previous recipe to connect again to the server, as the certificate is still valid. The main reason to change a certificate from `Valid` to `Expired` in the `indext.txt` file is to allow us to generate and hand out a new certificate using the exact same name.

Intermediary CAs

This recipe shows how to set up an intermediary CA and how to configure OpenVPN to make use of an intermediary CA. The OpenVPN `easy-rsa` scripts also include functionality to set up an intermediary CA. The advantage of an intermediary CA (or sub CA) is that the top-level CA (also known as the root CA) can be guarded more closely. The intermediary CAs can be distributed to the people responsible for generating the server and client certificates.

Getting ready

Set up the client and server certificates using the first recipe from *Chapter 2*. In this recipe, the server computer was running CentOS 5 Linux and OpenVPN 2.1.1. The client was running Fedora 12 Linux and OpenVPN 2.1.1.

How to do it...

1. First, we create the intermediary CA certificate:

   ```
   $ cd /etc/openvpn/cookbook/
   $ . ./vars
   $ ./build-inter IntermediateCA
   ```

2. Verify that this certificate can indeed act as a Certificate Authority:

   ```
   $ openssl x509 -text -noout -in keys/IntermediateCA.crt \
     | grep -C 1 CA
             X509v3 Basic Constraints:
                 CA:TRUE
         Signature Algorithm: sha1WithRSAEncryption
   ```

3. Next, we create a new `keys` directory for our intermediary CA (the current directory is still `/etc/openvpn/cookbook`):

   ```
   $ mkdir -m 700 -p IntermediateCA/keys
   $ cp [a-z]* IntermediateCA
   $ cd IntermediateCA
   ```

4. Edit the `vars` file and change the EASY_RSA line to:

   ```
   export EASY_RSA=/etc/openvpn/cookbook/IntermediateCA
   ```

5. Source this new `vars` file and set up the `keys` directory:

   ```
   $ . ./vars
   $ ./clean-all
   ```

```
$ cp ../keys/IntermediateCA.crt keys/ca.crt
$ cp ../keys/IntermediateCA.key keys/ca.key
```

5. Now, we are ready to create our first intermediary certificate:

```
$ ./build-key IntermediateClient
```

6. Verify that the certificate has the new Intermediary CA as its issuer:

```
$ openssl x509 -subject -issuer -noout -in \
  keys/IntermediateClient.crt
    subject= /C=NL/O=Cookbook/CN=IntermediateClient/...
    issuer= /C=NL/O=Cookbook/CN=IntermediateCA/...
```

7. And finally, we verify that the certificate is indeed a valid certificate. In order to do this we need to "stack" the root CA (public) certificate and the intermediary CA certificate into a single file:

```
$ cd /etc/openvpn/cookbook
$ cat keys/ca.crt IntermediaryCA/ca.crt > ca+subca.pem
$ openssl verify -CAfile ca+subca.pem IntermediateClient.crt
IntermediateClient.crt: OK
```

How it works...

The intermediary CA certificate has the "right" to act as a certificate authority, meaning that it can sign new certificates itself. The intermediary CA needs a directory structure for this, which is very similar to the root CA directory structure. First, we set up this directory structure and then we copy over all the necessary files. After that we create a client certificate and verify that it is a valid certificate. In order to perform this validation, the entire certificate chain from the root-level CA to the intermediary CA to the client certificate need to be present. This is why the root CA public certificate and the intermediary CA public certificate are stacked into a single file. This single file is then used to perform the entire certificate chain validation.

There's more...

Certificates that have been issued by an intermediary CA also need to be revoked by the same CA. This means that with multiple CAs you will also have to use multiple CRLs. Fortunately, CRLs can be stacked just like CA certificates: simply `cat` the file together, as will be explained in the next recipe.

Multiple CAs: stacking, using --capath

The goal of this recipe is to create an OpenVPN setup where the client certificates are signed by a "client-only" CA and the server certificate is signed by a different "server-only" CA. This provides an extra level of operational security, where one person is allowed to create only client certificates whereas another is allowed to generate only a server certificate. This ensures that the client and server certificates can never be mixed for a Man-in-the-Middle attack.

Getting ready

Set up the server certificate using the first recipe from *Chapter 2*. Use the client certificate and the intermediary CA certificate from the previous recipe. For this recipe, the server computer was running CentOS 5 Linux and OpenVPN 2.1.1. The client was running Fedora 12 Linux and OpenVPN 2.1.1.

How to do it...

1. Create the server configuration file:

```
tls-server
proto udp
port 1194
dev tun

server 192.168.200.0 255.255.255.0

ca       /etc/openvpn/cookbook/ca+subca.pem
cert     /etc/openvpn/cookbook/server.crt
key      /etc/openvpn/cookbook/server.key
dh       /etc/openvpn/cookbook/dh1024.pem
tls-auth /etc/openvpn/cookbook/ta.key 0

persist-key
persist-tun
keepalive 10 60

user  nobody
group nobody

daemon
log-append /var/log/openvpn.log
```

Save it as `example4-9-server.conf`.

2. Start the server:

```
[root@server]# openvpn --config example4-9-server.conf
```

3. Next, create the client configuration file:

```
client
proto udp
remote openvpnserver.example.com
port 1194

dev tun
nobind

ca        /etc/openvpn/cookbook/ca.crt
cert      /etc/openvpn/cookbook/IntermediateClient.crt
key       /etc/openvpn/cookbook/IntermediateClient.key
tls-auth /etc/openvpn/cookbook/ta.key 1

ns-cert-type server
```

Save it as `example4-9-client.conf`. Note that we did not specify the `ca+subca.pem` file in the client configuration.

4. Start the client:

```
[root@client]# openvpn --config example4-9-client.conf
```

5. In the server log files, you can now see the client connecting using the certificate that was created by the Intermediary CA:

```
... openvpnclient:49283 [IntermediateClient] Peer Connection
Initiated with openvpnclient:49283
```

How it works...

When the client connects to the server, the client (public) certificate is sent to the server for verification. The server needs to have access to the full certificate chain in order to do the verification, therefore, we stack the root CA certificate and the intermediary CA (or sub-CA) certificate together. This allows the client to connect to the server.

Vice versa, when the client connects, the server (public) certificate is also sent to the client. As the server certificate was originally signed by the root CA, we do not need to specify the full certificate stack here.

Note that if we had forgotten to specify the `ca+subca.pem` file in the OpenVPN server configuration file, we would have received an error:

```
openvpnclient:49286 VERIFY ERROR: depth=0, error=unable to get local
issuer certificate:
/C=NL/O=Cookbook/CN=IntermediateClient/...
```

There's more...

Apart from stacking the CA certificates, it is also possible to stack the CRLs or to use an entirely different mechanism to support multiple CA certificates and their corresponding CRLs.

Stacking CRLs

If CRLs are used in this configuration, then the CRLs from both the root CA and the intermediary CA need to be stacked:

```
$ cd /etc/openvpn/cookbook
$ cat keys/crl.pem IntermediateCA/keys/crl.pem > crl-stack.pem
```

They can then be included in the OpenVPN server configuration using:

```
crl-verify /etc/openvpn/cookbook/crl-stack.pem
```

Using the --capath directive

Another way to include multiple CAs and CRLs in the OpenVPN server configuration is to use the following directive:

```
capath /etc/openvpn/cookbook/ca-dir
```

This directory needs to contain all CA certificates and CRLs using a special naming convention:

 ▶ All CA certificates must have a name equal to the 'hash' of the CA certificate, and must end with `.0`
 ▶ All CRLs must have a name equal to the 'hash' of the CA certificate, and must end with `.r0`

For our root CA and intermediary CA, this would require:

```
$ cd /etc/openvpn/cookbook
$ mkdir ca-dir
$ openssl x509 -hash -noout -in keys/ca.crt
    bcd54da9
```

This hexadecimal number `bcd54da9` is the hash of the root CA certificate:

```
$ cp keys/ca.crt   ca-dir/bcd54da9.0
$ cp keys/crl.pem ca-dir/bcd54da9.r0
```

Similarly, for the intermediary CA certificiate:

```
$ openssl x509 -hash -noout -in IntermediateCA/keys/ca.crt
    1f5e4734
$ cp IntermediateCA/keys/ca.crt   ca-dir/1f5e4734.0
$ cp IntermediateCA/keys/crl.pem ca-dir/1f5e4734.r0
```

When using many different CA certificates and corresponding CRLs, this method is far easier to manage then the "stacked" files.

5
Two-factor Authentication with PKCS#11

In this chapter, we will cover:

- ▸ Initializing a hardware token
- ▸ Getting a hardware token ID
- ▸ Using a hardware token
- ▸ Using the management interface to list PKCS#11 certificates
- ▸ Selecting a PKCS#11 certificate using the management interface
- ▸ Generating a key on the hardware token
- ▸ Private method for getting a PKCS#11 certificate
- ▸ Pin caching example

Introduction

In this chapter, we will focus on the support for two-factor authentication for OpenVPN. Two-factor authentication is based on the idea that in order to use a system (like a VPN), you need to provide two things:

- ▸ something you **know** that is a password
- ▸ something you **possess** that is a smartcard or hardware token

Starting with version 2.1, OpenVPN supports two-factor authentication by providing PKCS#11 support on Windows, Mac OS X, and Linux. PKCS#11 is an industry standard for communicating with smartcards or hardware tokens, and there are both open source and commercial drivers available. The major difficulty when supporting two-factor authentication is the software support on different platforms. While most hardware token vendors provide drivers for Microsoft Windows, there are far fewer cards and tokens supported on Linux. For this chapter, we have made use of an Aladdin eToken Pro USB hardware token (http://www.aladdin.com), which is well supported on Windows, Mac OS X, and Linux, allowing a user to transparently switch between different operating systems using the same hardware token.

The first recipe in this chapter will go into the details of initializing a hardware token on Linux. If this first recipe cannot be completed successfully (or if no suitable third-party PKCS#11 library is available for Linux), then the token can be considered "not supported on Linux". However, the remaining recipes of this chapter can still succeed on other platforms.

Please note that OpenVPN depends purely on a working PKCS#11 driver. When selecting a hardware device, it will be important to verify whether the device is supported on the platforms needed, not if it will work with OpenVPN itself.

 It should be noted that most issues that come up when configuring OpenVPN to use a hardware token on Linux are related to the poor support of these tokens on Linux.

Initializing a hardware token

In this recipe, we initialize an Aladdin eToken PRO 32K hardware token on Linux using the proprietary driver software from Aladdin (pkiclient). Initialization consists of the following steps:

1. Format the hardware token
2. Copy a private key to the token
3. Copy the corresponding public X509 certificate to the token

This recipe does not use OpenVPN at all, but it is a required step for the remaining recipes of this chapter.

Getting ready

Install PCSC-lite 1.4.4 or higher, OpenSC 0.11.4 or higher, and the Aladdin pkiclient driver. For this recipe, the computer used was running Fedora 12 Linux, PCSC-lite 1.5.2, OpenSC 0.11.12, and PKI Client 5.00.

Set up the client and server certificates using the first recipe from *Chapter 2, Client-server IP-only Networks*. Keep the client certificate and private key files `client1.crt` and `client1.key` at hand.

How to do it...

1. First, bring up the eToken PKI Client properties window and click on **Initialize eToken**. This will bring up the following dialog box:

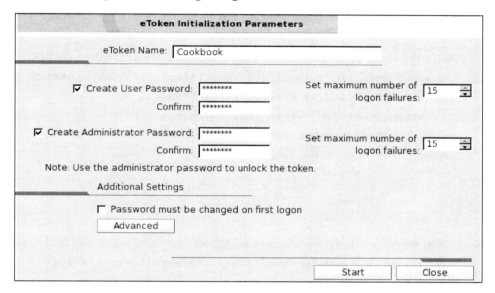

2. Choose a user password and an administrator password. The user password is used by end-users to access the hardware token, whereas the administrator password can be used for administrative tasks, such as resetting the user password.

3. Deselect **Password must be changed on first logon**, then click on **Start**.

   The token will now be initialized, wiping out all previous contents. This initialization phase is normally the crucial phase in determining whether a token is supported on Linux.

   After this step has completed successfully, close the PKI Client Properties window and continue in a terminal window.

4. Convert the private key `client1.key` to DER format and copy it to the token:

```
$ openssl rsa -in client1.key -out client1key.der -outform der
$ pkcs11-tool --module /usr/lib64/libeTPkcs11.so \
  -w client1key.der --type privkey --login \
  --id 20100703 --label "Client1"
```

```
Please enter User PIN: [enter pin]
Generated private key:
Private Key Object; RSA
   label:      Client1
   ID:         20100703
   Usage:      decrypt, sign, unwrap
```

The parameters `label` and `id` should be the same for both the private key and the certificate. Note the path of the PKCS#11 library, `/usr/lib64/libeTPkcs11.so`, which indicates that this recipe was run on a 64-bit machine. For a 32-bit architecture, the library path would have been `usr/lib/libeTPkcs11.so`.

5. Next, convert the certificate `client1.crt` to DER format and copy it as well:

    `$ openssl x509 -in client1.crt -out client1cert.der -outform der`

    `$ pkcs11-tool --module /usr/lib64/libeTPkcs11.so \`

    `-w client1cert.der --type cert --login \`

    `--id 20100703 --label "Client1"`

    ```
    Please enter User PIN: [enter pin]
    Generated certificate:
    Certificate Object, type = X.509 cert
    label:      Client1
    ID:         20100703
    ```

6. Finally, we verify that the files have been copied successfully to the token:

    `$ pkcs11-tool --module /usr/lib64/libeTPkcs11.so -O --login`

    ```
    Please enter User PIN: [enter pin]
    Private Key Object; RSA
       label:      Client1
       ID:         20100703
       Usage:      decrypt, sign, unwrap
    Certificate Object, type = X.509 cert
       label:      Client1
    ID:         20100703
    ```

Both the private key and the certificate are on the token.

How it works...

After the initialization phase, we manipulate the token using the `pkcs11-tool` tool from the OpenSC package. This tool offers a command-line interface to manipulate a hardware token using an external PKCS#11 module. In this recipe, the PKCS#11 module is supplied by the Aladdin `pkiclient` driver software.

The `pkcs11-tool` utility can only copy private keys and certificates to a hardware token if they are in so-called DER format. Hence, we first convert the `client.key` and `client.crt` files to this format using the `openssl` command.

There's more...

Public and private objects

The certificate stored on the hardware token is considered as a public object. Even if we did not log in to the token we can still view it:

```
$ pkcs11-tool --module /usr/lib64/libeTPkcs11.so -O
    Certificate Object, type = X.509 cert
      label:      Client1
      ID:         20100703
```

In a later recipe, we will see how we can disable this functionality.

OpenSC versus Aladdin PKI Client driver

In this recipe, we used the proprietary Aladdin PKI Client driver software to initialize the token. This also means that all access to the token has to be done using this driver.

The open source package OpenSC, from which the `pkcs11-tool` command is used, also supplies a PKCS#11 driver, `opensc-pkcs11.so`. However, it is not possible to initialize a token using the Aladdin driver software and then access it using the PKCS11 module that comes with the OpenSC package.

The main reason why the Aladdin PKI Client driver was chosen is that this driver works better on the computer used for this recipe. However, this is highly dependent on the operating system installation.

Getting a hardware token ID

Before we can configure OpenVPN to make use of the hardware token, we must first determine what the hardware token ID is. This hardware token ID looks quite complicated at first, hence a separate recipe is included for this purpose.

Getting ready

Keep the hardware token from the previous recipe at hand. Install OpenVPN 2.1. In this recipe, the computer used was running Fedora 12 Linux, pcsc-lite 1.5.2, opensc-0.11.12, PKI Client 5.00, and OpenVPN 2.1.1.

How to do it...

Use the following command to list the PKCS#11 IDs that are available to OpenVPN:

```
$ openvpn --show-pkcs11-ids /usr/lib64/libeTPkcs11.so
    The following objects are available for use.
    Each object shown below may be used as parameter to
    --pkcs11-id option please remember to use single quote mark.

    Certificate
            DN:                 /C=NL/O=Cookbook/CN=openvpnclient1/…
            Serial:             02
            Serialized id:   Aladdin\x20Ltd\x2E/eToken/001a01a9/
    Cookbook/20100703
```

How it works...

OpenVPN loads the PKCS#11 library /usr/lib64/libETPkcs11.so and queries it for the certificates in a very similar fashion to the pkcs11-tool command from the previous recipe. The library /usr/lib64/libETPkcs11.so is part of Aladdin's PKI Client 5.00 client software.

Each certificate that is found is then translated into a **serialized ID** that is unique for each token and for each certificate found. The serialized ID for the token used in this recipe is:

```
Aladdin\x20Ltd\x2E/eToken/001a01a9/Cookbook/20100703
```

This can be read as follows:

- ▸ The token manufacturer is Aladdin\x20Ltd\x2E. The code \x20 is the hexadecimal representation of the space character. Similarly, the code \x2E is the hexadecimal representation of the character '.' (period).

- ▸ The token model is eToken.

- ▸ The token serial number is 001a01a9. This serial number is unique for each Aladdin eToken token.

- ▸ The token name is Cookbook. The token name is usually chosen when the token is initialized.

- ▸ The certificate ID to use is 20100703. This is the same ID that was used to copy the private key and X509 certificate to the token in the previous recipe.

There's more...

In this section, we will address the automatic selection of a certificate on a hardware token and on the choice of the PKCS#11 library.

What about automatic selection?

A logical question to ask is whether it is possible to automatically choose a certificate on a hardware token. Currently, this is not possible, mostly due to security concerns. Automatically choosing a certificate on the first hardware token that is entered is considered a bad security practice. As we are attempting to improve security using two-factor authentication, this is not allowed.

PKCS#11 libraries

The library `/usr/lib64/libETPkcs11.so` is part of Aladdin's PKI Client 5.00 client software for 64-bit Linux. For a 32-bit Linux architecture, the library would have been `/usr/lib/libeTPkcs11.so`. On Windows, this library is usually found in `'%windir%\system32\etpkcs11.dll` or `C:\WINDOWS\system32\etpkcs11.dll`.

Other hardware token middleware can also be used. For example, the PKCS#11 library that is supplied by the OpenSC project is `/usr/lib64/opensc-pkcs11.so` (64-bit Linux). However, note that a PKCS#11 library from one project or vendor is usually incompatible when used with hardware tokens that have been initialized using the client software from another vendor. The choice of hardware device and the choice of the driver software for the hardware device depends greatly on which operating systems will be used and whether the same hardware device is used on different operating systems. For Windows users, the driver supplied with the hardware token often works better, but it also comes with licensing costs. If the driver software for a particular device is not available for Mac OS X or Linux, then the OpenSC driver is a better choice.

Using a hardware token

This recipe will demonstrate how to use a hardware token as a replacement for an X509 certificate and the corresponding private key.

Getting ready

We use the following network layout:

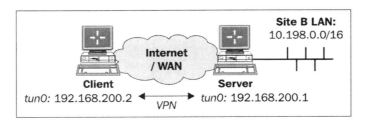

Keep the hardware token from the first recipe at hand. For this recipe, the server computer was running CentOS 5 Linux and OpenVPN 2.1.1. The client was running Fedora 12 Linux and OpenVPN 2.1.1. Keep the server configuration file `basic-udp-server.conf` from the *Chapter 2* recipe *Server-side routing* at hand.

How to do it...

1. Start the server using the configuration file `basic-udp-server.conf`:

   [root@server]# openvpn --config basic-udp-server.conf

2. Next, create the client configuration file:

   ```
   client
   proto udp
   remote openvpnserver.example.com

   port 1194

   dev tun
   nobind

   ca        /etc/openvpn/cookbook/ca.crt
   tls-auth /etc/openvpn/cookbook/ta.key 1

   ns-cert-type server

   pkcs11-providers /usr/lib64/libeTPkcs11.so
   pkcs11-id 'Aladdin\x20Ltd\x2E/eToken/001a01a9/Cookbook/20100703'
   ```

   The last directive `pkcs11-id` and the serialized ID `Aladdin\x20...` need to be specified on a single line. Save it as `example5-3-client.conf`.

3. Start the client:

   `[root@client]$ openvpn --config example5-3-client.conf`

   The client connection log is shown below:

```
┌────────────────────────────── Example 5-3 ──────────────────────────────┐
│ File  Edit  View  Terminal  Help                                         │
│ [client]# openvpn --config example5-3-client.conf                        │
│ Sat Jul  3 19:12:49 2010 OpenVPN 2.1.1 x86_64-redhat-linux-gnu [SSL] [LZO2] [EPOLL] [PKCS1 │
│ 1] built on Jan  5 2010                                                   │
│ Sat Jul  3 19:12:49 2010 PKCS#11: Adding PKCS#11 provider '/usr/lib64/libeTPkcs11.so'      │
│ Sat Jul  3 19:12:49 2010 NOTE: OpenVPN 2.1 requires '--script-security 2' or higher to cal │
│ l user-defined scripts or executables                                    │
│ Sat Jul  3 19:12:50 2010 Control Channel Authentication: using '/etc/openvpn/cookbook/ta.k │
│ ey' as a OpenVPN static key file                                         │
│ Sat Jul  3 19:12:50 2010 UDPv4 link local: [undef]                       │
│ Sat Jul  3 19:12:50 2010 UDPv4 link remote: 194.171.96.27:1194           │
│ Enter Cookbook token Password:                                           │
│ Sat Jul  3 19:12:58 2010 [openvpnserver] Peer Connection Initiated with 194.171.96.27:1194 │
│ Sat Jul  3 19:13:01 2010 TUN/TAP device tun1 opened                      │
│ Sat Jul  3 19:13:01 2010 /sbin/ip link set dev tun1 up mtu 1500          │
│ Sat Jul  3 19:13:01 2010 /sbin/ip addr add dev tun1 192.168.200.2/24 broadcast 192.168.200 │
│ .255                                                                      │
│ Sat Jul  3 19:13:01 2010 Initialization Sequence Completed               │
│ ▮                                                                         │
└──────────────────────────────────────────────────────────────────────────┘
```

After entering the hardware token password (`Enter the Cookbook token password`), the connection is established.

How it works...

We configure OpenVPN to make use of a PKCS#11 provider:

`pkcs11-providers /usr/lib64/libeTPkcs11.so`

Note that on a 32-bit system, we would have used:

`pkcs11-providers /usr/lib/libeTPkcs11.so`

With the serialized ID from the previous recipe, we instruct OpenVPN to use the certificate we copied to the token in the first recipe:

`pkcs11-id 'Aladdin\x20Ltd\x2E/eToken/001a01a9/Cookbook/20100703'`

This enables OpenVPN to make use of the certificate and private key stored on the hardware token, allowing it to establish a connection to the OpenVPN server.

There's more...

In this section, we will explain in more detail what is different when using a hardware token and what to be aware of when using the alternate OpenSC PKCS#11 driver in combination with OpenVPN.

What is different?

The major difference between using a hardware token and using a regular certificate and private key pair is in how security is established between the client and the peer. When a regular certificate and private key are used OpenVPN has full access to the private key using the OpenSSL library. The SSL handshake between client and server is performed entirely by OpenVPN itself by creating the session encryption keys using the private key.

When a hardware token is used, OpenVPN does not have access to the private key. The SSL handshake is performed in parts by OpenVPN and in parts by the hardware token. Especially, the session encryption keys are computed by the hardware token itself.

Using the OpenSC driver

When the PKCS#11 driver `opensc-pkcs11.so` from the OpenSC package is used, it is convenient to add the following to the OpenVPN configuration file, even if no scripts are used:

```
script-security 2 system
```

There is a bug in OpenVPN up to 2.1.4 when this line is not present, which causes rekeying to fail. This means that the OpenVPN session will stop functioning after the rekeying interval, which is normally set to 1 hour. The previous line of code is a work-around for this bug.

Using the management interface to list PKCS#11 certificates

This recipe will demonstrate how to list the available certificates using the management interface on the client side. Although no particular network layout is required, we have to set up a working VPN connection before we can fully use the management interface.

Getting ready

We use the following network layout:

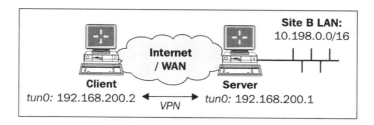

Keep the hardware token from the first recipe at hand. For this recipe, the server computer was running CentOS 5 Linux and OpenVPN 2.1.1. The client was running Fedora 12 Linux and OpenVPN 2.1.1. Keep the server configuration file `basic-udp-server.conf` from the *Chapter 2* recipe, *Server-side routing* at hand.

How to do it...

1. Start the server using the configuration file `basic-udp-server.conf`:

   [root@server]# openvpn --config basic-udp-server.conf

2. Next, create the client configuration file:

   ```
   client
   proto udp
   remote openvpnserver.example.com

   port 1194

   dev tun
   nobind

   ca      /etc/openvpn/cookbook/ca.crt
   tls-auth /etc/openvpn/cookbook/ta.key 1

   ns-cert-type server

   pkcs11-providers /usr/lib64/libeTPkcs11.so
   pkcs11-id 'Aladdin\x20Ltd\x2E/eToken/001a01a9/Cookbook/20100703'

   management 127.0.0.1 23000 stdin
   ```

   Save it as `example5-4-client.conf`.

3. Start the client:

```
[root@client]$ openvpn --config example5-4-client.conf
```

After the connection is established, telnet to the management interface from another terminal window on the client:

```
[client]$ telnet 127.0.0.1 23000
```

4. The first management command to try is:

```
pkcs11-id-count
```

This will return the number of certificates found on the hardware token.

5. The second command will return the first certificate on the hardware token that is configured for use in OpenVPN (counting starts at zero!):

```
pkcs11-id-get 0
```

This will output the serialized ID and the X509 certificate as a BASE64-encoded blob. This might not be very useful to an end-user but the management interface is also intended to be accessed programmatically. The results of the previous two commands are shown in the following figure:

```
Example 5-4
File  Edit  View  Terminal  Help
[client]# telnet 127.0.0.1 23000
Trying 127.0.0.1...
Connected to 127.0.0.1.
Escape character is '^]'.
ENTER PASSWORD:cookbook
SUCCESS: password is correct
>INFO:OpenVPN Management Interface Version 1 -- type 'help' for more info
pkcs11-id-count
>PKCS11-COUNT:2
pkcs11-id-get 0
>PKCS11ID-ENTRY:'0', ID:'Aladdin\x20Ltd\x2E/eToken/001a01a9/Cookbook/20100703', BLOB:'MIIE
tzCCAp+gAwIBAgIBAjANBgkqhkiG9w0BAQUFADBYMQswCQYDVQQGEwJOTDERMA8GA1UEChMIQ29va2Jvb2sxFDASBg
NVBAMTCONvb2tib29rIENBMSAwHgYJKoZIhvcNAQkBFhFqYW5qdXN0QG5pa2hlZi5ubDAeFw0xMDA1MDYxMjAwMDla
Fw0xMzAxMzAxMjAwMDlaMFsxCzAJBgNVBAYTAk5MMREwDwYDVQQKEwhDb29rYm9vazEXMBUGA1UEAxMOb3B1bnZwbm
NsaWVudDExIDAeBgkqhkiG9w0BCQEWEWphbmp1c3RAbmlraGVmLm5sMIGfMA0GCSqGSIb3DQEBAQUAA4GNADCBiQKB
gQDhouKcguk7UpXQeiU/j/fhB3fM2pSiAt7CB5sPFNHXMYo6wr6RIy4uStydnjIfKSmHpwmtiOM57AkNdusvqbqm4Q
mSv+m7pD3m1rbPeUFHPywv+OjhhRupV2P7eOfyIfHYYPJI5QrXGTUBUPen7eisZwO7RIesNzVRxWDS+r/sdQIDAQAB
o4IBCzCCAQcwCQYDVR0TBAIwADAtBglghkgBhvhCAQ0EIBYeRWFzeS1SU0EgR2VuZXJhdGVkIENlcnRpZmljYXRlMB
0GA1UdDgQWBBQlyKoO5EGNnfkxPG8UzndPDwCWCDCBiQYDVR0jBIGBMH+AFBM8t0dMBxMyZt6HwyT0ceoSbldKoVyk
WjBYMQswCQYDVQQGEwJOTDERMA8GA1UEChMIQ29va2Jvb2sxFDASBgNVBAMTCONvb2tib29rIENBMSAwHgYJKoZIhv
cNAQkBFhFqYW5qdXN0QG5pa2hlZi5ubIIJAKcT8GTJB5CsMBMGA1UdJQQMMAoGCCsGAQUFBwMCMAsGA1UdDwQEAwIH
gDANBgkqhkiG9w0BAQUFAAOCAgEAwjjqz1zM3ME850pL1GNwrOUrwWdSH2KMxzxp1iJtvIslbCXSIqTbDC85zUhFlz
w3qB4bLJEW23kFlQSR35F/Jp23mDy/vBoDVxgYCblHcxN4zKU87+ftkFK9zDlvKhjOeDvpSIeFkUREkXMXBPhmQWgG
y9Y6Ba0Va0dMJB79Q85aTWbzIcngUnfk5MMw8kw/Ol7d7EWuldV7zku0vVPcsFezfItU/+gpGox/zXjEmR1MEj8aKS
Pb6m6r+CJFceYvhix0vmGAEvSB7AHBoD/JwxhrxsKbD2BfsLa3L8CfgNM3EzRb22MKHZ+nITYQ/yYRiN6ALajHhhNx
ncwqhQ3Jpf9GeVTrGDwh449XjcR8k4KRIe0dmR95xb/V+Fd86N0wNtnw650lPSBXWJCJABSe2Md48AlBQy6y73lpko
LIJJoSBgvu5baBOleY84U3gXk6dSD2J+MbwkzfhNtwLssqpkpSsmuM3qwj0dVBYFuF0aRK8DoqL9yTmlUBiN+XsOJa
SsOSzbyKNthilTmgfwo6X0Fe4tlGU3chY/ZrFWzAJBUtGY5ZvRgrmI7nfbiMcVJfwrsgb299mwQ5WPs0UcHhxd55Al
+2I+s6zjGISDq2bJDbCIDmPZL4wuCKftRDTKnazCcOpgPcDxwgD0Us/+EZt+X8m0peU/Bknj3nv5vTCaQ='
```

How it works...

We configured OpenVPN to make use of a PKCS#11 provider:

```
pkcs11-providers /usr/lib64/libeTPkcs11.so
```

Then we enabled the management interface. This allows us to retrieve (public) information from the hardware token via the management interface. Note that if the certificate on the hardware token is marked private, then this recipe would fail. See the recipe *Private method for getting a PKCS#11 certificate* later in this chapter for details.

While this example may not have much practical use, it does show how OpenVPN can be controlled using the management interface. It is expected that both the management interface and the PKCS#11 interface will become more important in future versions of OpenVPN.

See also

The next recipe, *Selecting a PKCS#11 certificate using the management interface*, explains how to use the management interface to select and use a PKCS#11 certificate in OpenVPN.

Selecting a PKCS#11 certificate using the management interface

This recipe will demonstrate how the management interface can be used to select a certificate and a corresponding private key from a hardware token. This recipe is a continuation of the previous recipe. Although no particular network layout is required, we have to set up a working VPN connection before we can fully use the management interface.

Getting ready

We use the following network layout:

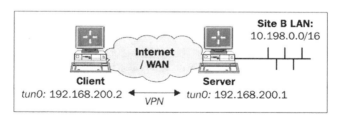

Keep the hardware token from the first recipe at hand. For this recipe, the server computer was running CentOS 5 Linux and OpenVPN 2.1.1. The client was running Fedora 12 Linux and OpenVPN 2.1.1. Keep the server configuration file `basic-udp-server.conf` from the *Chapter 2* recipe *Server-side routing* at hand.

How to do it...

1. Start the server using the configuration file `basic-udp-server.conf`:

   ```
   [root@server]# openvpn --config basic-udp-server.conf
   ```

2. Next, create the client configuration file:

   ```
   client
   proto udp
   remote openvpnserver.example.com

   port 1194

   dev tun
   nobind

   ca        /etc/openvpn/cookbook/ca.crt
   tls-auth /etc/openvpn/cookbook/ta.key 1

   ns-cert-type server

   pkcs11-providers /usr/lib64/libeTPkcs11.so
   pkcs11-id-management

   management 127.0.0.1 23000 stdin
   management-query-passwords
   management-hold
   management-signal
   management-forget-disconnect
   ```

   Save it as `example5-5-client.conf`.

3. Start the client:

   ```
   [root@client]# openvpn --config example5-5-client.conf
   ... OpenVPN 2.1.1 x86_64-redhat-linux-gnu [SSL] [LZO2] [EPOLL]
   [PKCS11] built on Jan  5 2010
   Enter Management Password: [choose a password]
   ```

   After the management password is entered, the OpenVPN client stops and waits for a connection on the management interface.

4. Next, we use `telnet` to connect to the management interface:

   [client]$ telnet 127.0.0.1 23000

   ```
   Connected to 127.0.0.1.
   Escape character is '^]'.
   ENTER PASSWORD: [enter the management password]
   SUCCESS: password is correct
   >INFO:OpenVPN Management Interface Version 1 -- type 'help' for
   more info
   >HOLD:Waiting for hold release
   ```

5. The OpenVPN client is now waiting for the `hold release` command before continuing:

   ```
   hold release
   SUCCESS: hold release succeeded
   ```

6. Next, the OpenVPN client is asking for the serialized PKCS#11 ID to use:

   ```
   >NEED-STR:Need 'pkcs11-id-request' string MSG:Please specify
   PKCS#11 id to use
   ```
   needstr pkcs11-id-request
   'Aladdin\x20Ltd\x2E/eToken/001a01a9/Cookbook/20100703'
   ```
   SUCCESS: 'pkcs11-id-request' needstr-string entered, but not yet
   verified
   ```

   And finally, the OpenVPN client is asking for the password of the hardware token:

   ```
   >PASSWORD:Need 'Cookbook token' password
   ```
   password 'Cookbook token' [hardware token password]
   ```
   SUCCESS: 'Cookbook token' password entered, but not yet verified
   ```

   After this, the VPN connection is established.

How it works...

We configured OpenVPN to make use of a PKCS#11 provider and to use the management interface to manage the PKCS#11 identities:

```
pkcs11-providers /usr/lib64/libeTPkcs11.so
pkcs11-id-management
```

We also configured OpenVPN to set up a management interface on port 23000 on `localhost` and to use this interface to query for passwords (`management-query-passwords`), to start and stop the client (`management-hold`), to send a signal to the client when the user disconnects from the management interface (`management-signal`), and to forget all cached passwords when the user disconnects (`management-forget-disconnect`):

```
management 127.0.0.1 23000 stdin
management-query-passwords
management-hold
management-signal
management-forget-disconnect
```

When the OpenVPN client starts, it waits for a user to connect on the management interface before continuing. After the user logs in on the client interface and types `hold release`, OpenVPN next queries for the pkcs11-id to use, which the user needs to supply using the `needstr` command. If the right pkcs11-id is entered, the user is requested to type the password for the hardware token on which the pkcs11-id is found. For this, the `password` command is used.

This example shows that OpenVPN can be controlled using the management interface. The management interface and the PKCS#11 interface will become more important in future versions of OpenVPN.

There's more...

The design philosophy behind the management interface is that the third-party managers can be written that control the OpenVPN client. Current manager applications (for example, the OpenVPN GUI application on Windows) parse the output of the OpenVPN client and supply responses using the system standard input and output mechanisms. This does not allow for much interactive control, which led to the development of the management interface. Most of the GUI tools on Linux, such as the OpenVPN plugin for the Gnome Network Manager, already make use of the management interface. The Windows OpenVPN GUI is being rewritten and it will also make use of the management interface.

Generating a key on the hardware token

In this recipe, we will generate a private key on the hardware token itself, after which we generate a certificate to match this private key. For security-sensitive purposes, this is one of the safest ways to generate a certificates/private-key pair, as the private key cannot be copied off the hardware token. It also means that if the hardware token fails or is stolen then the private key and corresponding certificate are lost.

Getting ready

Keep the hardware token from the previous recipe at hand. In this recipe the computer used was running Fedora 12 Linux, pcsc-lite 1.5.2, opensc-0.11.12, engine_pkcs11 0.1.4 and PKI Client 5.00, but the commands used should work with other PKCS#11 libraries as well. The `engine_pkcs11` library is the "engine" interface between the `openssl` command and a PKCS#11 driver. This package can be found on the OpenSC project website for Linux, Windows, and Mac OS X.

How to do it...

The `easy-rsa` scripts that are supplied with OpenVPN 2.1 support PKCS#11 management, but it requires some modification to the `vars` and `openssl.cnf` files.

1. First we modify the `vars` file:

   ```
   export EASY_RSA=/etc/openvpn/cookbook
   export OPENSSL="openssl"
   export KEY_CONFIG=`$EASY_RSA/whichopensslcnf $EASY_RSA`
   export KEY_DIR="$EASY_RSA/keys"
   export PKCS11TOOL="pkcs11-tool"
   export PKCS11_MODULE_PATH="/usr/lib64/libeTPkcs11.so"
   export PKCS11_PIN="[hardware token PIN]"
   export KEY_SIZE=1024
   export CA_EXPIRE=3650
   export KEY_EXPIRE=1000
   export KEY_COUNTRY="NL"
   export KEY_PROVINCE=
   export KEY_CITY=
   export KEY_ORG="Cookbook"
   export KEY_EMAIL="openvpn-ca@cookbook.example.com"
   ```

   Adjust the settings (`KEY_ORG`, `KEY_EMAIL`) to reflect your organization.

2. After this we source the `vars` file:

   ```
   $ . ./vars
   ```

3. Next we modify the `openssl.cnf` file that is supplied with the `easy-rsa` scripts. Uncomment the line 'pkcs11 = pkcs11_section' line and adjust the line 'dynamic_path' to reflect the location of the 'engine_pkcs11.so' file on your system. This library acts as the "glue" between the 'openssl' command and a PKCS#11 driver. The output below shows the location of the 'engine_pkcs11.so' file on 64-bit Fedora 12 Linux:

   ```
   pkcs11 = pkcs11_section
   dynamic_path = /usr/lib64/openssl/engines/engine_pkcs11.so`
   ```

On Windows this file is part of the OpenSC 'SCB' package and is named
'engine_pkcs11.dll'.

4. After this we start the 'build-key' script with extra command-line parameters:

```
$ ./build-key --pkcs11 /usr/lib64/libeTPkcs11.so \
  0 20100705 "Onboard" client5
```

The output of the command is quite long and is therefore cut into parts. First a
private key is generated on the token:

```
User PIN: Generating key pair on PKCS#11 token...
Key pair generated:
Private Key Object; RSA
   label:      Onboard
   ID:         20100705
   Usage:      decrypt, sign, unwrap
Public Key Object; RSA 1024 bits
   label:      Onboard
   ID:         20100705
   Usage:      encrypt, verify, wrap
```

Then the certificate creation process is started using a pkcs11 engine. This is very
similar to the certificate generation process from the first recipe of *Chapter 2,
Client-server IP-only Networks*, hence it is abbreviated:

```
    engine "pkcs11" set.
[...]
The Subject's Distinguished Name is as follows
countryName           :PRINTABLE:'NL'
organizationName      :PRINTABLE:'Cookbook'
commonName            :PRINTABLE:'client5'
emailAddress          :IA5STRING:'openvpn-ca@cookbook.example.com'
Certificate is to be certified until Mar 30 18:16:33 2013 GMT
(1000 days)
Sign the certificate? [y/n]:y


1 out of 1 certificate requests certified, commit? [y/n]y
Write out database with 1 new entries
Data Base Updated
```

And finally the certificate that was generated is copied back to the hardware token:

```
Generated certificate:
Certificate Object, type = X.509 cert
   label:      Onboard
   ID:         20100705
```

The certificate and private key pair are now ready for use with OpenVPN.

5. We can retrieve the serialized ID using:

```
$ openvpn --show-pkcs11-ids /usr/lib64/libeTPkcs11.so
```

```
Certificate
      DN:                   /C=NL/O=Cookbook/CN=client5/...
      Serial:               09
      Serialized id:
Aladdin\x20Ltd\x2E/eToken/001a01a9/Cookbook/20100705
```

How it works...

The following command specifies that a PKCS#11 module should be used to generate the private key for the certificate:

```
$ ./build-key --pkcs11 /usr/lib64/libeTPkcs11.so \
    0 20100705 "Onboard" client5
```

The parameters to the `--pkcs11` command-line options are (in order):

▸ **Library**: The location of the PKCS#11 library to use.

▸ **Slot**: The slot number of the hardware token. This is usually '0' unless multiple hardware tokens are plugged in at the same time.

▸ **ID**: The ID of the private key and certificate on the token. This is the same ID that shows up at the end of the serialized id output in the recipe "Getting a hardware token ID" earlier in this chapter.

▸ **Label**: The label of the private key and certificate on the token. This label is not really used by OpenVPN but it is useful to track different certificate/private key pairs on a token.

The last parameter `client5` is the name of the client certificate to generate, similar to the "normal" command:

```
$ ./build-key client5
```

With these parameters the `build-key` command first generates a private key on the token (and corresponding public key, but this is not used by OpenVPN). After that the normal certificate generation process is started using an openssl PKCS#11 engine. The `engine_pkcs11.so` library is used for this. When the certificate is signed by the Certificate Authority (CA) the certificate is converted to DER format and copied back to the hardware token. The certificate is now ready to be used by OpenVPN.

Private method for getting a PKCS#11 certificate

In this recipe we will configure OpenVPN to use a private certificate on a hardware token. Normally, the certificates which are stored on a hardware token are publicly accessible, as a certificate is 'public' anyways. Some tokens allow the user to protect the certificates, so that the token password is always needed to retrieve it. OpenVPN supports this kind of hardware token.

Getting ready

We use the following network layout:

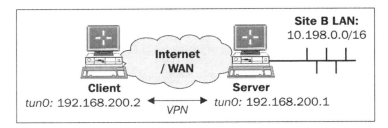

Keep the hardware token from the first recipe at hand. For this recipe, the server computer was running CentOS 5 Linux and OpenVPN 2.1.1. The client was running Fedora 12 Linux and OpenVPN 2.1.1. Keep the server configuration file `basic-udp-server.conf` from the *Chapter 2* recipe *Server-side routing* at hand.

How to do it...

1. First, we store the certificate `client2.crt` and corresponding private key `client2.key` on the token with protection (attribute `CKA_PRIVATE`) enabled. This is done using the pkcs11-tool command-line option `--private`:

```
$ openssl rsa -in client2.key -out client2key.der -outform der
$ pkcs11-tool --module /usr/lib64/libeTPkcs11.so \
    -w client2key.der --type privkey --login \
    --id 123456 --label "Client2"
$ openssl x509 -in client2.crt -out client2cert.der -outform der
$ pkcs11-tool --module /usr/lib64/libeTPkcs11.so \
    -w client2cert.der --type cert --login \
    --id 123456  --label "Client2" --private
```

2. Start the OpenVPN server using the configuration file 'basic-udp-server.conf':

   [root@server]# openvpn --config basic-udp-server.conf

3. Next, create the client configuration file:

   ```
   client
   proto udp
   remote openvpnserver.example.com

   port 1194

   dev tun
   nobind

   ca        /etc/openvpn/cookbook/ca.crt
   tls-auth /etc/openvpn/cookbook/ta.key 1

   ns-cert-type server

   pkcs11-providers /usr/lib64/libeTPkcs11.so
   pkcs11-id 'Aladdin\x20Ltd\x2E/eToken/001a01a9/Cookbook/123456'

   pkcs11-cert-private 1
   ```

   And save it as example5-7-client.conf.

4. Start the client:

   [root@client]# openvpn --config example5-7-client.conf

   ```
   UDPv4 link local: [undef]
   UDPv4 link remote: 194.171.96.27:1194
   Enter Cookbook token Password:
   [openvpnserver] Peer Connection Initiated with
   openvpnserver:1194
   TUN/TAP device tun0 opened
   /sbin/ip link set dev tun0 up mtu 1500
   /sbin/ip addr add dev tun0 192.168.200.3/24 broadcast
   192.168.200.255
   Initialization Sequence Completed
   ```

After entering the hardware token password ('Enter the Cookbook token password') the connection is established.

How it works...

The following directive tells OpenVPN to log in to the token before attempting to retrieve any information from it:

```
pkcs11-cert-private 1
```

This will allow OpenVPN to use the certificate and corresponding private key in a similar fashion to the *Using a hardware token* recipe.

There's more...

Each hardware token and PKCS#11 module provider has different security features, for example, PIN Pads and biometric devices. OpenVPN can deal with a variety of them using the following directives:

```
pkcs11-protected-authentication 1
pkcs11-private-mode <mask>
```

The first is used primarily for keypads and biometric devices. The second contains <mask>, which is encoded as a hexadecimal number consisting of the following:

- ► 0 : try to determine automatically (this is the default)
- ► 1: use the `sign` operation on the card to access the private key
- ► 2: use the `sign recover` operation on the card to access the private key
- ► 4: use the `decrypt` operation on the card to access the private key
- ► 8: use the `unwrap` operation on the card to access the private key

This allows OpenVPN to access the private key when starting the SSL handshake with the remote VPN endpoint. Each hardware token and/or PKCS#11 module provider has its own setting.

See also

- ► The recipe *Using a hardware token* mentioned earlier in this chapter explains the basic setup and interaction with a hardware token.

Pin caching example

By default, OpenVPN caches the hardware token password (or token PIN) for as long as the session lasts. In this recipe, we will configure OpenVPN to "forget" the token PIN after a certain period for even better security. The downside is that the client will fail to reconnect and will exit if it is restarted after this caching period.

Getting ready

We use the following network layout:

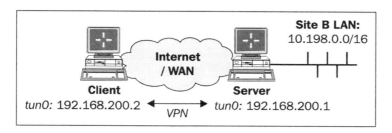

Keep the hardware token from the first recipe at hand. For this recipe, the server computer was running CentOS 5 Linux and OpenVPN 2.1.1. The client was running Fedora 12 Linux and OpenVPN 2.1.1. Keep the server configuration file `basic-udp-server.conf` from the *Chapter 2* recipe *Server-side routing* at hand.

How to do it...

1. Start the server using the configuration file 'basic-udp-server.conf':

    [root@server]# openvpn --config basic-udp-server.conf

2. Next, create the client configuration file:

    ```
    client
    proto udp
    remote openvpnserver.example.com

    port 1194

    dev tun
    nobind

    ca        /etc/openvpn/cookbook/ca.crt
    tls-auth /etc/openvpn/cookbook/ta.key 1

    ns-cert-type server

    pkcs11-providers /usr/lib64/libeTPkcs11.so
    pkcs11-id 'Aladdin\x20Ltd\x2E/eToken/001a01a9/Cookbook/20100703'

    pkcs11-pin-cache 300
    ```

The directive `pkcs11-id` and the serialized id `Aladdin\x20...` need to be specified on a single line. Save it as `example5-8-client.conf`.

3. Start the client:

```
[root@client]# openvpn --config example5-8-client.conf
[...]
Initialization Sequence Completed
```

The PIN code is now cached for 300 seconds. If we cause the OpenVPN client to restart within that period, then it will automatically reconnect.

4. First, we retrieve the process ID of the OpenVPN process and then we use the `kill` command to send a restart (USR1) signal:

```
[root@client]# ps -elf | grep '[o]penvpn'
4 S root      3647 3003  0 80   0 - 34458 poll_s 01:25 pts/1
00:00:00 openvpn --config example5-8-client.confopenvpn –config
example5-8-client.conf

[root@client]# kill –USR1 3647
```

The OpenVPN client log will show a successful reconnect. However, if the client is restarted after 300 seconds then the re-connect will fail and the client will terminate.

5. We wait for more than 300 seconds and then use the same `kill` command to restart the client:

```
[root@client]# kill –USR1 3647
```

The OpenVPN client log will now show:

```
... SIGUSR1[hard,] received, process restarting
... NOTE: OpenVPN 2.1 requires '--script-security 2' or higher to call
user-defined scripts or executables
... PKCS#11: Cannot get certificate object
... PKCS#11: Cannot get certificate object
... PKCS#11: Unable get rsa object
... Cannot load certificate "Aladdin\x20Ltd\x2E/eToken/001a01a9/
Cookbook/20100703" using PKCS#11 interface
... Error: private key password verification failed
... Exiting
```

How it works...

The following directive tells OpenVPN to "forget" any cached PIN codes after N seconds:

```
pkcs11-pin-cache N
```

If the client needs to reconnect after that period it will fail and will exit.

There's more...

When the PKCS#11 driver 'opensc-pkcs11.so' from the OpenSC package is used, it is convenient to add the following to the OpenVPN configuration file, even if no scripts are used:

```
script-security 2 system
```

There is a bug in OpenVPN up to 2.1.4 when this line is not present, which causes rekeying to fail. This means that the OpenVPN session will stop functioning after the rekeying interval, which is normally set to 1 hour. The above line is a work-around for this bug.

See also

▶ The recipe *Using a hardware token* earlier in this chapter, which explains the basic setup and interaction with a hardware token.

6
Scripting and Plugins

In this chapter, we will cover:

- ▸ Using a client-side up/down script
- ▸ Windows login greeter
- ▸ Using client-connect /client-disconnect scripts
- ▸ Using a `learn-address` script
- ▸ Using a `tls-verify` script
- ▸ Using an `auth-user-pass-verify` script
- ▸ Script order
- ▸ Script security and logging
- ▸ Using the `down-root` plugin
- ▸ Using the PAM authentication plugin

Introduction

One of the most powerful features of OpenVPN is its scripting capability and the ability to extend OpenVPN itself through the use of plugins. Using client-side scripting, the connection process can be tailored to the site-specific needs, such as setting up advanced routing options or mapping network drives. With server-side scripting, it is possible to assign a custom IP address to different clients, or to extend the authentication process by adding an extra username and password check. Plugins are very useful when integrating OpenVPN authentication into existing authentication frameworks, such as PAM, LDAP, or even Active Directory.

In this chapter, the focus will be on scripting, both at the client side and at the server side and on a few often-used plugins.

Using a client-side up/down script

In this recipe, we will use very simple up and down scripts on the client side to show how OpenVPN calls these scripts. By logging messages to a file, as well as the environment variables, we can easily see which information OpenVPN provides to the up and down scripts.

Getting ready

Install OpenVPN 2.1 or higher on two computers. Make sure the computers are connected over a network. Set up the client and server certificates using the first recipe from *Chapter 2*. For this recipe, the server computer was running Fedora 12 Linux and OpenVPN 2.1.1. The client was running Windows XP SP3 and OpenVPN 2.1.1.

How to do it...

1. Create the server configuration file:

```
proto udp
port 1194
dev tun
server 192.168.200.0 255.255.255.0

ca        /etc/openvpn/cookbook/ca.crt
cert      /etc/openvpn/cookbook/server.crt
key       /etc/openvpn/cookbook/server.key
dh        /etc/openvpn/cookbook/dh1024.pem
tls-auth /etc/openvpn/cookbook/ta.key 0

persist-key
persist-tun
keepalive 10 60

topology subnet

user   nobody
group nobody   # nogroup on some distros

daemon
log-append /var/log/openvpn.log
```

save it as example6-1-server.conf.

2. Start the server:

```
[root@server]# openvpn --config example6-1-server.conf
```

3. Create the client configuration file:

```
client
proto udp
remote openvpnserver.example.com
port 1194

dev tun
nobind

ca       "c:/program files/openvpn/config/ca.crt"
cert     "c:/program files/openvpn/config/client2.crt"
key      "c:/program files/openvpn/config/client2.key"
tls-auth "c:/program files/openvpn/config/ta.key" 1

ns-cert-type server

script-security 2
up   "c:\\program\ files\\openvpn\\scripts\\updown.bat"
down "c:\\program\ files\\openvpn\\scripts\\updown.bat"
```

Note the backslashes: when specifying the `ca`, `cert`, `key`, and `tls-auth` directives, forward slashes can be used, but not for the `up` and `down` scripts! Save it as `example6-1.ovpn`.

4. Next, on the Windows client, create the batch file `updown.bat`:

```
@echo off
echo === BEGIN '%script_type%' script === >> c:\temp\openvpn.log
echo Script name: [%0] >> c:\temp\openvpn.log
echo Command line argument 1: [%1] >> c:\temp\openvpn.log
echo Command line argument 2: [%2] >> c:\temp\openvpn.log
echo Command line argument 3: [%3] >> c:\temp\openvpn.log
echo Command line argument 4: [%4] >> c:\temp\openvpn.log
echo Command line argument 5: [%5] >> c:\temp\openvpn.log
echo Command line argument 6: [%6] >> c:\temp\openvpn.log
echo Command line argument 7: [%7] >> c:\temp\openvpn.log
echo Command line argument 8: [%8] >> c:\temp\openvpn.log
echo Command line argument 9: [%9] >> c:\temp\openvpn.log
set >> c:\temp\openvpn.log
echo === END '%script_type%' script === >> c:\temp\openvpn.log
```

5. Finally, start the OpenVPN client:

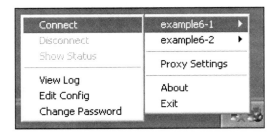

After the client successfully connects to the OpenVPN server, the log file
`c:\temp\openvpn.log` contains an output similar to the following:

```
=== BEGIN 'up' script ===
Script name: ["c:\program files\openvpn\scripts\updown.bat"]
Command line argument 1: [Local Area Connection 2]
Command line argument 2: [1500]
Command line argument 3: [1541]
Command line argument 4: [192.168.200.2]
Command line argument 5: [255.255.255.0]
Command line argument 6: [init]
Command line argument 7: []
Command line argument 8: []
Command line argument 9: [] 7
...
script_type=up
[dump of environment variables]
...
=== END 'up' script ===
```

When the client disconnects from the server, the script is called again, with the exact same
command-line parameters, but now the `script_type` is set to `down`.

Note that the first command-line argument contains the name of the `TUN` device. On Linux
and Mac OS systems, this will generally be `tun0` or `tun1` but on Windows platforms, it is the
actual name of the TAP-Win32 adapter.

How it works...

After the initial connection is made with the OpenVPN server, but before the VPN is fully
established, the OpenVPN client calls the `up` script. If the `up` script returns with an exit
code not equal to zero, the connection sequence is aborted.

Similarly, when the connection is shut down the `down` script is executed after the VPN
connection has been stopped.

Note the use of the double backslashes (\\) in the up and down directives: OpenVPN translates the backslash character internally and hence it needs to be specified twice. The backslash between c:\\program and files is required as otherwise OpenVPN cannot find the up and down scripts.

There's more...

In this section, we will see some more advanced tricks when using up and down scripts, including a sample script to verify the remote hostname of a VPN server.

Environment variables

The script used in this recipe merely writes out all the environment variables to a file. These environment variables contain useful information about the remote server, such as the certificate common_name. An extension to this script would be to check whether the certificate common_name matches the remote hostname. The IP address of the remote hostname is available as trusted_ip.

Calling the 'down' script before the connection terminates

The down script is executed after the actual connection to the OpenVPN server has been stopped. It is also possible to execute the script during the disconnect phase **before** the connection to the server is dropped. To do this, add the following directive to the client configuration file:

```
down-pre
```

Advanced: verify the remote hostname

A more advanced usage of an up script would be to verify that the remote hostname matches the remote IP address, similar to the way that a web browser verifies the address of secure websites. On Linux systems, this can easily be done using a shell script as an up script:

```
#!/bin/bash

# reverse DNS lookup
server_name=`host $untrusted_ip | \
  sed -n 's/.*name pointer \(.*\)\./\1/p'`
if [ "$server_name" != "$common_name" ]
then
    echo "Server certificate does not match hostname."
    echo "Aborting"
    exit 1
fi
```

But on Windows, this is trickier to achieve without resorting to tools such as 'PowerShell' or 'Cygwin'.

Windows login greeter

This recipe is a continuation of the previous recipe. It will demonstrate how to push a message from the OpenVPN server to the client during the connection phase. This message can be used as a legal warning or as a disclaimer message. In order to do this, we use the `setenv-safe` directive, which is available in OpenVPN 2.1 and higher. This directive can be pushed out to clients, in contrast with the more commonly-used `setenv` directive.

Getting ready

Install OpenVPN 2.1 or higher on two computers. Make sure the computers are connected over a network. Set up the client and server certificates using the first recipe from *Chapter 2, Client-server IP-only Networks*. For this recipe, the server computer was running Fedora 12 Linux and OpenVPN 2.1.1. The client was running Windows XP SP3 and OpenVPN 2.1.1. Keep the server configuration file, `example6-1-server.conf`, from the previous recipe at hand.

How to do it...

1. Append a line to the server configuration file `example6-1-server.conf`:

   ```
   push "setenv-safe MSG 'This is a message from the OpenVPN server'"
   ```

   Note that this is a single line. Save it as `example6-2-server.conf`.

2. Start the server:

   ```
   [root@server]# openvpn --config example6-2-server.conf
   ```

3. Next, create the client configuration file:

   ```
   client
   proto udp
   remote openvpnserver.example.com
   port 1194

   dev tun
   nobind

   ca       "c:/program files/openvpn/config/ca.crt"
   cert     "c:/program files/openvpn/config/client2.crt"
   key      "c:/program files/openvpn/config/client2.key"
   tls-auth "c:/program files/openvpn/config/ta.key" 1

   script-security 2 system
   up   "c:\\openvpn\\cookbook\\example6-2.vbs"
   ```

   Save it as `example6-2.ovpn`.

4. Next, create the Visual Basic Script, `example6-2.vbs`:

```
Set oShell = CreateObject( "WScript.Shell" )
msg=oShell.ExpandEnvironmentStrings("%OPENVPN_MSG%")
MsgBox msg, , "Welcome"
```

Save it in `c:\openvpn\cookbook`, or more importantly in a location with no spaces in the directory name. Start the OpenVPN client. During the connection phase, a message box will pop up:

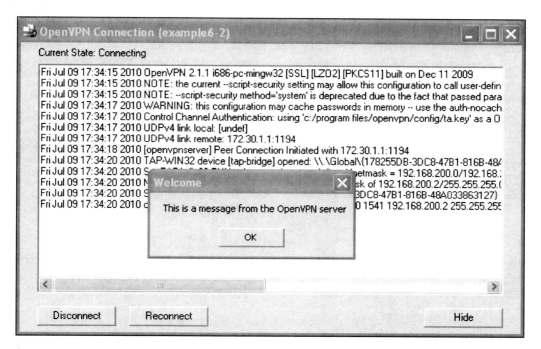

How it works...

The following server directive pushes the statement `setenv-safe MSG ...` to the connecting client:

```
push "setenv-safe MSG 'This is a message from the OpenVPN server'"
```

The client carries out the directive as if the following was specified:

```
setenv-safe MSG 'This is a message from the OpenVPN server'
```

The `setenv-safe` directive prepends `OPENVPN_` to all the environment variables prior to setting them to avoid conflicts with the existing system variables.

The following directive is required so that we can execute the Visual Basic script directly:

```
script-security 2 system
```

If we had specified it without the `system`, the OpenVPN client would not have been able to execute the VBS file, as it is not a real executable program.

The Visual Basic script picks up the new environment variable and displays a message box with the text.

There's more...

There are a few things to keep in mind when developing scripts for the Windows platform.

Spaces in filenames

An oddity of running scripts is related to the use of spaces in filenames: it is not easy to place a script in a directory with a space in it, nor should the script itself have a space in the filename. OpenVPN gets confused which part of the command is the actual script and which part comprises the command-line parameters to the script. Therefore, it is best to avoid spaces in the full pathnames for scripts altogether. With OpenVPN 2.1, we could also have used:

```
cd "c:\\program files\\openvpn\\scripts"
up "example6-2.vbs"
```

Another option is to always use the OpenVPN GUI application. This application switches to the directory `C:\Program Files\OpenVPN\config` prior to launching the OpenVPN. So, a script can also be referenced using:

```
up "..\\scripts\\example6-2.vbs"
```

Yet another option is to specify the path to the Windows scripting executable directly. You can then pass the name of the actual script as the first argument, which can then be stored in a directory containing spaces:

```
up   "%windir%\\system32\\wscript.exe
  \"c:\\program files\\openvpn\\scripts\\example6-2.vbs\""
```

Note that this statement is a single line.

setenv or setenv-safe

Normally, the following directive is used to set an environment variable that will be available to any script that OpenVPN calls:

```
setenv env-var value
```

However, the `setenv` directive cannot be pushed to a client from the server side. The `setenv-safe` directive, which was introduced in OpenVPN 2.1, can be pushed.

Security considerations

This recipe can be used to show a disclaimer or legal text when a user sets up a VPN connection. However, it is trivial for a user to circumvent this by modifying the client configuration file. If more stringent security is required, an application should be developed that can interact with the OpenVPN server itself.

Using client-connect/client-disconnect scripts

This recipe will demonstrate how to set up a client-connect script that gets executed on the server side when a new client connects. Similarly, a `client-disconnect` script can be specified that is executed when a client disconnects from the server. Client-connect and client-disconnect scripts can be used for several purposes:

- ▸ Extra authentication
- ▸ Opening and closing firewall ports
- ▸ Assigning specific IP address to special clients
- ▸ Writing out connection-specific configuration lines for a client

In this recipe, we will use a client-connect script to push a custom message to an OpenVPN client, based on the time of the day when the client connects.

Getting ready

Install OpenVPN 2.1 or higher on two computers. Make sure the computers are connected over a network. Set up the client and server certificates using the first recipe from _Chapter 2_. For this recipe, the server computer was running CentOS 5 Linux and OpenVPN 2.1.1. The client was running Windows XP SP3 and OpenVPN 2.1.1. Keep the server configuration file `example6-1-server.conf` from the first recipe of this chapter at hand.

How to do it...

1. Append the following lines to the `example6-1-server.conf` server configuration file:

```
script-security 2
client-connect      /etc/openvpn/cookbook/example6-3-connect.sh
```

   Save it as `example6-3-server.conf`.

2. Next , create the connect script:

```
#!/bin/bash

hour=`/bin/date +"%H"`
if [ $hour -lt 6 ]
then
    msg1="You're up at a weird hour"
elif [ $hour -le 12 ]
then
    msg1="Good morning"
elif [ $hour -lt 18 ]
then
    msg1="Good afternoon"
else
    msg1="Good evening"
fi

OPENVPN_MSG1="$msg1 $common_name"
OPENVPN_MSG2=`/bin/date +"Local time at the VPN server is
%H:%M:%S"`

# now write out the extra configuration lines to $1
echo "push \"setenv-safe MSG1 '$OPENVPN_MSG1'\"" > $1
echo "push \"setenv-safe MSG2 '$OPENVPN_MSG2'\"" >> $1
```

Save this file as `example6-3-connect.sh`.

3. Make sure the script is executable:

    [root@server]# chmod 755 example6-3-connect.sh

4. Start the server:

    [root@server]# openvpn --config example6-3-server.conf

5. The client configuration file is very similar to the one from the previous recipe:

```
client
proto udp
remote openvpnserver.example.com
port 1194

dev tun
nobind

ca       "c:/program files/openvpn/config/ca.crt"
cert     "c:/program files/openvpn/config/client2.crt"
```

```
key      "c:/program files/openvpn/config/client2.key"
tls-auth "c:/program files/openvpn/config/ta.key" 1

script-security 2 system
up   "c:\\openvpn\\cookbook\\example6-3.vbs"
```

Save it as `example6-3.ovpn`.

6. Create the VB Script file:

```
Set oShell = CreateObject( "WScript.Shell" )
msg1=oShell.ExpandEnvironmentStrings("%OPENVPN_MSG1%")
msg2=oShell.ExpandEnvironmentStrings("%OPENVPN_MSG2%")
MsgBox msg1 + vbcrlf + msg2, , "Welcome"
```

Save it as `c:\openvpn\cookbook\example6-3.vbs`.

7. Start the OpenVPN client:

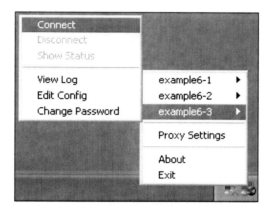

During the connection phase a message box will pop up:

How it works...

When a client connects, the OpenVPN server executes the `client-connect` script with several environment variables set that are related to the client connecting. The script writes out two lines to the connect-specific configuration file, which is passed as the first and only parameter to the `client-connect` script. This configuration file is then processed by the OpenVPN server as if it's a normal configuration file. The two lines that we use are:

```
push "setenv-safe MSG1 '$OPENVPN_MSG1'"
push "setenv-safe MSG2 '$OPENVPN_MSG2'"
```

This means that two environment variables are pushed out to the client. These environment variables are picked up by the OpenVPN client and are displayed in a dialog box using a Windows VBS script.

There's more...

In this section, we focus on `client-disconnect` and the many environment variables that are available to all OpenVPN scripts.

'client-disconnect' scripts

A `client-disconnect` script can be specified using:

```
client-disconnect /etc/openvpn/cookbook/disconnect.sh
```

This script is executed when the client disconnects from the server. Be aware that when a client first disconnects and a `explicit-exit-notify` is **not** specified on the client side, then the OpenVPN server will first try to reconnect several times to the client. If a client does not respond after several attempts then the `client-disconnect` script will be executed. Depending on the server configuration, this might be several minutes after the client has actually disconnected.

Environment variables

There is a multitude of environment variables available inside a client-connect and client-disconnect script. It is very instructive to write a `client-connect` script that does a little more than:

```
#!/bin.bash
env >> /tmp/log
```

Also, similar to the `up` and `down` script, is the environment variable `script_type` that contains the type of script as configured in the server configuration file. This gives the server administrator the option to write a single script for both `client-connect` and `client-disconnect`.

Absolute paths

Note that an absolute path is used for the script. Relative paths are allowed, but especially for the OpenVPN server, it is more secure to use absolute paths. Assuming that the OpenVPN server is always started in the same directory is a bad security practice. An alternative is to use:

```
cd /etc/openvpn/cookcook
client-connect example6-3-connect.sh
```

Using a 'learn-address' script

This recipe will demonstrate how to set up a `learn-address` script that is executed on the server side when there is a change in the address of a connecting client. Learn-address scripts can be used to dynamically set up firewalling rules for specific clients or to adjust routing tables.

In this recipe, we will use a `learn-address` script to open up a firewall and to set up masquerading for a client. When the client disconnects, the firewall is closed again and the 'iptables' masquerading rule is removed.

Getting ready

Install OpenVPN 2.1 or higher on two computers. Make sure the computers are connected over a network. Set up the client and server certificates using the first recipe from *Chapter 2*. In this recipe, the server computer was running CentOS 5 Linux and OpenVPN 2.1.1. The client was running Windows XP SP3 and OpenVPN 2.1.1. For the client, keep the client configuration file `basic-udp-client.ovpn` from the *Chapter 2* recipe *Using an 'ifconfig-pool' block* at hand.

How to do it...

1. Create the server configuration file:

```
proto udp
port 1194
dev tun

server 192.168.200.0 255.255.255.0

ca      /etc/openvpn/cookbook/ca.crt
cert    /etc/openvpn/cookbook/server.crt
key     /etc/openvpn/cookbook/server.key
dh      /etc/openvpn/cookbook/dh1024.pem
```

```
tls-auth /etc/openvpn/cookbook/ta.key 0

persist-key
persist-tun
keepalive 10 60

topology subnet

daemon
log-append /var/log/openvpn.log
script-security 2
learn-address /etc/openvpn/cookbook/example6-4-learn-address.sh
push "redirect-gateway def1"
```

Save it as `example6-4-server.conf`. Note that this server configuration file does not have the lines `user nobody` and `group nobody` (nor `group nogroup`).

2. Next, create the `learn-address` script:

```
#!/bin/bash

# $1 = action (add, update, delete)
# $2 = IP or MAC
# $3 = client_common name

if [ "$1" = "add" ]
then
    /sbin/iptables -I FORWARD -i tun0 -s $2 -j ACCEPT
    /sbin/iptables -I FORWARD -o tun0 -d $2 -j ACCEPT
    /sbin/iptables -t nat -I POSTROUTING -s $2 -o wlan0 -j
MASQUERADE
elif [ "$1" = "delete" ]
then
    /sbin/iptables -D FORWARD -i tun0 -s $2 -j ACCEPT
    /sbin/iptables -D FORWARD -o tun0 -d $2 -j ACCEPT
    /sbin/iptables -t nat -D POSTROUTING -s $2 -o wlan0 -j
MASQUERADE
fi
```

Save this file as `example6-4-learn-address.sh`.

3. Make sure the script is executable and start the OpenVPN server:

```
[root@server]# chmod 755 example6-4-learn-address.sh

[root@server]# openvpn --config example6-4-server.conf
```

4. Start the client using the Windows GUI using the basic configuration file:

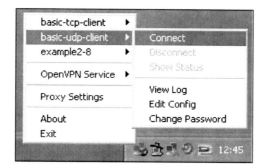

5. After the client connects to the server, check the 'iptables' firewall rules on the server:

[root@server]# iptables -L FORWARD -n -v

```
Chain FORWARD (policy ACCEPT 4612K packets, 1761M bytes)
 pkts bytes target     prot opt in      out      source
destination
     0     0 ACCEPT     all  -- *       tun0     0.0.0.0/0
192.168.200.2
     0     0 ACCEPT     all  -- tun0    *        192.168.200.2
0.0.0.0/0
```

[root@server]# iptables -t nat -L POSTROUTING -n -v

```
Chain POSTROUTING (policy ACCEPT 336K packets, 20M bytes)
 pkts bytes target     prot opt in      out      source
destination
     0     0 MASQUERADE all  -- *       wlan0    192.168.200.2
0.0.0.0/0
```

6. Disconnect the client, wait for a few minutes, and then verify that the 'iptables' rules have been removed.

How it works...

When a client connects to the OpenVPN server or disconnects from it, the OpenVPN server executes the learn-address script with several command-line arguments:

- ▸ $1: Action (add, update, delete).
- ▸ $2: IP or MAC. For tun-based network, this is the client IP address. For tap-based networks, this is the client (virtual) MAC address.
- ▸ $3: client_common name.

In this recipe, the `learn-address` is used to open up the firewall for the connecting client and to set up the masquerading rules for the client so that the clients can reach the other machines on the server-side LAN.

There's more...

In the following section, some details of the use of the `user nobody` directive and the `update` action of the `learn-address` script are given.

User 'nobody'

As stated earlier, this server configuration does not include the following lines:

```
user nobody
group nobody
```

(Or, `group nogroup` on some Linux distributions). If we had added these lines, then the OpenVPN server process would be running as user `nobody`. This user does not have the required rights to open and close firewall ports using 'iptables', hence they were removed in this example.

The 'update' action

The `learn-address` script is also called when the OpenVPN server detects an address change on the client side. This can happen most often in a 'TAP'-based network when an external DHCP server is used. The `learn-address` script can then adjust routing tables or firewalling rules based on the new client IP address.

Using a 'tls-verify' script

OpenVPN has several layers at which the credentials of a connecting client are verified. It is even possible to add a custom layer to the verification process by specifying a `tls-verify` script. In this recipe, we will demonstrate how such a script can be used to allow access only for a particular certificate.

Getting ready

Install OpenVPN 2.1 or higher on two computers. Make sure the computers are connected over a network. Set up the client and server certificates using the first recipe from *Chapter 2, Client-server IP-only network.* For this recipe, the server computer was running CentOS 5 Linux and OpenVPN 2.1.1. The client was running Windows 2000 and OpenVPN 2.1.1. Keep the client configuration file, `basic-udp-client.ovpn,` from the *Chapter 2* recipe *Using an 'ifconfig-pool' block* at hand.

How to do it...

1. Create the server configuration file:

```
proto udp
port 1194
dev tun

server 192.168.200.0 255.255.255.0

ca         /etc/openvpn/cookbook/ca.crt
cert       /etc/openvpn/cookbook/server.crt
key        /etc/openvpn/cookbook/server.key
dh         /etc/openvpn/cookbook/dh1024.pem
tls-auth /etc/openvpn/cookbook/ta.key 0

persist-key
persist-tun
keepalive 10 60

topology subnet

user    nobody
group nobody  # nogroup on some distros
daemon
log-append /var/log/openvpn.log

script-security 2
tls-verify /etc/openvpn/cookbook/example6-5-tls-verify.sh
```

Save it as `example6-5-server.conf`.

2. Next, create the `tls-verify` script:

```
#!/bin/bash

[ $# -lt 2 ] && exit 1

# if the depth is non-zero , continue processing
[ "$1" -ne 0 ] && exit 0

allowed_cns=`sed 's/ /_/g' $0.allowed`
for i in $allowed_cns
do
```

```
    [ "$2" = "$i" ] && exit 0
done
# catch-all
exit 1
```

Save this file as `example6-5-tls-verify.sh`.

3. Make sure the script is executable:

   [root@server]# chmod 755 example6-5-tls-verify.sh

4. Finally, create the list of allowed certificates:

   [root@server]# echo "/C=NL/O=Cookbook/CN=openvpnclient1/ emailAddress=openvpn-ca@cookbook.example.com" > /etc/openvpn/ cookbook/example6-5-tls-verify.sh.allowed

   Note that this is a one-line command.

5. Start the OpenVPN server:

   [root@server]# openvpn --config example6-5-server.conf

6. Start the client with the Windows GUI using the basic configuration file:

   The client should be able to connect normally.

7. Now, on the OpenVPN server, remove the file `/etc/openvpn/cookbook/ example6-5-tls-verify.sh.allowed` and reconnect. This time the server log will show the following:

```
CN not found in /etc/openvpn/cookbook/example6-5-tls-verify.
sh.allowed, denying access
… openvpnclient1:9007 TLS_ERROR: BIO read tls_read_plaintext
error: error:140890B2:SSL routines:SSL3_GET_CLIENT_CERTIFICATE:no
certificate returned
… openvpnclient1:9007 TLS Error: TLS object -> incoming plaintext
read error
… openvpnclient1:9007 TLS Error: TLS handshake failed
```

This means that the client is denied access by the OpenVPN server.

How it works...

When a client connects to the OpenVPN server, the `tls-verify` script is executed several times to verify the entire certificate chain of the connecting client. In this recipe, we look for the end-user certificate, which is the equivalent of the `client1.crt` file. When this end-user certificate is found in the `example6-5-tls-verify.sh.allowed` file, the script returns 0, indicating a successful verification. If it is not found, a message is printed to the OpenVPN log and the script returns 1. The OpenVPN server then denies the access to this particular client.

There's more...

In this recipe, we focus only on the end-user certificate using a simple lookup table. Of course, this could also have been achieved in many other ways (for example, by using a `client-config-dir` file). With a `tls-verify` script, it is also possible to disallow all the certificates from a particular certificate authority (CA). In more complex setups, where client certificates can be signed by many different CAs, it is sometimes very useful to temporarily refuse access to all the certificates from a particular CA. For example, to deny access to all certificates that are signed with the "Cookbook CA" from *Chapter 2*, Client-server IP-only Networks, the following script could be used:

```
#!/bin/bash

[ $# -lt 2 ] && exit 1
CA=`echo $2 | sed -n 's/.*\/CN=\(.*\)\/.*/\1/p'`
[ "$CA" = "Cookbook CA" ] && exit 1
```

Using an 'auth-user-pass-verify' script

Next to certificates and private keys, OpenVPN also offers the option to use a username and password mechanism for verifying client access. In this recipe, we will demonstrate how to set up an `auth-user-pass-verify` script, which is executed on the server side when a client connects. This script can be used to look up a user in a database or file and can also be used to verify that the right password was specified.

Getting ready

Install OpenVPN 2.1 or higher on two computers. Make sure the computers are connected over a network. Set up the client and server certificates using the first recipe from *Chapter 2*. For this recipe, the server computer was running CentOS 5 Linux and OpenVPN 2.1.1. The client was running Fedora 12 Linux and OpenVPN 2.1.1. Keep the server configuration file `example6-1-server.conf` from the recipe *Using a Client-side up/down script* at hand.

How to do it...

1. Append a line to the server configuration file `example6-1-server.conf`:

   ```
   script-security 2
   auth-user-pass-verify /etc/openvpn/cookbook/example6-6-aupv.sh
   via-file
   ```

   Note that the last line is a single line. Save it as `example6-6-server.conf`.

2. Create the `auth-user-pass-verify` script:

   ```bash
   #!/bin/bash

   # the username+password is stored in a temporary file
   # pointed to by $1
   username=`head -1 $1`
   password=`tail -1 $1`

   if grep "$username:$password" $0.passwd > /dev/null 2>&1
   then
     exit 0
   else
     if grep "$username" $0.passwd > /dev/null 2>&1
     then
       echo "auth-user-pass-verify: Wrong password entered for user
   '$username'"
     else
       echo "auth-user-pass-verify: Unknown user '$username'"
     fi
     exit 1
   fi
   ```

   Save it as `example6-6-aupv.sh`.

3. Set up a (very unsafe!) password file:

   ```
   [server]$ cd /etc/openvpn/cookbook
   [server]$ echo "cookbook:koobcook" > example6-6-aupv.sh.passwd
   ```

4. Make sure the `auth-user-pass-verify` script is executable, then start the server:

   ```
   [root@server]#$ chmod 755 example6-6-aupv.sh
   [root@server]# openvpn --config example6-6-server.conf
   ```

5. Next, create the client configuration file:

   ```
   client
   proto udp
   remote openvpnserver.example.com
   ```

```
port 1194

dev tun
nobind

ca        /etc/openvpn/cookbook/ca.crt
cert      /etc/openvpn/cookbook/client1.crt
key       /etc/openvpn/cookbook/client1.key
tls-auth /etc/openvpn/cookbook/ta.key 1

ns-cert-type server

auth-user-pass
```

Save it as `example6-6-client.conf`.

6. Start the client:

   ```
   [root@client]# openvpn --config example6-6-client.conf
   ```

7. First, the OpenVPN client will ask for the username and password:

   ```
   Enter Auth Username: cookbook
   Enter Auth Password: koobcook
   ```

   Then, if the right password is entered, the connection is established as normal.

8. Next, try to reconnect using a different username:

   ```
   Enter Auth Username: janjust
   Enter Auth Password: whatever
   ```

   The server log will now show:

   ```
   auth-user-pass-verify: Unknown user 'janjust'
   … openvpnclient:50834 TLS Auth Error: Auth Username/Password
   verification failed for peer
   ```

   And the client is refused access.

How it works...

The OpenVPN client first prompts the user for the Auth username and password. Note that the password is sent to the server over a secure channel, but the password itself is not hashed or encrypted. The server-side `auth-user-pass-verify` script is passed the username and password in a file on two lines. The script then looks up the username in its password file and verifies whether the right password was specified. If so, then the script exits with exit code 0, indicating success. Otherwise, an exit code of 1 is returned, causing the server to abort the client connection.

There's more...

In the following section, we'll see some details about how a password can be specified and can be passed from the server to the `auth-user-pass-verify` script.

Specifying the username and password in a file on the client

OpenVPN has the option to specify the username and password in a file on the client. For this, OpenVPN needs to be compiled with a special flag. Normally, this flag is not enabled, and hence when `auth-user-pass /etc/openvpn/cookbook/password-file` is specified, the OpenVPN client refuses to start the following:

```
... Sorry, 'Auth' password cannot be read from a file
... Exiting
```

Note that it is unsafe to allow the password to be stored on the client (in plaintext format!), so there is a good reason that this option is disabled by default. However, the OpenVPN manual page suggests that it is possible.

Passing the password via environment variables

In this recipe, we used:

```
auth-user-pass-verify example6-6-aupv.sh via-file
```

This configured the OpenVPN server to pass the client-supplied username and password via a temporary file. This temporary file is accessible only to the server process and hence this is a safe mechanism to pass the encrypted password to the `auth-user-pass-verify` script.

It is also possible to pass the username and password to the `auth-user-pass-verify` script via environment variables:

```
auth-user-pass-verify example6-6-aupv.sh via-env
```

The advantage of this is that no extra files need to be created. The downside is that passing a password via plaintext and via the environment is slightly less secure: it is easier (but not easy!) to snoop the environment of another process than it is to read a secure file owned by another user.

Script order

With all the possible scripts that can be configured on the OpenVPN server, it becomes important to determine the order in which these scripts are executed. In this recipe, we will find out what the order is, as well as the command-line parameters for each of these scripts.

Getting ready

Install OpenVPN 2.1 or higher on two computers. Make sure the computers are connected over a network. Set up the client and server certificates using the first recipe from *Chapter 2*. For this recipe, the server computer was running CentOS 5 Linux and OpenVPN 2.1.1. The client was running Fedora 12 Linux and OpenVPN 2.1.1. Keep the server configuration file `example6-1-server.conf` from the first recipe of this chapter at hand. Keep the client configuration file from the previous recipe at hand.

How to do it...

1. Append a line to the server configuration file `example6-1-server.conf`:

   ```
   script-security 2
   cd /etc/openvpn/cookbook
   up                      example6-7-script.sh
   route-up                example6-7-script.sh
   down                    example6-7-script.sh
   client-connect          example6-7-script.sh
   client-disconnect       example6-7-script.sh
   learn-address           example6-7-script.sh
   tls-verify              example6-7-script.sh
   auth-user-pass-verify example6-7-script.sh via-env
   ```

   Save it as `example6-7-server.conf`.

2. Create the following script:

   ```
   #!/bin/bash

   exec >> /tmp/example6-7.log 2>&1
   date +"%H:%M:%S: START $script_type script ==="
   echo "argv = $0 $@"
   echo "user = `id -un`/`id -gn`"
   date +"%H:%M:%S: END $script_type script ==="
   ```

   Save it as `example6-7-script.sh`.

3. Make sure the script is executable and then start the server:

   ```
   [root@server]# chmod 755 example6-7-script.sh
   [root@server]# openvpn --config example6-7-server.conf
   ```

4. Next, start the client:

   ```
   [root@client]# openvpn --config example6-6-client.conf
   ```

   The Auth username and password can be chosen arbitrarily, as they are not used.

5. After successfully connecting to the server, disconnect the client and wait for a few minutes until the server recognizes that the client has disconnected. Now, stop the OpenVPN server as well.

A log file will be created in `/tmp/example6-7.log`, parts of which are shown here:

```
18:45:45: START up script ===
18:45:45: START route-up script ===
18:46:26: START tls-verify script ===
18:46:26: START tls-verify script ===
18:46:27: START user-pass-verify script ===
18:46:27: START client-connect script ===
18:46:27: START learn-address script ===
argv = example6-7-script.sh add 192.168.200.2 openvpnclient1
18:47:14: START client-disconnect script ===
18:47:20: START learn-address script ===
argv = example6-7-script.sh delete 192.168.200.2
18:47:20: START down script ===
```

How it works...

There are many script hooks built into OpenVPN. When the OpenVPN server starts up and when a client connects and then disconnects, these scripts are executed one by one. The order is (for OpenVPN 2.1):

- up as user `root`.

- route-up as user `root`; afterwards, root privileges are dropped and OpenVPN switches to the user `nobody` as specified in the server configuration.

- tls-verify. The CA certificate that was used to sign the client certificate is passed for verification.

- tls-verify. The client certificate itself is passed.

- user-pass-verify.

- client-connect.

- learn-address with action `add`.

At this point, the client has successfully established a VPN connection. Now, when the client disconnects:

- client-disconnect

- learn-address with action `delete`

And when the server shuts down:

- down; note that this is run as user `nobody`!

There's more...

When writing scripts, it is very important to keep the script execution time in mind. The design of OpenVPN 2 is very monolithic: everything (except plugins, which we will come to later in this chapter) is run under a single thread. This means that while a script is executing, the whole OpenVPN server is temporarily unavailable for all other clients: the routing of packets stop, other clients cannot connect or disconnect and even the management interface is not responding. So, it is very important to ensure that all the server-side scripts execute very quickly.

This design flaw has been recognized, but it is not expected that there will be a major change until the arrival of OpenVPN 3.

Script security and logging

One of the major differences between OpenVPN 2.0 and 2.1 is related to the security when running scripts. With OpenVPN 2.0, all scripts were executed using a 'system' call and the entire set of server environment variables was passed to each script. With OpenVPN 2.1, the `script-security` configuration directive is introduced and the default for executing scripts is now the `execv` call, which is more secure. Also, it is wise to log output of your scripts for security reasons. With script logging output, including timestamps, it becomes much easier to track down problems and possible security incidents.

In this recipe, we will focus on the different options for the `script-security` configuration directive and on the methods to ease the logging of script output.

Getting ready

Install OpenVPN 2.1 or higher on two computers. Make sure the computers are connected over a network. Set up the client and server certificates using the first recipe from *Chapter 2*. For this recipe, the server computer was running CentOS 5 Linux and OpenVPN 2.1.1. The client was running Fedora 12 Linux and OpenVPN 2.1.1. Keep the server configuration file `example6-1-server.conf` from the first recipe at hand.

How to do it...

1. Start the OpenVPN server using the configuration file from the first recipe:

   ```
   [root@server]# openvpn --config example6-1-server.conf
   ```

2. Create the client configuration file:

   ```
   client
   proto udp
   remote openvpnserver.example.com
   ```

```
port 1194

dev tun
nobind

ca         /etc/openvpn/cookbook/ca.crt
cert       /etc/openvpn/cookbook/client1.crt
key        /etc/openvpn/cookbook/client1.key
tls-auth /etc/openvpn/cookbook/ta.key 1

ns-cert-type server

up "/etc/openvpn/cookbook/example6-8-up.sh arg1 arg2"
```

Save it as `example6-8-client.conf`. Notice the lack of the `script-security` directive.

3. Create the `up` script:

```
#!/bin/bash

exec >> /etc/openvpn/cookbook/example6-8.log 2>&1
date +"%H:%M:%S: START $script_type script ==="
echo "argv = [$0] [$1] [$2] [$3] [$4]"
pstree $PPID
date +"%H:%M:%S: END $script_type script ==="
```

Save it as `example6-8-up.sh` and make sure it is executable.

4. Start the OpenVPN client:

```
[client]$ openvpn --config example6-8-client.conf
```

The client appears to connect successfully until the `up` script needs to be executed:

```
... /etc/openvpn/cookbook/example6-8-up.sh [arguments]

... openvpn_execve: external program may not be called unless '--
script-security 2' or higher is enabled.  Use '--script-security 3
system' for backward compatibility with 2.1_rc8 and earlier.  See
--help text or man page for detailed info.
... script failed: external program fork failed
... Exiting
```

5. When we repeat the above with an extra command-line parameter `--script-security 2`, the client can connect successfully:

```
[client]$ openvpn --config example6-8-client.conf  \
    --script-security 2
```

The log file `/etc/openvpn/cookbook/example6-8.log` now shows:

```
19:07:22: START up script ===
argv = [/etc/openvpn/cookbook/example6-8-up.sh] [arg1] [arg2] [tun0]
[1500]
openvpn---example6-8-up.s---pstree
19:07:22: END up script ===
```

If we repeat the above exercise with `--script-security 3` or `--script-security 2 system` directives, we would get a similar output.

How it works...

In order to execute the scripts on either the client or the server, the directive, `script-security 2` (or 3) must be specified, otherwise, OpenVPN 2.1 or higher will refuse to start. The following parameters can be specified for the `script-security` directive:

► 0: No external programs can be called. This means that OpenVPN cannot successfully start up, except on Microsoft Windows under certain circumstances.

► 1: Only built-in external programs (such as `/sbin/ifconfig`, `/sbin/ip` on Linux, `netsh.exe`, and `route.exe` on Windows) can be called.

► 2: Built-ins and scripts can be called.

► 3: Same as 2, but now passwords can be passed to scripts via environment variables as well.

There is a second parameter for the `script-security` directive:

► `execve`: Call external programs using the `execve` call. This is the default.

► `system`: Call external programs using the `system` call.

The difference between the two is a minor one, yet there are subtle differences, especially, when spaces are used in path- or filenames.

There's more...

There are subtle differences between running scripts on Linux/NetBSD/Mac OS and on Windows. On Windows, the system call `CreateProcess` is used by default. If `script-security 2 system` is used a `system` call is used. The biggest difference is seen when spaces are used in path- or filenames. OpenVPN often gets confused which part of a statement is the actual executable and which part are command-line parameters. The following script runs fine when using `--script-security 2`:

```
up "c:\\program\ files\\openvpn\\scripts\\example6-8-up.bat"
```

However, when `--script-security 2 system` is used, an error is reported:

```
c:\program' is not recognized as an internal or external command
```

Using the 'down-root' plugin

OpenVPN supports a plugin architecture, where external plugins can be used to extend the functionality of OpenVPN. Plugins are special modules or libraries that adhere to the OpenVPN Plugin API. One of these plugins is the `down-root` plugin, which is available only on Linux. This allows the user to run specified commands as user `root` when OpenVPN shuts down. Normally, the OpenVPN process drops root privileges (if the `--user` directive is used) for security reasons. While this is a good security measure, it makes it hard to undo some of the actions that an `up` script can perform, which is run as user `root`. For this, the `down-root` plugin was developed. This recipe will demonstrate how the `down-root` plugin can be used to remove a file that was created by an `up` script.

Getting ready

Set up the server certificates using the first recipe from *Chapter 2*, Client-server IP-only. For this recipe, the server computer was running CentOS 5 Linux and OpenVPN 2.1.1. No client computer was required.

How to do it...

1. Create the server configuration file:

```
proto udp
port 1194
dev tun

server 192.168.200.0 255.255.255.0

ca      /etc/openvpn/cookbook/ca.crt
cert    /etc/openvpn/cookbook/server.crt
```

```
key       /etc/openvpn/cookbook/server.key
dh        /etc/openvpn/cookbook/dh1024.pem
tls-auth  /etc/openvpn/cookbook/ta.key 0

persist-key
persist-tun
keepalive 10 60

topology subnet

user   nobody
group nobody   # nogroup on some distros

daemon
log-append /var/log/openvpn.log

script-security 2
cd /etc/openvpn/cookbook
up "example6-9.sh"
plugin ./openvpn-down-root.so "./example6-9.sh --down"

suppress-timestamps
verb 5
```

Save it as `example6-9-server.conf`.

2. Next, create the `up` script, which we will also use for the `down-root` plugin:

```
#!/bin/sh
if [ "$script_type" = "up" ]
then
  touch /tmp/example6-9.tempfile
fi
if [ "$1" = "--down" ]
then
  rm /tmp/example6-9.tempfile
fi
```

Save it as `example6-9.sh` and make sure it is executable.

3. Start the OpenVPN server:

```
[root@server]# openvpn --config example6-9-server.conf
```

The server log file will now show:

```
PLUGIN_CALL: POST ./openvpn-down-root.so/PLUGIN_UP status=0
example6-9.sh tun0 1500 1541 192.168.200.1 192.168.200.2 init
```

This indicates the plugin has started. The fact that there were no error codes right after the up script was executed indicates that it ran successfully.

4. Verify that the file /tmp/example6-9.tempfile was created on the server.

5. Next, stop the server. The server log will now show:

```
PLUGIN_CALL: POST ./openvpn-down-root.so/PLUGIN_DOWN status=0
PLUGIN_CLOSE: ./openvpn-down-root.so
```

6. Verify that the file /tmp/example6-9.tempfile has been removed.

How it works...

The down-root plugin is registered at system startup when the OpenVPN server process is still running with root privileges. Plugins are spawned off in a separate thread, meaning that when the main OpenVPN process drops its root privileges, the plugins will still have full root access. When OpenVPN shuts down, the plugin is called and it removes the file created by the user root when the server started.

An interesting part of the server log file is:

```
/sbin/ifconfig tun0 0.0.0.0
SIOCSIFADDR: Permission denied
SIOCSIFFLAGS: Permission denied
Linux ip addr del failed: external program exited with error status:
255
PLUGIN_CALL: POST ./openvpn-down-root.so/PLUGIN_DOWN status=0
PLUGIN_CLOSE: ./openvpn-down-root.so
```

This indicates that the OpenVPN process was indeed not capable of running the command /sbin/ifconfig tun0 0.0.0.0, proving that root privileges had been successfully dropped. The plugin was then called, which did have root privileges, so that it could remove the root-owned file in /tmp.

Note that it is required to specify a path starting with './' for both the plugin itself and the script that the plugin runs. If the leading './' is not specified on Linux or Mac OS, then OpenVPN will not be able to find the plugin nor the script that the plugin needs to run, as the current directory ('.') normally is not part of the PATH environment variable.

Also note that the up script is called with an environment variable script_type set but that this is not true for plugins. To overcome this, an extra parameter was added so that the same script could be used as both the up and down-root scripts.

There's more...

Plugins are supported on Linux, Net/FreeBSD, and on Windows. The following script callbacks can be intercepted using a plugin:

- ► up
- ► down
- ► route-up
- ► ipchange
- ► tls-verify
- ► auth-user-pass-verify
- ► client-connect
- ► client-disconnect
- ► learn-address

See also

- ► The next recipe, *Using the PAM authentication plugin*, which explains how to use an OpenVPN plugin to authenticate remote VPN clients.

Using the PAM authentication plugin

A very useful plugin for OpenVPN is a plugin to validate a username using the Linux/UNIX PAM authentication system. PAM stands for Pluggable Authentication Modules and is a very modular system for allowing users access to system resources. It is used by most modern Linux and UNIX variants, offering a very flexible and extendible system for authenticating and authorizing users. In this recipe, we will use the PAM authentication plugin as a replacement of an auth-user-pass-verify script to validate a remote user's credentials against the system PAM configuration.

Getting ready

Set up the client and server certificates using the first recipe from *Chapter 2, Client-server IP-only Networks*. For this recipe, the server computer was running CentOS 5 Linux and OpenVPN 2.1.1. The client was running Windows 2000 and OpenVPN 2.1.1.

How to do it...

1. Create the server configuration file:

```
proto udp
port 1194
dev tun

server 192.168.200.0 255.255.255.0

ca       /etc/openvpn/cookbook/ca.crt
cert     /etc/openvpn/cookbook/server.crt
key      /etc/openvpn/cookbook/server.key
dh       /etc/openvpn/cookbook/dh1024.pem
tls-auth /etc/openvpn/cookbook/ta.key 0

persist-key
persist-tun
keepalive 10 60

topology subnet

user   nobody
group nobody  # nogroup on some distros

daemon
log-append /var/log/openvpn.log

verb 5
suppress-timestamps

plugin /etc/openvpn/cookbook/openvpn-auth-pam.so "login login
USERNAME password PASSWORD"
```

Note that the last line of the server configuration file is a single line. Save it as `example6-10-server.conf`.

2. Start the OpenVPN server:

```
[root@server]# openvpn --config example6-10-server.conf
```

The server log file will now show:

```
AUTH-PAM: BACKGROUND: INIT service='login'
PLUGIN_INIT: POST /etc/openvpn/cookbook/openvpn-auth-pam.so
'[/etc/openvpn/cookbook/openvpn-auth-pam.so] [login] [login]
[USERNAME] [password] [PASSWORD]' intercepted=PLUGIN_AUTH_USER_
PASS_VERIFY
```

This indicates that the PAM plugin successfully initialized in the background.

3. Next, create the client configuration file:

```
client
proto udp
remote openvpnserver.example.com
port 1194

dev tun
nobind

ca        "c:/program files/openvpn/config/ca.crt"
cert      "c:/program files/openvpn/config/client1.crt"
key       "c:/program files/openvpn/config/client1.key"
tls-auth "c:/program files/openvpn/config/ta.key" 1

auth-user-pass
```

Save it as example6-10.ovpn.

4. Start the OpenVPN client. The OpenVPN GUI on Windows will first prompt for the Auth username and password:

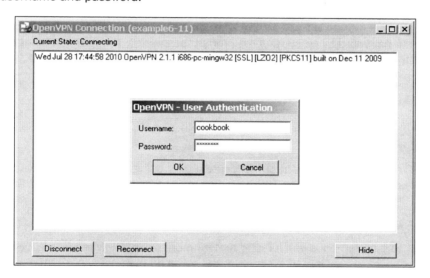

On the server used in this recipe, a special user cookbook was created. After typing in the username and password, the connection to the server is successfully established. The OpenVPN server log shows:

```
AUTH-PAM: BACKGROUND: received command code: 0
AUTH-PAM: BACKGROUND: USER: cookbook
AUTH-PAM: BACKGROUND: my_conv[0] query='login:' style=2
AUTH-PAM: BACKGROUND: name match found, query/match-string ['login:',
'login'] = 'USERNAME'
```

```
AUTH-PAM: BACKGROUND: my_conv[0] query='Password: ' style=1
AUTH-PAM: BACKGROUND: name match found, query/match-string ['Password:
', 'password'] = 'PASSWORD'
... openvpnclient:50887 PLUGIN_CALL: POST /etc/openvpn/cookbook/openvpn-
auth-pam.so/PLUGIN_AUTH_USER_PASS_VERIFY status=0
... openvpnclient:50887 TLS: Username/Password authentication succeeded
for username 'cookbook'
```

This shows that the user was successfully authenticated using PAM.

How it works...

The PAM authentication plugin intercepts the `auth-user-pass-verify` callback. When the OpenVPN client connects and passes along the username and password, the plugin wakes up. It queries the PAM subsystem by looking at the "login" module (this is the first parameter for the `openvpn-auth-pam.so` file). The other parameters are used by the auth-pam plugin to know which input to expect from the PAM subsystem:

```
login USERNAME password PASSWORD
```

The PAM "login" subsystem will ask for the username by presenting the prompt "login" and will ask for the password by presenting the prompt "password". The auth-pam plugin uses this information to know where to fill in the username (`USERNAME`) and password (`PASSWORD`).

After the user has been successfully authenticated by the PAM subsystem, the connection is established.

There's more...

It would also have been possible to authenticate a user using an 'auth-user-pass-verify' script, which queries the PAM subsystem. There are two major advantages to using the PAM plugin for this:

▶ It is not required to use the 'script-security' directive at all.

▶ The plugin method is much faster and far more scalable. When many users try to connect to the OpenVPN server at the same time, the VPN performance would be greatly affected when using an `auth-user-pass-verify` script, as for each connecting a user, a separate process needs to be started, during which the OpenVPN's main thread is installed.

See also

▶ The previous recipe, *Using the 'down-root' plugin*, in which the basics of using OpenVPN plugins are explained.

7
Troubleshooting OpenVPN: Configurations

In this chapter, we will cover:

- ▸ Cipher mismatches
- ▸ TUN versus TAP mismatches
- ▸ Compression mismatches
- ▸ Key mismatches
- ▸ Troubleshooting MTU and `tun-mtu` issues
- ▸ Troubleshooting network connectivity
- ▸ Troubleshooting `client-config-dir` issues
- ▸ How to read the OpenVPN log files

Introduction

The topic of this chapter and the next is troubleshooting OpenVPN. This chapter will focus on troubleshooting OpenVPN misconfigurations, whereas the next chapter will focus on the all-too-common routing issues that occur when setting up a VPN.

The recipes in these chapters will therefore deal first with breaking the things. We will then provide the tools on how to find and solve the configuration errors. Some of the configuration directives used in this chapter have not been demonstrated before, so even if you are not interested in breaking things this chapter will still be insightful.

Cipher mismatches

In this recipe, we will change the cryptographic ciphers that OpenVPN uses. Initially, we will change the cipher only on the client side, which will cause the initialization of the VPN connection to fail. The primary purpose of this recipe is to show the error messages that appear, not to explore the different types of ciphers that OpenVPN supports.

Getting ready

Install OpenVPN 2.0 or higher on two computers. Make sure the computers are connected over a network. Set up the client and server certificates using the first recipe from *Chapter 2*. For this recipe, the server computer was running CentOS 5 Linux and OpenVPN 2.1.1. The client was running Fedora 13 Linux and OpenVPN 2.1.1. Keep the configuration file basic-udp-server.conf from the *Chapter 2* recipe *Server-side routing* at hand, as well as the client configuration file basic-udp-client.conf.

How to do it...

1. Start the server using the configuration file basic-udp-server.conf:

    ```
    [root@server]# openvpn --config basic-udp-server.conf
    ```

2. Next, create the client configuration file by appending a line to the basic-udp-client.conf file:

    ```
    cipher CAST5-CBC
    ```

    Save it as example7-1-client.conf.

3. Start the client, after which the following message will appear in the client log:

    ```
    [root@client]# openvpn --config example7-1-client.conf
    ... WARNING: 'cipher' is used inconsistently, local='cipher CAST5-
    CBC', remote='cipher BF-CBC'
    ... [openvpnserver] Peer Connection Initiated with server-ip:1194
    ... TUN/TAP device tun0 opened
    ... /sbin/ip link set dev tun0 up mtu 1500
    ... /sbin/ip addr add dev tun0 192.168.200.2/24 broadcast
    192.168.200.255
    ... Initialization Sequence Completed
    ... Authenticate/Decrypt packet error: cipher final failed
    ```

And, similarly, on the server side:

```
... client-ip:52461 WARNING: 'cipher' is used inconsistently,
local='cipher BF-CBC', remote='cipher CAST5-CBC'
... client-ip:52461 [openvpnclient1] Peer Connection Initiated with
openvpnclient1:52461
... openvpnclient1/client-ip:52461 Authenticate/Decrypt packet
error: cipher final failed
... openvpnclient1/client-ip:52461 Authenticate/Decrypt packet
error: cipher final failed
```

The connection will not be successfully established, but it will also not be disconnected immediately.

How it works...

During the connection phase, the client and the server negotiate several parameters needed to secure the connection. One of the most important parameters in this phase is the encryption cipher, which is used to encrypt and decrypt all the messages. If the client and server are using different ciphers, then they are simply not capable of talking to each other.

By adding the following configuration directive to the server configuration file, the client and the server can communicate again:

```
cipher CAST5-CBC
```

There's more...

OpenVPN supports quite a few ciphers, although support for some of the ciphers is still experimental. To view the list of supported ciphers, type:

$ openvpn --show-ciphers

This will list all ciphers with both variables and fixed cipher length. The ciphers with variable cipher length are very well supported by OpenVPN, the others can sometimes lead to unpredictable results.

TUN versus TAP mismatches

A common mistake when setting up a VPN based on OpenVPN is the type of adapter that is used. If the server is configured to use a TUN-style network but a client is configured to use a TAP-style interface, then the VPN connection will fail. In this recipe, we will show what is typically seen when this common configuration error is made.

Getting ready

Install OpenVPN 2.0 or higher on two computers. Make sure the computers are connected over a network. Set up the client and server certificates using the first recipe from *Chapter 2, Client-server IP-only Networks*. For this recipe, the server computer was running CentOS 5 Linux and OpenVPN 2.1.1. The client was running Fedora 13 Linux and OpenVPN 2.1.1. Keep the configuration file, `basic-udp-server.conf`, from the *Chapter 2* recipe *Server-side routing* at hand, as well as the client configuration file `basic-udp-client.conf`.

How to do it...

1. Start the server using the configuration file `basic-udp-server.conf`:

   [root@server]# openvpn --config basic-udp-server.conf

2. Next, create the client configuration:

   ```
   client
   proto udp
   remote openvpnserver.example.com
   port 1194

   dev tap
   nobind

   ca        /etc/openvpn/cookbook/ca.crt
   cert      /etc/openvpn/cookbook/client1.crt
   key       /etc/openvpn/cookbook/client1.key
   tls-auth /etc/openvpn/cookbook/ta.key 1

   ns-cert-type server
   ```

   Save it as `example7-2-client.conf`.

3. Start the client:

   [root@client]# openvpn --config example7-2-client.conf

   The client log willl show:

   ```
   … WARNING: 'dev-type' is used inconsistently, local='dev-type
   tap', remote='dev-type tun'
   … WARNING: 'link-mtu' is used inconsistently, local='link-mtu
   1573', remote='link-mtu 1541'
   … WARNING: 'tun-mtu' is used inconsistently, local='tun-mtu 1532',
   remote='tun-mtu 1500'
   ```

```
... [openvpnserver] Peer Connection Initiated with server-ip:1194
... TUN/TAP device tap0 opened
... /sbin/ip link set dev tap0 up mtu 1500
... /sbin/ip addr add dev tap0 192.168.200.2/24 broadcast
192.168.200.255
... Initialization Sequence Completed
```

At this point, you can try pinging the server, but it will respond with an error:

[client]$ ping 192.168.200.1

```
PING 192.168.200.1 (192.168.200.1) 56(84) bytes of data.
From 192.168.200.2 icmp_seq=2 Destination Host Unreachable
From 192.168.200.2 icmp_seq=3 Destination Host Unreachable
From 192.168.200.2 icmp_seq=4 Destination Host Unreachable
```

How it works...

A TUN-style interface offers a point-to-point connection over which only TCP/IP traffic can be tunneled. A TAP-style interface offers the equivalent of an Ethernet interface that includes extra headers. This allows a user to tunnel other types of traffic over the interface. When the client and the server are misconfigured, the expected packet size is different:

... WARNING: 'tun-mtu' is used inconsistently, local='tun-mtu 1532', remote='tun-mtu 1500'

This shows that each packet that is sent through a TAP-style interface is 32 bytes larger than the packets sent through a TUN-style interface.

By correcting the client configuration, this problem is resolved.

Compression mismatches

OpenVPN supports on-the-fly compression of the traffic that is sent over the VPN tunnel. This can improve the performance over a slow network line, but it does add a little overhead. When transferring uncompressible data (such as ZIP files), the performance actually decreases slightly.

If the compression is enabled on the server but not on the client, then the VPN connection will fail.

Getting ready

Install OpenVPN 2.0 or higher on two computers. Make sure the computers are connected over a network. Set up the client and server certificates using the first recipe from *Chapter 2, Client-server IP-only Networks*. For this recipe, the server computer was running CentOS 5 Linux and OpenVPN 2.1.1. The client was running Fedora 13 Linux and OpenVPN 2.1.1. Keep the configuration file, `basic-udp-server.conf`, from the *Chapter 2* recipe *Server-side routing* at hand, as well as the client configuration file `basic-udp-client.conf`.

How to do it...

1. Append a line to the server configuration file `basic-udp-server.conf`:

    `comp-lzo`

    Save it as `example7-3-server.conf`.

2. Start the server:

    `[root@server]# openvpn --config example7-3-server.conf`

3. Next, start the client:

    `[root@client]# openvpn --config basic-udp-client.conf`

    The connection will initiate but when data is sent over the VPN connection, the following messages will appear:

    `Initialization Sequence Completed`

    `... write to TUN/TAP : Invalid argument (code=22)`

    `... write to TUN/TAP : Invalid argument (code=22)`

How it works...

During the connection phase, no compression is used to transfer information between the client and the server. One of the parameters that is negotiated is the use of compression for the actual VPN payload. If there is a configuration mismatch between the client and the server, then both the sides will get confused by the traffic that the other side is sending.

With a network fully comprising OpenVPN 2.1 clients and an OpenVPN 2.1 server, this can be fixed for all the clients by just adding another line:

    push "comp-lzo"

There's more...

OpenVPN 2.0 did not have the ability to push compression directives to the clients. This means that an OpenVPN 2.0 server does not understand this directive, nor do OpenVPN 2.0 clients. So, if an OpenVPN 2.1 server pushes out this directive to an OpenVPN 2.0 client, the connection will fail.

Key mismatches

OpenVPN offers extra protection for its TLS control channel in the form of HMAC keys. These keys are exactly the same as the static "secret" keys used in *Chapter 1, Point-to-Point Networks*, for point-to-point style networks. For multi-client style networks, this extra protection can be enabled using the `tls-auth` directive. If there is a mismatch between the client and the server related to this `tls-auth` key, then the VPN connection will fail to get initialized.

Getting ready

Install OpenVPN 2.0 or higher on two computers. Make sure the computers are connected over a network. Set up the client and server certificates using the first recipe from *Chapter 2, Client-server IP-only Networks*.. For this recipe, the server computer was running CentOS 5 Linux and OpenVPN 2.1.1. The client was running Fedora 13 Linux and OpenVPN 2.1.1. Keep the configuration file, `basic-udp-server.conf`, from the *Chapter 2* recipe *Server-side routing* at hand, as well as the client configuration file `basic-udp-client.conf`.

How to do it...

1. Start the server using the configuration file `basic-udp-server.conf`:

   ```
   [root@server]# openvpn --config basic-udp-server.conf
   ```

2. Next, create the client configuration:

   ```
   client
   proto udp
   remote openvpnserver
   port 1194

   dev tun
   nobind

   ca          /etc/openvpn/cookbook/ca.crt
   ```

```
cert      /etc/openvpn/cookbook/client1.crt
key       /etc/openvpn/cookbook/client1.key
tls-auth /etc/openvpn/cookbook/ta.key
```

```
ns-cert-type server
```

Note the lack of the second parameter for `tls-auth`. Save it as `example7-4-client.conf` file.

3. Start the client:

    `[root@client]# openvpn --config example7-4-client.conf`

    The client log will show no errors, but the connection will not be established either. In the server log we'll find:

    ... `Initialization Sequence Completed`

    ... `Authenticate/Decrypt packet error: packet HMAC authentication failed`

    ... `TLS Error: incoming packet authentication failed from client-ip:54454`

This shows that the client `openvpnclient1` is connecting using the wrong `tls-auth` parameter and the connection is refused.

How it works...

At the very first phase of the connection initialization, the client and the server verify each other's HMAC keys. If an HMAC key is not configured correctly, then the initialization is aborted and the connection will fail to establish. As the OpenVPN server is not able to determine whether the client is simply misconfigured or whether a malicious client is trying to overload the server, the connection is simply dropped. This causes the client to keep listening for the traffic from the server, until it eventually times out.

In this recipe, the misconfiguration consisted of the missing parameter 1 behind:

```
tls-auth /etc/openvpn/cookbook/ta.key
```

The second parameter to the `tls-auth` directive is the direction of the key. Normally, the following convention is used:

*   0: from server to client
*   1: from client to server

This parameter causes OpenVPN to derive its HMAC keys from a different part of the `ta.key` file. If the client and server disagree on which parts the HMAC keys are derived from, the connection cannot be established. Similarly, when the client and server are deriving the HMAC keys from different `ta.key` files, the connection can also not be established.

Chapter 1's recipe, *Multiple secret keys*, in which the format and usage of the OpenVPN secret keys is explained in detail.

Troubleshooting MTU and tun-mtu issues

One of the more advanced features of OpenVPN is the ability to tune the network parameters of both the TUN (or TAP) adapter and the parameters of the encrypted link itself. This is a frequent cause of configuration mistakes, leading to low performance or even the inability to successfully transfer data across the VPN tunnel. This recipe will show what happens if there is an MTU (Maximum Transfer Unit) mismatch between the client and the server and how this mismatch can cause the VPN tunnel to fail only under certain circumstances.

Getting ready

Install OpenVPN 2.0 or higher on two computers. Make sure the computers are connected over a network. Set up the client and server certificates using the first recipe from *Chapter 2, Client-server IP-only Networks..* For this recipe, the server computer was running CentOS 5 Linux and OpenVPN 2.1.1. The client was running Fedora 13 Linux and OpenVPN 2.1.1. Keep the configuration file `basic-udp-server.conf` from the *Chapter 2* recipe *Server-side routing* at hand, as well as the client configuration file `basic-udp-client.conf`.

How to do it...

1. Start the server using the configuration file `basic-udp-server.conf`:

    [root@server]# openvpn --config basic-udp-server.conf

2. Next, create the client configuration file by appending a line to the `basic-udp-client.conf` file:

    tun-mtu 1400

    Save it as `example7-5-client.conf`.

3. Start the client and look at the client log:

    [root@client]# openvpn --config example7-5-client.conf

    ```
    ... WARNING: 'link-mtu' is used inconsistently, local='link-mtu
    1441', remote='link-mtu 1541'
    ... WARNING: 'tun-mtu' is used inconsistently, local='tun-mtu 1400',
    remote='tun-mtu 1500'
    ... [openvpnserver] Peer Connection Initiated with server-ip:1194
    ... TUN/TAP device tun0 opened
    ```

```
... /sbin/ip link set dev tun0 up mtu 1400
... /sbin/ip addr add dev tun0 192.168.200.2/24 broadcast
192.168.200.255
... Initialization Sequence Completed
```

There are a few warnings when the tunnel comes up, but the connection is initialized.

4. It is possible to send a traffic over the link, which we can verify using the `ping` command:

   [client]$ ping -c 2 192.168.200.1

   ```
   PING 192.168.200.1 (192.168.200.1) 56(84) bytes of data.
   64 bytes from 192.168.200.1: icmp_seq=1 ttl=64 time=30.6 ms
   64 bytes from 192.168.200.1: icmp_seq=2 ttl=64 time=30.7 ms
   ```

5. However, when sending larger packets, for example:

   [client]$ ping -s 1450 192.168.200.1

   Then, the following messages appear in the client log file:

   ... Authenticate/Decrypt packet error: packet HMAC authentication failed

   ... Authenticate/Decrypt packet error: packet HMAC authentication failed

The same thing will happen if the client tries to download a large file.

How it works...

The MTU or Maximum Transfer Unit determines how large packets can be that are sent over the tunnel without breaking up (fragmenting) the packet into multiple pieces. If the client and the server disagree on this MTU size, then the server will send packets to the client that are simply too large. This causes an HMAC failure (if `tls-auth` is used, as in this recipe) or the part of the packet that is too large is thrown away.

There's more...

On the Windows platform, it is not easy to change the MTU setting for the Tap-Win32 adapter that OpenVPN uses. The directive `tun-mtu` can be specified but the Windows version of OpenVPN cannot alter the actual MTU setting, as Windows did not support this until Windows Vista. OpenVPN, however, does not yet have the capability of altering the MTU size on Windows Vista or Windows 7.

See also

▶ *Chapter 9, Performance Tuning*, which gives some hints and examples on how to optimize the `tun-mtu` directive.

Troubleshooting network connectivity

This recipe will focus on the type of log messages that are typically seen when the OpenVPN configurations are fine, but the network connectivity is not. In most cases, this is due to a firewall blocking access to either the server or the client. In this recipe, we explicitly block access to the server and then try to connect to it.

Getting ready

Install OpenVPN 2.0 or higher on two computers. Make sure the computers are connected over a network. Set up the client and server certificates using the first recipe from *Chapter 2, Client-server IP-only Networks*. For this recipe, the server computer was running CentOS 5 Linux and OpenVPN 2.1.1. The client was running Fedora 13 Linux and OpenVPN 2.1.1. Keep the configuration file, `basic-udp-server.conf`, from the *Chapter 2* recipe *Server-side routing* at hand, as well as the client configuration file `basic-udp-client.conf`.

How to do it...

1. Start the server using the configuration file `basic-udp-server.conf`:

    `[root@server]# openvpn --config basic-udp-server.conf`

2. On the server, explicitly block access to OpenVPN using iptables:

    `[root@server]# iptables -I INPUT -p udp --dport 1194 -j DROP`

3. Next, start the client using the configuration file `basic-udp-client.conf`:

    `[root@client]# openvpn --config basic-udp-client.conf`

The client will try to connect the server using the UDP protocol. After a while, a timeout will occur because no traffic is getting through and the client will restart:

```
... TLS Error: TLS key negotiation failed to occur within 60 seconds
(check your network connectivity)
... TLS Error: TLS handshake failed
... SIGUSR1[soft,tls-error] received, process restarting
```

Abort the client and stop the server.

How it works...

When OpenVPN is configured to use the default UDP protocol, the client will wait for an answer from the server for 60 seconds. If no answer was received, the connection is restarted. As we are explicitly blocking UDP traffic, the timeout occurs and the client is never able to connect.

The amount of time the client waits for the connection to start is controlled using the directive:

```
hand-window N
```

Here, N is the number of seconds to wait for the initial handshake to complete. The default value is 60 seconds.

Of course, the connection can be repaired by removing the firewall rule.

There's more...

One of the major differences between the UDP protocol and the TCP protocol is the way connections are established: every TCP connection is started using a TCP handshake by both the client and the server. If the handshake fails, then the connection is not established. There is no need to wait for traffic coming back from the server, as the connection itself is dropped:

```
... Attempting to establish TCP connection with openvpnserver:1194
[nonblock]
... TCP: connect to openvpnserver:1194 failed, will try again in 5 seconds:
Connection refused
```

Troubleshooting 'client-config-dir' issues

In this recipe, we will demonstrate how to troubleshoot issues related to the use of the directive client-config-dir. This directive can be used to specify a directory for so-called CCD files. CCD files can contain OpenVPN directives to assign a specific IP address to a client, based on the client's certificate. Experience has shown that it is easy to misconfigure this directive. In this recipe, we will make one of the common misconfigurations and then show how to troubleshoot it.

Getting ready

Install OpenVPN 2.0 or higher on two computers. Make sure the computers are connected over a network. Set up the client and server certificates using the first recipe from *Chapter 2, Client-server IP-only Networks*.. For this recipe, the server computer was running CentOS 5 Linux and OpenVPN 2.1.1. The client was running Fedora 13 Linux and OpenVPN 2.1.1. Keep the configuration file, basic-udp-server.conf, from the *Chapter 2*'s recipe *Server-side routing* at hand, as well as the client configuration file basic-udp-client.conf.

How to do it...

1. Append the following lines to the configuration file basic-udp-server.conf:

    ```
    client-config-dir /etc/openvpn/cookbook/clients
    ccd-exclusive
    ```

    Save it as example7-7-server.conf.

2. Make sure the directory `/etc/openvpn/cookbook/clients` is accessible only to root:

   `[root@server]# chown root /etc/openvpn/cookbook/clients`

   `[root@server]# chmod 700 /etc/openvpn/cookbook/clients`

3. Start the server:

   `[root@server]# openvpn --config example7-7-server.conf`

4. Next, start the client using the configuration file `basic-udp-client.conf`:

   `[root@client]# openvpn --config basic-udp-client.conf`

Then, the client will fail to connect with a message:

```
... [openvpnserver] Peer Connection Initiated with server-ip:1194
... AUTH: Received AUTH_FAILED control message
```

The server log file is a bit confusing: first, it mentions that there was a problem reading the CCD file `openvpnclient1` but then it states that the client is connected:

```
... client-ip:42692 TLS Auth Error: --client-config-dir authentication
failed for common name 'openvpnclient1' file='/etc/openvpn/cookbook/
clients/openvpnclient1'
... client-ip:42692 [openvpnclient1] Peer Connection Initiated with
client-ip:42692
```

The VPN connection has not been properly initiated, however.

How it works...

The following directives are used by the OpenVPN server to look in the directory `/etc/openvpn/cookbook/clients` for a CCD file with the name (CN) of the client certificate:

```
client-config-dir /etc/openvpn/cookbook/clients
ccd-exclusive
```

The purpose of the second directive, `ccd-exclusive`, is to only allow clients for which a CCD file is present. If a CCD file for a client is not present, the client will be denied the access.

The name of the client certificate is listed in the server log:

```
... client-ip:42692 TLS Auth Error: --client-config-dir authentication
failed for common name 'openvpnclient1'
```

But, it can also be retrieved using:

```
openssl x509 -subject -noout -in client1.crt
```

Look for the first part starting with `/CN=` and convert all spaces to underscores.

The OpenVPN server process is running as user nobody and because we have set very restrictive permissions on the directory `/etc/openvpn/cookbook/clients`, this user is not capable of reading any files in that directory. When the client with certificate `openvpnclient1` connects, the OpenVPN server is not capable of reading the CCD file (even though it might be there). Because of the `ccd-exclusive` directive, the client is then denied access.

There's more...

In this section, we will explain how to increase the logging verbosity and what some of the most common `client-config-dir` mistakes are.

More verbose logging

Increasing the verbosity of logging is often helpful when troubleshooting `client-config-dir` issues. With `verb 5` and the right permissions, you will see the following log file entries in the OpenVPN server log:

```
openvpnclient1/client-ip:39814 OPTIONS IMPORT: reading client specific
options from: /etc/openvpn/cookbook/clients/openvpnclient1
```

If this message is **not** present in the server log, then it is safe to assume that the CCD file has **not** been read.

Other frequent client-config-dir mistakes

There are a few frequent `client-config-dir` mistakes:

 ▶ A non-absolute path is used to specify the `client-config-dir`, for example:

   `client-config-dir clients`.

   This might work in some cases, but you have to be very careful when starting the server or when combining this with directives such as `--chroot` or `--cd`. Especially when the `--chroot` directive is used, all paths, including the absolute path, will be relative to the `chroot` path.

 ▶ The CCD file itself must be correctly named, without any extension. This typically tends to confuse the Windows users. Look in the server log to see what the OpenVPN server thinks; the `/CN= name` is of the client certificate. Also, be aware that OpenVPN rewrites some characters of the `/CN= name`, such as spaces. For the full list of characters that will be remapped, see the manual page, section *String Types and Remapping*.

 ▶ The CCD file and the **full** path to it must be readable to the user under which the OpenVPN server process is running (usually `nobody`).

▶ *Chapter 2*'s recipe, *Using client-config-dir files*, which explains the basic usage of client configuration files.

How to read the OpenVPN log files

Troubleshooting an OpenVPN setup often comes down to reading and interpreting the OpenVPN log file correctly. In this recipe, no new features of OpenVPN will be introduced, but a detailed walk-through of an OpenVPN log file will be given. The setup from the recipe *Troubleshooting MTU and tun-mtu issues* earlier in this chapter will be used as a starting point.

Getting ready

Use the same setup as in the recipe *Troubleshooting MTU and tun-mtu issues* earlier in this chapter. For this recipe, the server computer was running CentOS 5 Linux and OpenVPN 2.1.1. The client was running Fedora 13 Linux and OpenVPN 2.1.1. Keep the configuration file, `basic-udp-server.conf`, from the *Chapter 2* recipe *Server-side routing* at hand. For the client, keep the configuration file, `example7-5-client.conf`, from the recipe *Troubleshooting MTU and tun-mtu issues* at hand.

How to do it...

1. Start the server using the configuration file `basic-udp-server.conf`:

   ```
   [root@server]# openvpn --config basic-udp-server.conf
   ```

2. Next, start the client with an increased verbosity setting and without timestamps in the log file:

   ```
   [root@client]# openvpn --config example7-5-client.conf \
      --verb 7 --suppress-timestamps
   ```

   The connection will initiate, but it will not be possible to send large packets.

3. Trigger an error by typing:

   ```
   [client]$ ping -c 1 192.168.200.1
   [client]$ ping -c 1 -s 1450 192.168.200.1
   ```

4. Abort the client. The log file will have become large quite quickly.

5. Open the log file using a text editor and browse through it. An explanation of the general structure of the log file is given in the next section.

How it works...

The first part of the log file contains the configuration as specified in the configuration file and from the command-line parameters. This is the section starting with:

```
Current Parameter Settings:
  config = 'example7-5-client.conf'
```

It ends with the following line:

```
OpenVPN 2.1.1 x86_64-redhat-linux-gnu [SSL] [LZO2] [EPOLL] [PKCS11]
built on Jan  5 2010
```

This section is about 250 lines long depending on the configuration and it contains what OpenVPN thinks is the configuration. Check this section carefully to make sure that you agree.

The next interesting section is:

```
Control Channel Authentication: using '/etc/openvpn/cookbook/ta.key'
as a OpenVPN static key file
Outgoing Control Channel Authentication: Using 160 bit message hash
'SHA1' for HMAC authentication
Outgoing Control Channel Authentication: HMAC KEY: 51cc24c0 …
Outgoing Control Channel Authentication: HMAC size=20 … Incoming
Control Channel Authentication: Using 160 bit …
Incoming Control Channel Authentication: HMAC KEY: 1c748f91 …
Incoming Control Channel Authentication: HMAC size=20 …
```

This part shows that a `tls-auth` key is read and used and that the two separate HMAC keys are derived. The keys are actually printed in the log file, so you can reference them with the output from the server log file. The server incoming key should be the same as the client outgoing key and vice versa. The misconfiguration from the recipe *Key mismatches* earlier in this chapter would have appeared here.

Right after this section is the warning that is the root cause of the misconfiguration from the recipe *Troubleshooting MTU and tun-mtu issues* earlier in this chapter:

```
WARNING: normally if you use --mssfix and/or --fragment, you should
also set --tun-mtu 1500 (currently it is 1400)
```

Log file messages starting with `WARNING` should always be given special attention to. In some cases, they can be ignored but in this case it was the root cause of the VPN connection not working properly.

After this warning come a whole range of messages of the following form:

```
DPv4 WRITE [50] to server-ip:1194: P_ACK_V1 kid=0 pid=[ #74 ] [ 37 ]
UDPv4 READ [108] from server-ip:1194: P_CONTROL_V1 kid=0 pid=[ #73 ] [
] pid=38 DATA len=66
```

These messages are all part of the initial handshake between the client and the server to exchange configuration information, encryption keys, and other information for setting up the VPN connection. Right after this is another hint about the misconfiguration:

```
WARNING: 'link-mtu' is used inconsistently, local='link-mtu 1441',
remote='link-mtu 1541'
WARNING: 'tun-mtu' is used inconsistently, local='tun-mtu 1400',
remote='tun-mtu 1500'
```

We skip forward over a lot of TLS_prf messages to come to the processing of the configuration directives pushed by the server:

```
PUSH: Received control message: 'PUSH_REPLY,route-gateway
192.168.200.1,topology subnet,ping 10,ping-restart 60,ifconfig
192.168.200.2 255.255.255.0'
```

This is another important line to check for, as it shows what the server has actually pushed to the client. Verify that this actually matches what you thought the server should push.

After this the local TUN adapter is opened and initialized and the first packets can begin to flow.

The first ping command worked fine, as we can see from this part:

```
TUN READ [84]
...
UDPv4 WRITE [125] to server-ip:1194: P_DATA_V1 kid=0 DATA len=124
UDPv4 READ [125] from server-ip:1194: P_DATA_V1 kid=0 DATA len=124
TLS: tls_pre_decrypt, key_id=0, IP=server-ip:1194
TUN WRITE [84]
```

The TUN READ is the ping command being read from the TUN interface, followed by a write over the encrypted channel to the remote server. Notice the difference in packet size: the packet sent over the encrypted tunnel is 125 bytes, which is 41 bytes larger than the original packet read from the TUN interface. This exactly matches the difference between the link-mtu and tun-mtu as shown earlier in the log file.

Next comes the section where the ping -s 1450 breaks down. A ping of 1450 bytes cannot be read in one piece if the MTU of the interface is set to 1400, hence two TUN READS are necessary to capture all data:

```
TUN READ [1396]
...
UDPv4 WRITE [1437] to server-ip:1194: P_DATA_V1 kid=0 DATA len=1436
TUN READ [102]
...
UDPv4 WRITE [141] to server-ip:1194: P_DATA_V1 kid=0 DATA len=140
```

Notice that the data is actually sent as two separate packets to the server. This is perfectly normal behaviour, as the packet needs to be fragmented. Calculation of the packet sizes versus the MTU sizes breaks down in this case, as the second packet is not a complete IP packet.

The server receives the large `ping` command and sends an equally large reply. As the server has an MTU setting of 1500, there is no need to fragment the data, so it arrives at the client as a single packet:

```
UDPv4 READ [1441] from server-ip:1194: P_DATA_V1 kid=0 DATA len=1440
TLS: tls_pre_decrypt, key_id=0, IP=server-ip:1194
Authenticate/Decrypt packet error: packet HMAC authentication failed
```

The client, however, is expecting a packet with a maximum size of 1400 bytes. It is not able to properly decode the larger packet and write out the `packet HMAC authentication failed` message.

Finally, when we abort the client, we see an `interrupted system call` message (in this case, *Ctrl-C* was used to abort the client, plus a range of clean-up message before the client actually stops:

```
event_wait : Interrupted system call (code=4)
PID packet_id_free
...
TCP/UDP: Closing socket
Closing TUN/TAP interface
/sbin/ip addr del dev tun0 192.168.200.2/24
PID packet_id_free
SIGINT[hard,] received, process exiting
```

If the client configuration had included:

```
user nobody
```

Then we would also have seen messages of the form:

```
SIOCSIFADDR: Permission denied
SIOCSIFFLAGS: Permission denied
Linux ip addr del failed: external program exited with error status:
255
```

In this case, these are harmless.

There's more...

On UNIX-based operating systems, it is also possible to send the OpenVPN log output via `syslog`. This allows a system administrator to effectively manage a large set of computers using a single system logging interface. To send log messages via `syslog`, replace the directive `log-append` with:

```
syslog [name]
```

Here, `name` is an optional parameter to specify the name of the OpenVPN instance in the syslog log files. This is particularly useful if there are multiple instances of OpenVPN running on a single host and they are all using `syslog` to log their output and error messages.

8

Troubleshooting OpenVPN: Routing

In this chapter, we will cover the following troubleshooting topics:

- ▶ The missing return route
- ▶ Missing return routes when `iroute` is used
- ▶ All clients function except the OpenVPN endpoints
- ▶ Source routing
- ▶ Routing and permissions on Windows
- ▶ Troubleshooting client-to-client traffic routing
- ▶ Understanding the `MULTI: bad source` warnings
- ▶ Failure when redirecting the default gateway

Introduction

The topic of this chapter and the previous one is troubleshooting the OpenVPN. This chapter focuses on the all-too-common routing issues that occur when setting up a VPN. As more than half of the questions asked on the `openvpn-users` mailing list can be traced back to routing issues, this chapter intends to provide answers to some of the more frequent routing misconfigurations.

The recipes in these chapters will therefore deal with first, breaking the things, and then, providing the tools on how to find and solve the configuration errors.

The missing return route

After setting up OpenVPN successfully for the very first time, it is very common to misconfigure the network routes for the VPN. In this recipe, we will first set up a basic TUN-style VPN as is done in *Chapter 2, Client-server IP-only networks*. At first, routing will not work until the right routes are added. The purpose of this recipe is to describe how to troubleshoot such a routing error.

Getting ready

We use the following network layout:

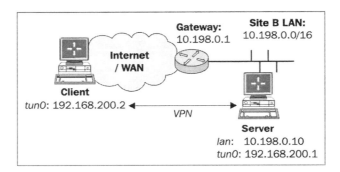

Install OpenVPN 2.0 or higher on two computers. Make sure the computers are connected over a network. Set up the client and server certificates using the first recipe from *Chapter 2, Client-server IP-only Networks*. For this recipe, the server computer was running CentOS 5 Linux and OpenVPN 2.1.1. The client was running Fedora 13 Linux and OpenVPN 2.1.1. Keep the configuration file, `basic-udp-server.conf`, from the *Chapter 2* recipe *Server-side routing* at hand, as well as the client configuration file, `basic-udp-client.conf`, from the same recipe.

How to do it...

1. Start the server using the configuration file `basic-udp-server.conf`:

   [root@server]# openvpn --config basic-udp-server.conf

2. Next, start the client:

   [root@client]# openvpn --config basic-udp-client.conf

   ...

   ... Initialization Sequence Completed

3. At this point, it is possible to ping the remote VPN IP and all the interfaces that are on the VPN server themselves:

    [client]$ ping -c 2 192.168.200.1

    ```
    PING 192.168.200.1 (192.168.200.1) 56(84) bytes of data.
    64 bytes from 192.168.200.1: icmp_seq=1 ttl=64 time=25.2 ms
    64 bytes from 192.168.200.1: icmp_seq=2 ttl=64 time=25.1 ms
    ```
    [client]$ ping -c 2 10.198.0.10

    ```
    PING 10.198.0.10 (10.198.0.10) 56(84) bytes of data.
    64 bytes from 10.198.0.10: icmp_seq=1 ttl=64 time=24.7 ms
    64 bytes from 10.198.0.10: icmp_seq=2 ttl=64 time=25.0 ms
    ```

    If either of these 'pings' fail, then the VPN connection has not been established successfully and there is no need to continue.

4. If no routes have been added to the server-side gateway, then all other hosts on the remote `10.198.0.0/16` network will be unavailable:

    [client]$ ping 10.198.0.1

    ```
    PING 10.198.0.1 (10.198.0.1) 56(84) bytes of data.
    ^C
    --- 10.198.0.1 ping statistics ---
    1 packets transmitted, 0 received, 100% packet loss, time 764ms
    ```

5. If we add a route on the LAN gateway of the remote network to explicitly forward all the VPN traffic to the VPN server, then we can reach all machines on the remote LAN (like it was done in the *Chapter 2* recipe, *Server-side routing*):

    [gateway]> ip route add 192.168.200.0/24 via 10.198.0.10

    Here, `10.198.1.1` is the LAN IP address of the VPN server. In this case, the remote LAN gateway is running Linux. The exact syntax for adding a static route to the gateway will vary with the model and operating system of the gateway.

6. Now, all the machines are reachable:

    [client]$ ping 10.198.0.1

    ```
    PING 10.198.0.1 (10.198.0.1) 56(84) bytes of data.
    64 bytes from 10.198.0.1: icmp_seq=1 ttl=63 time=27.1 ms
    64 bytes from 10.198.0.1: icmp_seq=2 ttl=63 time=25.0 ms
    ```

How it works...

When the VPN client attempts to make a connection to a host on the server-side LAN, packets are sent with a source and destination IP address:

▶ Source IP = 192.168.200.2: this address is the VPN tunnel's IP address

▶ Destination IP = IP of the host we're trying to contact

The remote host will want to reply with a packet, with the source and destination IP addresses swapped. When the remote host wants to send the packet, it does not know where to send it to, as the address 192.168.200.2 is our private VPN address. It then forwards the packet to the LAN gateway. However, the LAN gateway also does not know where to return the packets to, and will forward them out to its default gateway. When the packets reach a router that is connected directly to the Internet that router usually will decide to drop (throw away) the packets, causing the host to become unreachable.

By adding a route on the remote LAN gateway—telling it that all the traffic for the network `192.168.200.0/24` should be forwarded to the VPN server—the packets are sent back to the right machine. The VPN server will forward the packets back to the VPN client and the connection is established.

The step to ping the remote VPN endpoint first and then the server-LAN IP (10.198.0.10) may seem superfluous at first but they are crucial when troubleshooting routing issues. If these steps already fail, then there is no need to look at the missing routes.

There's more...

In this section, we will focus on different solutions to the problem described in this recipe.

Masquerading

A quick and dirty solution to the above issue is outlined in the *Chapter 2* recipe *Server-side routing*. In the *There's More...* section of that recipe, masquerading is used to make it appear as if all the traffic is coming from the OpenVPN server itself. This is perfect if you have no control over the remote LAN gateway, but it is not a very clean routing solution. Certain applications do not behave very well when NAT'ted. Also, from a security logging point of view, it is sometimes better to avoid NAT'ting, as you are mapping multiple IP addresses onto a single one, thereby losing information.

Adding routes on the LAN hosts

Instead of adding a route to the remote LAN gateway, it is also possible to add a route on each of the remote LAN hosts that the VPN client needs to reach. This solution is perfect if the VPN client only needs to be able to reach a limited set of server-side hosts, but it does not scale very well.

See also

 ▶ *Chapter 2*'s recipe, *Server-side routing*, which contains the basic setup for routing the traffic from the server-side LAN.

Missing return routes when 'iroute' is used

This recipe is a continuation of the previous one. After ensuring that a single VPN client can reach the server-side LAN, the next step is to make sure that other hosts behind the VPN client can reach the hosts on the server side LAN.

In this recipe, we will first set up a VPN as is done in the *Chapter 2* recipe *Routing: subnets on both sides*. If no return routes are set up, then the hosts on the client-side LAN will not be able to reach the hosts on the server-side LAN and vice versa. By adding the appropriate routes, the issue is resolved.

Getting ready

We use the following network layout:

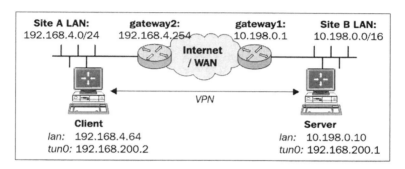

Install OpenVPN 2.0 or higher on two computers. Make sure the computers are connected over a network. Set up the client and server certificates using the first recipe from *Chapter 2, Client-server IP-only Networks*. For this recipe, the server computer was running CentOS 5 Linux and OpenVPN 2.1.1. The client was running Fedora 13 Linux and OpenVPN 2.1.1. Keep the configuration file, `example2-5-server.conf`, from the *Chapter 2* recipe, *Routing: subnets on both sides*, at hand, as well as the client configuration, `basic-udp-client.conf`, from the *Chapter 2* recipe *Server-side routing*.

How to do it...

1. Start the server:

   ```
   [root@server]# openvpn --config example2-5-server.conf
   ```

2. Next, start the client:

   ```
   [root@client]# openvpn --config basic-udp-client.conf
   ...
   ... Initialization Sequence Completed
   ```

3. At this point, it is possible to ping the remote VPN IP and all the interfaces that are on the VPN server itself, and vice versa:

```
[client]$ ping -c 2 192.168.200.1
PING 192.168.200.1 (192.168.200.1) 56(84) bytes of data.
64 bytes from 192.168.200.1: icmp_seq=1 ttl=64 time=25.2 ms
64 bytes from 192.168.200.1: icmp_seq=2 ttl=64 time=25.1 ms
```

```
[client]$ ping -c 2 10.198.0.10
PING 10.198.0.1 (10.198.0.10) 56(84) bytes of data.
64 bytes from 10.198.0.10: icmp_seq=1 ttl=64 time=24.7 ms
64 bytes from 10.198.0.10: icmp_seq=2 ttl=64 time=25.0 ms
```

```
[server]$ ping -c 2 192.168.200.2
PING 192.168.200.2 (192.168.200.2) 56(84) bytes of data.
64 bytes from 192.168.200.2: icmp_seq=1 ttl=64 time=25.0 ms
64 bytes from 192.168.200.2: icmp_seq=2 ttl=64 time=24.6 ms
[server]$ ping -c 2 192.168.4.64
PING 192.168.4.64 (192.168.4.64) 56(84) bytes of data.
64 bytes from 192.168.4.64: icmp_seq=1 ttl=64 time=25.2 ms
64 bytes from 192.168.4.64: icmp_seq=2 ttl=64 time=24.3 ms
```

4. The routing table on the server shows that the remote network is routed correctly:

```
[server]$ netstat -rn | grep tun0
192.168.4.0    192.168.200.1 255.255.255.0 UG 0 0 0 tun0
192.168.200.0 0.0.0.0        255.255.255.0 U  0 0 0 tun0
```

5. When we try to ping a remote host on the server-side LAN it fails, as it was the case in the previous recipe. Vice versa, when we try to ping a client-side LAN host from a host on the server-side LAN, we see:

```
[siteB-host]$ ping -c 2 192.168.4.66
PING 192.168.4.66 (192.168.4.66) 56(84) bytes of data.

--- 192.168.4.66 ping statistics ---
2 packets transmitted, 0 received, 100% packet loss, time 999ms
```

6. By adding the appropriate routes on the gateways at both the sides, the routing is restored. First, the gateway on the server-side LAN:

```
[gateway1]> ip route add 192.168.4.0/24 via 10.198.0.10
```

Here, `10.198.0.10` is the LAN IP address of the VPN server.

7. Next, the gateway/router on the client-side LAN:

```
[gateway2]> ip route add 10.198.0.0/16 via 192.168.4.64
```

Here, `192.168.4.64` is the LAN IP address of the VPN client.

After this, the hosts on the LANs can reach other.

How it works...

Similar to the previous recipe, when a host on the Site A's LAN attempts to make a connection to a host on the Site B's LAN packets that are sent with a source and destination IP address:

▶ Source IP = 192.168.4.64 : Site A's LAN address

▶ Destination IP = 10.198.1.12: Site B's LAN address

The remote host will want to reply with a packet with the source and destination IP addresses swapped. When the remote host wants to send the packet, it forwards the packet to the LAN gateway. However, the LAN gateway also does not know where to return the packets to, and will forward them out to its default gateway. When the packets reach a router that is connected directly to the Internet then the router usually will decide to drop (throw away) the packets, causing the host to become unreachable.

A similar problem occurred in the previous recipe, but now the IP addresses of the packets are the actual Site A's and Site B's LAN IP addresses.

By adding the appropriate routes on both the sides, the problem is alleviated.

When troubleshooting this sort of routing issue, it is very important to start at the innermost network (the actual VPN, in this case) and then work your way outwards:

▶ First make sure the VPN endpoints can see each other

▶ Make sure the VPN client can reach the server LAN IP and vice versa

▶ Make sure the VPN client can reach a host on the server-side LAN

▶ Make sure a host on the server-side LAN can see the VPN client

▶ Make sure a host on the client-side LAN can see the VPN server

▶ Finally, make sure a host on the client-side LAN can see a host on the server-side LAN and vice versa

There's more...

Again, a quick and a dirty solution to the above issue is outlined in the *Chapter 2*'s recipe *Server-side routing*. In that recipe, masquerading is used to make it appear as if all the traffic is coming from the OpenVPN server itself. Especially, when connecting subnets over a VPN this is not advisable, as masquerading makes it impossible to tell which client is connecting to which server and vice versa. Therefore, a fully-routed setup is preferred in this case.

See also

▶ *Chapter 2*'s recipe, *Routing: subnets on both sides,* which explains in detail how to set up routing on both the client and the server side.

All clients function except the OpenVPN endpoints

This recipe is again a continuation of the previous one. The previous recipe explained how to troubleshoot routing issues when connecting a client-side LAN (or subnet) to a server-side LAN. However, in the previous recipe, an omission in the routing configuration was made on purpose. In this recipe, we will focus on troubleshooting this quite common omission.

Getting ready

We use the following network layout:

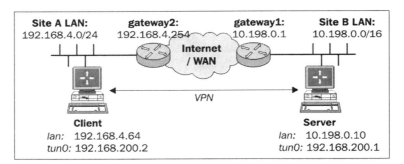

Install OpenVPN 2.0 or higher on two computers. Make sure the computers are connected over a network. Set up the client and server certificates using the first recipe from *Chapter 2, Client-server IP-only Networks.* For this recipe, the server computer was running CentOS 5 Linux and OpenVPN 2.1.1. The client was running Fedora 13 Linux and OpenVPN 2.1.1. Keep the configuration file, `example2-5-server.conf`, from the *Chapter 2* recipe *Routing: subnets on both sides* at hand, as well as the client configuration, `basic-udp-client.conf`, from the *Chapter 2* recipe *Server-side routing.*

How to do it...

1. Start the server:

   ```
   [root@server]# openvpn --config example2-5-server.conf
   ```

2. Next, start the client:

```
[root@client]# openvpn --config basic-udp-client.conf

...
... Initialization Sequence Completed
```

3. Add the appropriate routes on the gateways at both the sides:

```
[gateway1]> ip route add 192.168.4.0/24 via 10.198.0.10
[gateway2]> ip route add 10.198.0.0/16 via 192.168.4.64
```

   After this, all the hosts on the LANs can reach other.

4. We verify this by pinging various machines on the LANs on either of the sides:

```
[client]$ ping -c 2 10.198.0.10
[server]$ ping -c 2 192.168.4.64
[siteA-host]$ ping -c 2 10.198.0.1
[siteB-host]$ ping -c 2 192.168.4.66
```

   All of them work. However, when the VPN server tries to ping a host on the client-side LAN, it fails:

```
[server]$ ping -c 2 192.168.4.66
PING 192.168.4.66 (192.168.4.66) 56(84) bytes of data.

--- 192.168.4.66 ping statistics ---
2 packets transmitted, 0 received, 100% packet loss, time 1009ms
```

   Similarly, the client can only reach the LAN IP of the server and not any of the other hosts.

5. On Linux and UNIX hosts, it is possible to explicitly specify the source IP address:

```
[server]$ ping -I 10.198.0.10 -c 2 192.168.4.66
PING 192.168.4.66 (192.168.4.66) 56(84) bytes of data.
64 bytes from 192.168.4.66: icmp_seq=1 ttl=63 time=25.5 ms
64 bytes from 192.168.4.66: icmp_seq=2 ttl=63 time=24.3 ms
```

   That works! So, there is a problem with the source address of the packets.

6. By adding an extra route for the VPN subnet itself, to the gateways on both the ends, this issue is resolved:

```
[gateway1]> ip route add 192.168.200.0/24 via 10.198.0.10
[gateway2]> ip route add 192.168.200.0/24 via 192.168.4.64
```

7. Now, the VPN server can reach all the hosts on the client's subnet and vice versa:

```
[server]$ ping -c 2 192.168.4.66
PING 192.168.4.66 (192.168.4.66) 56(84) bytes of data.
64 bytes from 192.168.4.66: icmp_seq=1 ttl=63 time=25.3 ms
64 bytes from 192.168.4.66: icmp_seq=2 ttl=63 time=24.9 ms
```

How it works...

To troubleshoot issues like these, it is very handy to write out all the source addresses and the destination addresses of the LANs involved. In this case, the problem occurs when the VPN server wants to connect to a host on the client-side LAN. On the VPN server, the packet that is sent to the client-side host is sent out of the VPN interface directly. Therefore, the source address of this packet is set to the IP address of the VPN interface itself. Thus, the packet has the following IP addresses:

▶ Source IP = 192.168.200.1: VPN server's IP address

▶ Destination IP = 192.168.4.66: Site A's LAN address

The remote host will want to reply with a packet with the source and destination IP addresses swapped. When the remote host wants to send the packet, it forwards the packet to the LAN gateway. However, the LAN gateway also does not know where to return the packets to, and will forward them out to its default gateway. When the packets reach a router that is connected directly to the Internet that router usually will decide to drop (throw away) the packets, causing the host to become unreachable.

This problem occurs only on the VPN server and VPN client. On all other hosts on the client-side and server-side LAN, the LAN IP address is used and routing works as configured in the previous recipe.

By adding the appropriate routes on both the sides the problem is resolved.

There's more...

A good use of NAT'ing in this recipe would be to remove any references to the VPN IP range from the routing tables. This can be done by just masquerading the VPN endpoint addresses. If this is done, the extra routes are no longer needed on the gateways on both the LANs. For example, by adding a NAT'ing rule on the server:

```
[root@server]# iptables -t nat -I POSTROUTING -i tun0 -o eth0 \
   -s 192.168.200.0/24 -j MASQUERADE
```

And, similarly on the following client:

```
[root@client]# iptables -t nat -I POSTROUTING -i tun0 -o eth0 \
   -s 192.168.200.0/24 -j MASQUERADE
```

The extra routes on the gateways are no longer needed.

Note that this is easily done on Linux and UNIX-based operating systems but it requires more effort on Windows.

See also

> ▶ Chapter 2's recipe, *Routing: subnets on both sides,* which explain in detail how to set up routing on both the client and the server side.

Source routing

As the network configurations grow more complex, the requirement for more advanced features such as the source routing features, increases. Source routing is typically used whenever a server is connected to a network (or the Internet) using two network interfaces (see the following image). In this case, it is important to ensure that the connections that are started on one of the interfaces are kept to that interface. If the incoming traffic for a (VPN) connection is made on the first interface but the return traffic is sent back over the second interface, then VPN connections, amongst others, will fail, as we shall see in this recipe.

Source routing is an advanced feature of most of the modern operating systems. In this recipe, we will show how to set up source routing using the Linux `iproute2` tools, but the same can be achieved on other operating systems using similar tools.

Getting ready

We use the following network layout:

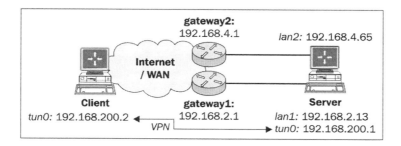

Install OpenVPN 2.0 or higher on two computers. Make sure the computers are connected over a network. Make sure the server has two separate network connections to a router or to the Internet. Set up the client and server certificates using the first recipe from *Chapter 2, Client-server IP-only Networks*. For this recipe, the server computer was running CentOS 5 Linux and OpenVPN 2.1.1 and was connected to a router with two IP addresses: **192.168.4.65** and **192.168.2.13**; the default gateway for the system was **192.168.2.1**, which means that the traffic will leave the interface with IP address **192.168.2.13** by default. The secondary gateway had IP address **192.168.4.1**. Keep the configuration file, `basic-udp-server.conf`, from the *Chapter 2* recipe *Server-side routing* at hand. The client was running Windows XP SP3 and OpenVPN 2.1.1. Keep the client configuration file, `basic-udp-client.ovpn`, from the *Chapter 2* recipe *Using an 'ifconfig-pool' block* at hand. The client IP address was **192.168.2.10** with default route **192.168.2.1**.

How to do it...

1. Start the server using the configuration file `basic-udp-server.conf`:

   ```
   [root@server]# openvpn --config basic-udp-server.conf
   ```

2. Next, start the client.

(In this configuration, the remote server address `openvpnserver.example.com` resolves to `192.168.4.65`.)

The connection will fail to start and the client OpenVPN log file will show the following message repeated a few times:

```
Wed Aug 25 16:24:28 2010 TCP/UDP: Incoming packet rejected from
192.168.2.13:1194[2], expected peer address: 192.168.4.65:1194
(allow this incoming source address/port by removing --remote or
adding --float)
```

3. By adding a source routing rule to return all the traffic, which:

   ❑ Comes in on one interface (`192.168.4.65`) from a host on the other interface (the subnet `'192.168.2.0/24'`)

   ❑ Wants to leave the interface (`192.168.2.0/24`)

to the router associated with the incoming subnet (`192.168.4.1`), the connection is restored:

```
[root@server]# ip route add to default table 100 dev eth0 \
                via 192.168.4.1
[root@server]# ip rule add from 192.168.2.10 priority 50 \
                table 100
[root@server]# ip rule add to 192.168.2.10 priority 50 \
                table 100
```

Now, the client can successfully connect to the VPN server.

How it works...

When a connection is made from the client `192.168.2.10` to the VPN server `192.168.4.65`, the return route is chosen to be the shortest one possible, which in the setup described here is `192.168.2.1`. The server operating system will set the return IP address of the packets to `192.168.2.13`, as that is the IP address of the interface associated with that network. This confuses the OpenVPN client, as it connects to host `192.168.4.65` but gets return traffic from `192.168.2.13`. By explicitly forcing traffic to go out the other interface (`192.168.4.65`), this asymmetric routing issue is resolved.

The exact syntax of the source routing rules is highly dependent on the exact network configuration, but the general idea of the three commands outlined in the section *How to do it* is to:

▶ Create a routing table with ID `100` and set the default gateway device for this table to `eth0`, which has IP address `192.168.4.65`

▶ Create a routing rule that any traffic which comes from client `192.168.2.10` is redirected to the routing table

▶ Create a routing rule that any traffic which wants to leave to client `192.168.2.10` is redirected to the routing table

The routing rules would need to be tweaked for a live situation, as these rules block out certain other types of network traffic, but the principle is correct.

There's more...

More advanced routing control can be done using **LARTC** (**Linux Advanced Routing and Traffic Control**). A better approach would be to mark packets coming on the interface and only redirect the marked packets to the correct outgoing interface.

Routing and permissions on Windows

In this recipe, we will focus on the common error experienced by the users when the VPN client machine is running Windows without full privileges. Under certain circumstances, the OpenVPN client can connect successfully but the routes that are pushed out by the remote server are not correctly set up. This recipe will focus on how to troubleshoot and correct this error. This misconfiguration applies mostly to Windows XP and Windows 2003, as on Windows Vista/7 other privilege problems may occur.

Getting ready

Install OpenVPN 2.0 or higher on two computers. Make sure the computers are connected over a network. Make sure the server has two separate network connections to a router or to the Internet. Set up the client and server certificates using the first recipe from *Chapter 2*, Client-server IP-only Networks. For this recipe, the server computer was running CentOS 5 Linux and OpenVPN 2.1.1. Keep the configuration file `basic-udp-server.conf` from the *Chapter 2* recipe *Server-side routing* at hand. The client was running Windows XP SP3 and OpenVPN 2.1.1. Keep the client configuration file, *basic-udp-client.ovpn*, from the *Chapter 2* recipe *Using an ifconfig-pool block* at hand.

How to do it...

1. Log in as a non-privileged user, being a user without `Power User` or `Administrator` privileges.
2. Start the server using the configuration file `basic-udp-server.conf`:

   `[root@server]# openvpn --config basic-udp-server.conf`
3. Finally, start the client.

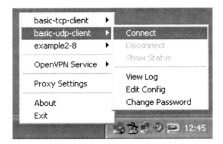

The connection will start and the OpenVPN GUI light will turn green. However, the client OpenVPN log file will show the following messages:

```
... C:\WINDOWS\system32\route.exe ADD 10.198.0.0 MASK 255.255.0.0
192.168.200.1
... ROUTE: route addition failed using CreateIpForwardEntry: Network
access is denied.   [status=65 if_index=2]
... Route addition via IPAPI failed [adaptive]
Thu Aug 26 16:47:53 2010 us=187000 Route addition fallback to route.
exe
```

If you attempt to reach a host on the server-side LAN, it will fail:

[WinClient]C:\>ping 10.198.0.1

```
Pinging 10.198.0.1 with 32 bytes of data:
Request timed out.
Ping statistics for 10.198.0.1:
    Packets: Sent = 1, Received = 0, Lost = 1 (100% loss),
```

The solution to this issue is to give the proper networking rights to the user. On Windows XP, this can be done by either adding the user to the group **Administrators** or by adding the user to the group's **Network Administrators**. The latter is preferred, as it gives the user the right to only modify some network settings and not the entire system configuration.

How it works...

The OpenVPN client tries to open the TAP-Win32 adapter, which is allowed in a default installation. However, when the server pushes out a route to the client using:

```
push "route 10.198.0.0 255.255.0.0"
```

Then, the OpenVPN client will not be able to actually add this route to the system routing tables. However, the VPN connection is successfully established and the GUI client shows a successful connection.

Note that even without the **push** route statement, the Windows OpenVPN GUI showed a green icon, suggesting the connection had started. Technically speaking, it is true that the connection has been established, but this should still be considered as a bug. However, the current OpenVPN GUI for Microsoft Windows is not actively maintained. The new GUI is currently under development and will hopefully address this issue.

There's more...

Windows XP and higher versions include a **Run As Administrator** service that allows a user to temporarily run a program with a higher privilege level. This mechanism was expanded in Windows Vista/7 and was made the default when launching applications. This has actually been the cause for numerous questions on the `openvpn-users` mailing list when running OpenVPN on these platforms. The **Run As** service can also be used on Windows XP, but it works differently than on Windows Vista/7.

See also

> ▶ *Chapter 10, OS Integration*, containing recipes on how to integrate OpenVPN into the Microsoft Windows operating system, amongst others.

Troubleshooting client-to-client traffic routing

In this recipe, we will troubleshoot a VPN setup where it is the intention that client-to-client traffic is enabled, but the server configuration directive 'client-to-client' is missing. In a TUN-style network, it is possible to allow client-to-client traffic without this directive and it even allows the server administrator to apply firewalling rules to the traffic between clients. In a TAP-style network, this is generally not possible, as will be explained in the *There's more...* section.

Getting ready

We use the following network layout:

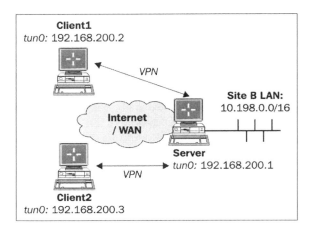

Install OpenVPN 2.0 or higher on three computers. Make sure the computers are connected over a network. Set up the client and server certificates using the first recipe from *Chapter 2, Client-server IP-only Networks*. For this recipe, the server computer was running CentOS 5 Linux and OpenVPN 2.1.1. The first client was running Fedora 13 Linux and OpenVPN 2.1.1. The second client was running Windows XP SP3 and was running OpenVPN 2.1.1. Keep the configuration file, `basic-udp-server.conf`, from the *Chapter 2* recipe *Server-side routing* at hand, as well as the client configuration file `basic-udp-client.conf` from the same recipe. For the Windows XP client, keep the client configuration file `basic-udp-client.ovpn` from the *Chapter 2* recipe *Using an 'ifconfig-pool' block* at hand.

How to do it...

1. Start the server using the configuration file, `basic-udp-server.conf`:

   [root@server]# openvpn --config basic-udp-server.conf

2. Next, start the Linux client.

   [root@client]# openvpn --config basic-udp-client.conf

3. And finally, start the Windows client:

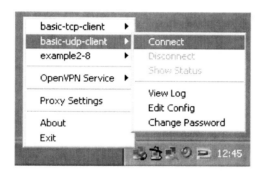

4. Next, try to ping the Windows client from the Linux client (make sure no firewalls are blocking the traffic):

   [client]$ ping -c 2 192.168.200.3

   ```
   PING 192.168.200.3 (192.168.200.3) 56(84) bytes of data.

   --- 192.168.200.3 ping statistics ---
   2 packets transmitted, 0 received, 100% packet loss, time 10999ms
   ```

   It is possible that the host is already reachable, but in that case the firewall on the server is very permissive.

5. At this point, it is instructive to set up `iptables` logging on the VPN server:

    [root@server]# iptables -I FORWARD -i tun+ -j LOG

    Then try the 'ping' again. This will result in the following messages in
    `/var/log/messages`:

    ```
    … openvpnserver kernel: IN=tun0 OUT=tun0 SRC=192.168.200.2
    DST=192.168.200.3 LEN=84 TOS=0x00 PREC=0x00 TTL=63 ID=0 DF
    PROTO=ICMP TYPE=8 CODE=0 ID=40808 SEQ=1
    … openvpnserver kernel: IN=tun0 OUT=tun0 SRC=192.168.200.2
    DST=192.168.200.3 LEN=84 TOS=0x00 PREC=0x00 TTL=63 ID=0 DF
    PROTO=ICMP TYPE=8 CODE=0 ID=40808 SEQ=2
    ```

The first client `192.168.200.2` is trying to reach the second client `192.168.200.3`. This issue can be resolved by adding the `client-to-client` configuration directive to the server configuration file and restarting the OpenVPN server, or it can be resolved by allowing tunnel traffic to be forwarded:

[server]# iptables -I FORWARD -i tun+ -o tun+ -j ACCEPT

[server]# echo 1 > /proc/sys/net/ipv4/ip_forward

How it works...

When the first OpenVPN client tries to reach the second client, packets are sent to the server itself. The OpenVPN server does not know how to handle these packets and hands them off to the kernel. The kernel forwards the packets based on whether routing is enabled and whether the firewall rules (`iptables`) allow it. If not, then the packet is simply dropped and the second client is never reached.

By adding the following directive, the OpenVPN server process deals with the client-to-client traffic internally, bypassing the kernel forwarding, and the firewalling rules:

```
client-to-client
```

The alternative solution, which is slightly more secure but also less scalable, is to properly set up routing in the Linux kernel.

There's more...

In a TAP-style network, the above `iptables` rule does not work. In a TAP-style network, all the clients are a part of the same broadcast domain. When the `client-to-client` directive is omitted and a client tries to reach another client, it first sends out 'arp who has' messages to find out the MAC address of the other client. The OpenVPN server will ignore these requests and will also not forward them to other clients, regardless of whether an `iptables` rule is set or not. Hence, the clients cannot easily reach each other without the `client-to-client` directive, unless tricks like proxy-ARP are used.

See also

▶ *Chapter 3*'s recipe, *Enabling Client-to-Client Traffic*, which explains how client-to-client traffic is set up in a TAP-style environment.

Understanding the 'MULTI: bad source' warnings

In this recipe, we focus again on a VPN configuration where we try to connect a client-side LAN to a server-side LAN. Normally, this is done by adding a `client-config-dir` directive to the OpenVPN server configuration, and then by adding the appropriate CCD file. However, if the CCD file is not found or is not readable, then the VPN connection will function properly, but the hosts on the client-side LAN will not be able to reach the hosts on the server-side LAN and vice versa. In this case, the OpenVPN server log file will show messages of the form `MULTI: bad source`, if the verbosity is set high enough.

In this recipe, we will first set up a VPN as is done in the *Chapter 2* recipe *Routing: subnets on both sides*, but with a missing CCD file for the client. Then, we will show how to trigger the `MULTI: bad source` warnings and what can be done to resolve the issue.

Getting ready

We use the following network layout:

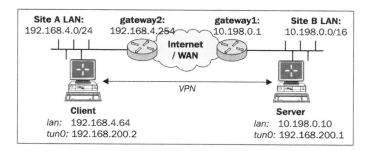

Install OpenVPN 2.0 or higher on two computers. Make sure the computers are connected over a network. Set up the client and server certificates using the first recipe from *Chapter 2, Client-server IP-only Networks*. For this recipe, the server computer was running CentOS 5 Linux and OpenVPN 2.1.1. The client was running Fedora 13 Linux and OpenVPN 2.1.1. Keep the configuration file, `basic-udp-server.conf`, from the *Chapter 2* recipe *Server-side routing* at hand. For the client, keep the configuration file `basic-udp-client.conf` *Chapter 2* recipe *Server-side routing* at hand. .

How to do it...

1. First, make sure the client CCD file is not accessible:

   [root@server]# chmod 700 /etc/openvpn/cookbook/clients

2. Start the server using the configuration file, `example2-5-server.conf`, and with increased verbosity:

   [root@server]# openvpn --config example2-5-server.conf --verb 5

3. Next, start the client to connect successfully:

   [root@client]# openvpn --config basic-udp-client.conf

   ```
   ...
   ... Initialization Sequence Completed
   ```

However, when a host on the client-side LAN tries to reach a machine on the server-side LAN, the following message appears in the OpenVPN server log file:

```
... openvpnclient1/client-ip:58370 MULTI: bad source address from client
[192.168.4.66], packet dropped
```

In this recipe, the root cause of the problem can be resolved as done in the *Chapter 7* recipe *Troubleshooting client-config-dir issues*: fix the permissions of the directory `/etc/openvpn/cookbook/clients` and reconnect the OpenVPN client.

How it works...

In order to connect a remote LAN to an OpenVPN server, two server-configuration directives are needed:

```
route remote-lan remote-mask
client-config-dir /etc/openvpn/cookbook/clients
```

And also a CCD file containing the name of the client certificate. The CCD file contains:

```
iroute remote-lan remote-mask
```

Without this, the OpenVPN server does not "know" which VPN client the remote network is connected to. If a packet comes in from a client that the OpenVPN server does not know about, then the packet is dropped and, with 'verb 5' or higher, the warning `MULTI: bad source` is printed.

There's more...

Apart from the warnings explained above, there is one other major reason for the `MULTI: bad source` messages to occur.

Other occurrences of the 'MULTI: bad source' message

Sometimes the `MULTI: bad source` message is printed in the OpenVPN server log file even when no client-side LAN is connected to the VPN client . This happens most often with VPN clients running Windows. When a file share is accessed over the VPN connection, Windows sometimes sends packets with a different source IP address than that of the VPN interface. These packets are not recognized by the OpenVPN server and the warning is printed. The solution to this issue is not known.

See also

▶ *Chapter 2*'s recipe, *Routing: subnets on both sides*, which explains the basics of setting up a `client-config-dir` setup.

▶ *Chapter 7*'s recipe, *Troubleshooting 'client-config-dir' issues*, which goes deeper into some of the frequently made mistakes when using the `client-config-dir` directive.

Failure when redirecting the default gateway

In this recipe, we will troubleshoot an infrequent yet very persistent issue that can occur when setting up a VPN connection. When the `redirect-gateway` directive is used to redirect the default gateway on an OpenVPN client, it sometimes causes the client to lose all the Internet connections. This particularly occurs when the client machine on which OpenVPN is running is connected to the rest of the network or with the Internet using a PPP-based connection, such as PPPoE or PPPoA, especially, when using a GPRS/UMTS connections via a mobile phone.

When this occurs, OpenVPN sometimes is not capable of determining the default gateway before it is redirected. After the default gateway is redirected to the OpenVPN tunnel, the whole tunnel collapses on itself, as all the traffic, including the encrypted tunnel traffic itself, is redirected into the tunnel, causing the VPN to lock up.

This recipe will show how to detect this situation and what can be done about it. In this recipe, we will not use a GPRS/UMTS connection but we will use a PPP-over-SSH connection, which behaves in a similar fashion and is more readily available.

Getting ready

We use the following network layout:

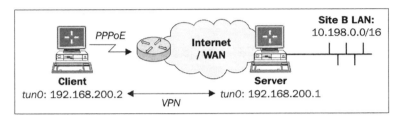

Install OpenVPN 2.0 or higher on two computers. Make sure the computers are connected over a network. Make sure the client is connected to the network using a PPP connection, as otherwise, the issue described in the title of this recipe will not occur. For this recipe, a PPP-over-SSH connection and the default route was altered to point to the `ppp0` device.

Set up the client and server certificates using the first recipe from *Chapter 2, Client-server IP-only Networks*. For this recipe, the server computer was running CentOS 5 Linux and OpenVPN 2.1.1. The client was running Fedora 13 Linux and OpenVPN 2.1.1. Keep the configuration file, `basic-udp-server.conf`, from the *Chapter 2* recipe *Server-side routing* at hand.

How to do it...

1. Start the server and add an extra parameter to direct the default gateway:

    ```
    [root@server]# openvpn --config basic-udp-server.conf \
        --push "redirect-gateway"
    ```

2. Create the client configuration file:

    ```
    client
    proto udp
    # next is the IP address of the VPN server via the
    # PPP-over-SSH link
    remote 192.168.222.1
    port 1194

    dev tun
    nobind
    ```

```
ca        /etc/openvpn/cookbook/ca.crt
cert      /etc/openvpn/cookbook/client1.crt
key       /etc/openvpn/cookbook/client1.key
tls-auth /etc/openvpn/cookbook/ta.key 1

user nobody
verb 5
```

Save it as example8-8-client.conf.

3. Check the system routes before starting the client:

   [root@client]# netstat -rn

   ```
   172.30.0.10   172.30.0.1    255.255.255.255 UGH 0 0 0 eth0
   192.168.222.1 0.0.0.0       255.255.255.255 UH  0 0 0 ppp0
   0.0.0.0       192.168.222.1 0.0.0.0             UG  0 0 0 ppp0
   ```

4. Now, start the client:

   [root@client]# openvpn --config example8-8-client.conf

   The connection will start but after a few seconds will stop and the log file will contain a warning message:

   ```
   ... OpenVPN ROUTE: omitted no-op route: 192.168.222.1/255.255.255.25
   5 -> 192.168.222.1
   ```

5. Check the system routes again:

   [client]$ netstat -rn

   ```
   172.30.0.19    172.30.0.1    255.255.255.255 UGH 0 0 0 eth0
   192.168.222.1  0.0.0.0       255.255.255.255 UH  0 0 0 ppp0
   192.16.186.192 0.0.0.0       255.255.255.192 U   0 0 0 eth0
   192.168.200.0  0.0.0.0       255.255.248.0   U   0 0 0 tun0
   10.198.0.0     192.168.200.1 255.255.0.0         UG  0 0 0 tun0
   0.0.0.0        192.168.200.1 0.0.0.0             UG  0 0 0 tun0
   ```

The default gateway is now the VPN tunnel but the original route to the gateway is now gone.

All the connections on the client have stopped. What's worse, when the OpenVPN client is aborted (by pressing *Ctrl-C* in the terminal window) the default route is not restored, as the OpenVPN process does not have the proper rights to do so:

```
TCP/UDP: Closing socket
/sbin/ip route del 10.198.0.0/16
RTNETLINK answers: Operation not permitted
ERROR: Linux route delete command failed: external program exited with
error status: 2
/sbin/ip route del 192.168.222.1/32
```

```
RTNETLINK answers: Operation not permitted
ERROR: Linux route delete command failed: external program exited with
error status: 2
/sbin/ip route del 0.0.0.0/0
RTNETLINK answers: Operation not permitted
ERROR: Linux route delete command failed: external program exited with
error status: 2
/sbin/ip route add 0.0.0.0/0 via 192.168.222.1
RTNETLINK answers: Operation not permitted
ERROR: Linux route add command failed: external program exited with
error status: 2
Closing TUN/TAP interface
```

The result is that the default gateway on the client machine is gone. The only solution is to reload the network adapter so that all the system defaults are restored.

The solution to the above problem is to use the following as is done in the *Chapter 2* recipe *Redirecting the default gateway*:

```
push "redirect-gateway def1"
```

How it works...

When the OpenVPN client initializes, it always tries to create a direct route to the OpenVPN server via the existing system gateway. Under certain circumstances this fails, mostly due to an odd network configuration. It is seen most often when the default gateway is a dial-up or PPPoE connection, which is used in certain ADSL/VDSL setups and especially when using GPRS/UMTS connections.

When the OpenVPN client is instructed to redirect all the traffic over the VPN tunnel, it normally sends the encrypted VPN traffic itself over a direct link to the OpenVPN server. You can think of the encrypted VPN traffic as "outside" of the tunnel. However, when this direct route is missing, then this "outside" traffic is also sent into the tunnel, creating a tunneling loop from which the VPN can never recover.

In the example used in this recipe, the situation is made worse by using the client configuration directive:

```
user nobody
```

This tells the OpenVPN process to drop all the privileges after starting. When the client is aborted because the tunnel is not functioning properly, the client is not capable of restoring the original gateway and the system is left in a non-functioning state:

```
[client]$ netstat -rn
    194.171.96.27   192.16.186.254 255.255.255.255 UGH 0 0 0 eth0
    192.168.222.1   0.0.0.0        255.255.255.255 UH  0 0 0 ppp0
    192.16.186.192  0.0.0.0        255.255.255.192 U   0 0 0 eth0
```

Only by adding a new default gateway can the network be restored.

The proper fix is to use:

```
push "redirect-gateway def1"
```

This will not overwrite the existing default gateway but which will add two extra routes:

```
0.0.0.0   192.168.200.1 128.0.0.0   UGH 0 0 0 tun0
128.0.0.0 192.168.200.1 128.0.0.0   UGH 0 0 0 tun0
```

both of which cover half the available network space. These two routes effectively replace the existing default route whilst not overwriting it.

There's more...

This "biting your own tail" problem was much more common when OpenVPN 2.0 was used. In OpenVPN 2.1 and higher, the detection of the default gateway was much improved and this problem now rarely occurs anymore. This is another good reason to upgrade all the clients (and preferably the server as well, of course) to OpenVPN 2.1 or higher.

See also

▶ *Chapter 2*'s recipe, *Redirecting the default gateway*, which explains how to properly redirect all traffic via the VPN tunnel.

9
Performance Tuning

In this chapter, we will cover the following troubleshooting topics:

- ▶ Optimizing performance using `ping`
- ▶ Optimizing performance using `iperf`
- ▶ OpenSSL cipher speed
- ▶ Compression tests
- ▶ Traffic shaping
- ▶ Tuning UDP-based connections
- ▶ Tuning TCP-based connections
- ▶ Analyzing performance using `tcpdump`

Introduction

This chapter focuses on getting the best performance out of an OpenVPN setup. There are several parameters that can be tuned on both the server side and the client side for getting the highest throughput and the lowest latency. However, the optimal settings of these parameters largely depend on the network layout. The recipes in this chapter will therefore provide guidelines on how to tune these parameters and how to measure the increase or decrease in performance. These guidelines can then be applied to other network layouts to find the optimal performance.

Optimizing performance using 'ping'

In this recipe, we will use the low-level `ping` command to determine the optimal Maximum Transfer Unit (MTU) size for our OpenVPN setup. Finding the right MTU size can have a tremendous impact on performance, especially, when using satellite links, or even some cable/ADSL providers. Especially, broadband connections using the PPPoE (PPP over Ethernet) protocol often have a non-standard MTU size. In a regular LAN setup, it is hardly ever required to optimize the MTU size, as OpenVPN's default settings are close to optimal.

Getting ready

Make sure the client and the server computers are connected over a network. For this recipe, the server computer was running CentOS 5 Linux. The client was running Fedora 13 Linux, but instructions for a Windows client are given as well.

How to do it...

1. We first verify that we can reach the server from the client:

   ```
   [client]$ ping -c 2 <openvpn-server-ip>
   ```

   This will send two ICMP ping packets to the server and two replies should be returned. If not, then a firewall or `iptables` rule is blocking ICMP traffic. Ensure that the server can be reached using `ping` before proceeding.

2. Next, try sending a large ping packet from the client to the server, with the `Don't Fragment` (DF) bit set. Strangely enough, on Linux, this is done using the parameter `-M do`.

   ```
   [client]$ ping -c 2 -M do -s 1600 <openvpn-server-ip>
   ```

   Normally, this command is not successful:

   ```
   From 172.30.0.128 icmp_seq=1 Frag needed and DF set (mtu = 1500)
   ```

   The maximum size of a packet that can be sent from this interface is 1500 bytes. From this, the Ethernet headers (normally 28 bytes) need to be subtracted, which means that the maximum size of an ICMP packet is 1472 bytes:

   ```
   [client]$ ping -c 2 -M do -s 1472 <openvpn-server-ip>
   PING 172.30.0.128 (172.30.0.128) 1472(1500) bytes of data.
   1480 bytes from 172.30.0.128: icmp_seq=1 ttl=128 time=0.630 ms
   1480 bytes from 172.30.0.128: icmp_seq=2 ttl=128 time=0.398 ms
   ```

3. For Windows clients, the syntax of the `ping` command is slightly different:

```
[winclient]C:> ping -f -l 1600 <openvpn-server-ip>
Packet needs to be fragmented but DF set.
```

And:

```
[winclient]C:> ping -f -l 1472 <openvpn-server-ip>
Pinging 172.30.0.1 with 1472 bytes of data:

Reply from 172.30.0.1: bytes=1472 time<1ms TTL=64
```

The payload size of 1472 bytes is actually the regular size for an Ethernet-based network, even though this recipe was performed over an ADSL2+ connection.

A good initial value for OpenVPN's `tun-mtu` setting is the maximum payload size plus the 28 bytes that were subtracted earlier. However, it does not mean this is the **optimal** value, as we will see in the later recipes.

How it works...

The ICMP protocol which the `ping` command uses has the option to set a flag `Don't Fragment` (DF). With this bit set, an ICMP packet may not be broken up into separate pieces before it reaches its destination. If the packet would need to be broken up by a router before it can be transmitted, it is dropped and an ICMP error code is returned. This provides with a very easy method to determine the largest packet that can be transmitted to the server and vice versa. Especially, in high-latency networks, for example, when a satellite link is used, it is very important to limit the number of packets and to maximize the size of each packet.

By smartly using the `ping` command, the maximum packet size can be determined. This size can then be used to further optimize the OpenVPN performance.

There's more...

In some network setups, ICMP traffic is filtered, rendering this recipe useless. If it is possible to reach the OpenVPN server, then the tunnel can also be used to find the maximum payload size:

▶ Start the OpenVPN server with the extra flags:

```
cipher none
auth none
```

Do the same for the OpenVPN client. Make sure compression is turned off (or simply not specified) and that the `fragment` option is not used. This will start a clear-text tunnel over which we can send ICMP packets of various sizes.

▶ Ping the remote end's VPN IP address, for example:

```
[client]$ ping -c 2 -M do -s 1472 192.168.200.1
```

When the ICMP packet becomes too large, the traffic will be dropped by an intermittent router. Lower the ICMP packet size until the ping returns successfully. From that value, the MTU size can be derived.

See also

▶ The recipe *Tuning UDP-based connections*, which will explain in more detail how to tune the performance of UDP-based setups.

▶ The recipe *Tuning TCP-based connections*, which goes deeper into the details of tuning TCP-based setups and also explains some of the intricacies of the MTU setting of the network adapter.

Optimizing performance using 'iperf'

This recipe is not really about OpenVPN but more about how to use the network performance measurement tool iperf in an OpenVPN setup. The iperf utility can be downloaded from http://sourceforge.net/projects/iperf/ for Linux, Windows, and MacOS.

In this recipe, we will run iperf outside of OpenVPN and over the VPN tunnel itself, after which the differences in performance will be explained.

Getting ready

We use the following network layout:

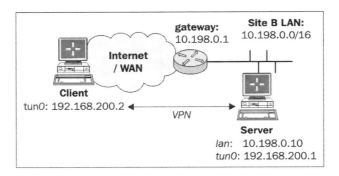

Install OpenVPN 2.0 or higher on two computers. Make sure the computers are connected over a network. Set up the client and server certificates using the first recipe from *Chapter 2, Client-server IP-only Networks*. For this recipe, the server computer was running CentOS 5 Linux and OpenVPN 2.1.1. The client was running Fedora 13 Linux and OpenVPN 2.1.1. Keep the configuration file `basic-udp-server.conf` from the *Chapter 2* recipe *Server-side routing* at hand, as well as the client configuration file `basic-udp-client.conf` from the same recipe.

How to do it...

1. Start the server:

   ```
   [root@server]# openvpn --config basic-udp-server.conf
   ```

2. Next, start the client:

   ```
   [root@client]# openvpn --config basic-udp-client.conf
   ...
   ... Initialization Sequence Completed
   ```

3. Next, we start `iperf` on the server:

   ```
   [server]$ iperf -s
   ```

4. First, we measure the performance outside the tunnel:

   ```
   [client]$ iperf -c <openvpn-server-ip>
   [  3]  0.0-10.0 sec  8.4 MBytes  807 kbits/sec
   ```

   This actually measures the performance of data being sent **TO** the server. The ADSL network used in this recipe has a theoretical upload limit of 1024 kilobits per second (kbps), which in practice results in a 800 kbps upload speed.

5. Next, we measure the performance inside the tunnel:

   ```
   [client]$ iperf -c 192.168.200.1
   [  3]  0.0-10.0 sec  8.2 MBytes  803 kbits/sec
   ```

   With this network setup, there is no measurable performance difference between traffic sent outside of the tunnel and traffic sent via the tunnel.

6. A second test is done over a 802.11n wireless network:

   ```
   [client]$ iperf -c <openvpn-server-ip>
   [  4]  0.0-10.8 sec  7.88 MBytes  6.10 Mbits/sec
   ```

   Versus:

   ```
   [client]$ iperf -c 192.168.200.1
   [  5]  0.0-11.3 sec  5.25 MBytes  3.91 Mbits/sec
   ```

Here, there is a noticeable drop in performance, suggesting that the OpenVPN is not configured optimally. There was a lot of noise on this wireless network, which makes it difficult to optimize.

How it works...

The `iperf` tool is very straightforward: it sets up a TCP connection (or UDP, if desired) and measures how fast it can send or receive data over this connection. Normally, traffic is tested in only one direction, although a dual test can be triggered using the `-d` flag. This option led to erratic behaviour on the CentOS 5 server, however.

There's more...

Tuning network performance depends heavily on both the network latency and the available bandwidth, as is outlined in more detail here.

Client versus server 'iperf' results

Both the client and the server `iperf` processes report the network throughput after a `iperf -c` session has ended. Practice shows that the numbers reported by the server used in this recipe were more accurate than the numbers reported by the client. On the ADSL2 network used when writing this recipe, the maximum upload speed is about 800 kbps. The client sometimes reported speeds larger than 1 mbps, whereas the server reported a more accurate 807 kbps.

Network latency

One of the main reasons for the lack of performance drop over the ADSL2 network versus the performance drop over the wireless network is due to network latency. On the ADSL2 network, the latency was very stable at about 38 ms. On the wireless network, the latency varied between 2 ms and 90 ms. Especially, this variation in latency can skew the `iperf` performance measurements, making it very hard to optimize the OpenVPN parameters.

Gigabit networks

Performance tests on gigabit networks show that the VPN itself is becoming the bottleneck. A normal TCP connection would show a transfer rate of 900 Mbps, whereas a TCP connection via an OpenVPN tunnel would not perform faster than about 320 Mbps. This test was performed with a Linux client and server, both running CentOS 5 Linux. The test suggested a performance bottleneck in the Linux TUN/TAP driver itself, rather than in OpenVPN itself.

OpenSSL cipher speed

OpenVPN uses OpenSSL to perform all cryptographic operations. This means that the performance of an OpenVPN client or server depends on how fast the incoming traffic can be decrypted and how fast the outgoing traffic can be encrypted. For a client with a single connection to the OpenVPN server, this is almost never an issue, but with an OpenVPN server with hundreds of clients, the cryptographic performance becomes very important.

In this recipe, we will show how to measure the performance of the OpenSSL cryptographic routines and how this measurement can be used to improve the performance of an OpenVPN server to which many clients connect.

Getting ready

This recipe is performed on a variety of computers:

- A laptop with Intel Core2 Duo T9300 processor running at 2.5 GHz, running Fedora Linux 13 64bit
- A server with Intel Xeon X5660 processor running at 2.8 GHz and with support for the AESNI instructions, running CentOS 5.5 64bit
- An older desktop computer with an AMD XP 1800+ processor running at 1.5 GHz, running Windows 2000 SP4

The recipe can easily be performed on MacOS as well. Each computer had OpenVPN 2.1 installed, with the accompanying OpenSSL libraries. The X5660 server had a patched version of OpenSSL 1.0.0a installed to add support for the AESNI instructions found in this processor.

How to do it...

On each system, the following OpenSSL commands are run:

```
$ openssl speed -evp bf-cbc
$ openssl speed -evp aes-128-cbc
$ openssl speed -evp aes-256-cbc
```

The first command tests the speed of the OpenVPN default BlowFish cryptographic cipher. The latter two test the performance of the 128 and 256-bit AES ciphers, which are very commonly used to secure websites. On the server with X5660 processor, the extra flag `-engine aesni` was used.

The results are displayed in the following table. All numbers in the tables are the bytes per second processed when encrypting a block of data. The size of the block of data is listed in the columns.

For the `BlowFish` cipher, the following results were recorded:

Type	16 bytes	64 bytes	256 bytes	1024 bytes	8192 bytes
Laptop	83536.57k	92731.18k	95851.54k	95426.22k	95862.84k
Server	99778.99k	109016.23k	111466.67k	111849.47k	112162.13k
Desktop	43275.10k	53286.38k	56698.94k	57690.84k	57959.89k

For the `AES128` cipher, the following results were recorded:

Type	16 bytes	64 bytes	256 bytes	1024 bytes	8192 bytes
Laptop	73268.26k	82778.39k	85588.05k	179870.91k	183104.85k
Server	708473.90k	748702.51k	758884.44k	762378.58k	755960.49k
Desktop	2562.10k	36724.69k	38093.24k	38330.40k	38485.37k

And for `AES256`:

Type	16 bytes	64 bytes	256 bytes	1024 bytes	8192 bytes
Laptop	53987.60k	59586.44k	60698.20k	130553.15k	132085.73k
Server	528984.16k	513814.54k	560398.93k	562632.92k	564687.49k
Desktop	25811.10k	28377.64k	29147.99k	29397.61k	29477.67k

How it works...

The output of the `openssl speed` command shows that the encryption and decryption performance is dependent on both the encryption key and the hardware used. Most OpenVPN packets are about 1500 bytes, so the column 1024 bytes is the most interesting column to look at.

The `BlowFish` cipher results are quite interesting if you take the processor speed into account: if you divide the `BlowFish` performance by the processor clock speed the numbers are very similar. This means that the `BlowFish` performance is bound purely by the processor clock speed. An older type processor running at a higher clock speed might actually outperform a newer processor with a slightly lower clock speed.

For the `AES128` and `AES256` ciphers, this is no longer true. Here the Core2 Duo and Xeon architectures are much faster than the older Pentium 4 and Athlon architectures. When the AESNI extensions found in the latest Intel processors are used, the performance jumps by a factor of 4. If an OpenVPN server is set up that must support many clients, then this cryptographic cipher is an excellent choice, provided that the server CPU supports these extensions.

There's more...

The choice of the cryptographic cipher on the performance of OpenVPN is minimal for a single client. Measurements done for this recipe indicate that the client CPU has a load of less than 8% when downloading a file at the highest speed over the VPN tunnel on a modern system. However, on the older desktop, the choice of cryptographic cipher does become important: upload speed drops from 760 kbps to 720 kbps when the `BlowFish` cipher changes to the `AES256` cipher. Especially, when older hardware or certain home router equipment is used, this can quickly become a bottleneck. Most home wireless routers capable of running OpenVPN, for example, the wireless routers that support the DD-WRT or OpenWRT distributions, have a processor speed of about 250 MHz. This processor speed can quickly become the bottleneck if this router is also used as an OpenVPN server, especially, when multiple clients connect simultaneously.

See also

▸ *Chapter 7*'s recipe, *Cipher mismatches*, which explains in more detail how to troubleshoot cipher mismatches in the client and server configuration files.

Compression tests

OpenVPN has built-in support for LZO compression, if compiled properly. All Windows binaries have LZO compression available by default. In this recipe, we will show what the performance is of using LZO compression when transferring both easily compressible data (such as web pages) and non-compressible data (such as photographs or binaries).

Getting ready

We use the following network layout:

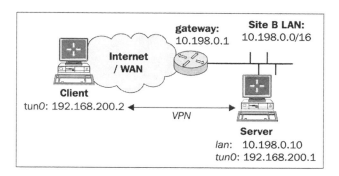

Install OpenVPN 2.0 or higher on two computers. Make sure the computers are connected over a network. Set up the client and server certificates using the first recipe from *Chapter 2, Client-server IP-only Networks*. For this recipe, the server computer was running CentOS 5 Linux and OpenVPN 2.1.1. The first client was running Fedora 13 Linux and OpenVPN 2.1.1. Keep the configuration file `basic-udp-server.conf` from the *Chapter 2* recipe *Server-side routing* at hand, as well as the client configuration file, `basic-udp-client.conf`, from the same recipe. The recipe was repeated with a second client running Windows XP SP3 and OpenVPN 2.1.1. For this client, keep the client configuration file, `basic-udp-client.ovpn`, from the *Chapter 2* recipe *Using an ifconfig-pool block* at hand.

How to do it...

1. Append the following line to the `basic-udp-server.conf` file:

    ```
    comp-lzo
    ```

    Save it as `example9-4-server.conf`.

2. Start the server:

    ```
    [root@server]# openvpn --config example9-4-server.conf
    ```

3. Similarly, for the client, add a line to the `basic-udp-client.conf` file:

    ```
    comp-lzo
    ```

    Save it as `example9-4-client.conf`.

4. Start the client:

    ```
    [root@client]# openvpn --config example9-4-client.conf
    ```

5. Next, we start `iperf` on the server:

    ```
    [server]$ iperf -s
    ```

6. First, we measure the performance when transferring data outside of the tunnel:

    ```
    [client]$ iperf -c <openvpn-server-ip>
    ```

    This results in a throughput of about 50 Mbps over an 802.11n wireless network.

7. Next, non-compressible data:

    ```
    [client]$ dd if=/dev/urandom bs=1024k count=60 of=random
    [client]$ iperf -c 192.168.200.1 -F random
    [  4]  0.0-10.0 sec  35.0 MBytes  29.3 Mbits/sec
    ```

    In the first step, we create a 60MB file with random data. Then, we measure the `iperf` performance when transferring this file.

8. And finally, compressible data (a file filled with zeroes):

```
[client]$ dd if=/dev/zeroes bs=1024k count=60 of=zeroes
[client]$ iperf -c 192.168.200.1 -F zeroes
[  5]  0.0- 5.9 sec  58.6 MBytes  83.3 Mbits/sec
```

The performance of the VPN tunnel when transferring compressible data such as text files and web pages is shown.

9. The same measurement can be made using a Windows PC. Add the following line to the `basic-udp-client.ovpn` file:

   ```
   comp-lzo
   ```

   Save it as `example9-4.ovpn`.

10. Start the client.

The results of the `iperf` measurement are slightly different:

▶ Outside the tunnel: 50 Mbps

▶ Non-compressible data: 16 Mbps

▶ Compressible data: 22 Mbps

Clearly, the OpenVPN configuration needs to be optimized, but that is outside the scope of this recipe. These results do show that for both Windows and Linux clients, there is a significant performance boost when the data that is sent over the tunnel is easily compressible.

How it works...

When compression is enabled, all packets that are sent over the tunnel are compressed before they are encrypted and transferred to the other side. Compression is done using the LZO library, which is integrated into OpenVPN. This compression is done on-the-fly, which means that the compression ratios achieved are not as good as when compressing the data in advance. When transferring text pages, the performance gain is nevertheless significant.

There's more...

When using compression, there are a few caveats to be aware of.

Pushing compression options

With OpenVPN, it is possible to push compression options from the server to the client using the directive:

```
comp-lzo
push "comp-lzo"
```

The caveat here is that this `push` directive is picked up by the OpenVPN 2.1 client **only** if it already has a line:

```
comp-lzo {yes|no|adaptive}
```

in the client configuration file. If this option is not present, the pushed directive is ignored and the connection actually fails to start.

Adaptive compression

When the following configuration directive is used, adaptive compression is enabled by default:

```
comp-lzo
```

When OpenVPN detects that a particular piece of data is not compressible it sends the data to the remote VPN endpoint without compressing it first. By specifying the following on both ends each packet is always compressed:

```
comp-lzo yes
```

Depending on the type of data that is transferred, the performance is slightly better.

Traffic shaping

In this recipe, we will use traffic shaping to limit the upload speed of an OpenVPN client. This can be used to throttle the bandwidth of a client to the server, or from client to client. Note that OpenVPN traffic shaping cannot be used to throttle the download speed of OpenVPN clients. Throttling download speeds can best be achieved using external traffic control tools, such as the 'tc' utility on Linux, which is part of the LARTC package.

Getting ready

We use the following network layout:

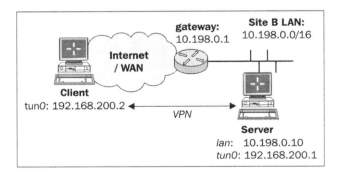

Install OpenVPN 2.0 or higher on two computers. Make sure the computers are connected over a network. Set up the client and server certificates using the first recipe from *Chapter 2, Client-server IP-only Networks*. For this recipe, the server computer was running CentOS 5 Linux and OpenVPN 2.1.1. The client was running Windows XP SP3 and OpenVPN 2.1.1. Keep the configuration file, `basic-udp-server.conf`, from the *Chapter 2* recipe *Server-side routing* at hand, as well as the client configuration file `basic-udp-client.ovpn` from the *Chapter 2* recipe *Using an ifconfig-pool block*.

How to do it...

1. Append the following line to the `basic-udp-server.conf` file:

   push "shaper 100000"

   This will throttle the upload speed of the VPN clients to 100,000 bytes per second (100 kbps). Save it as `example9-5-server.conf`.

2. Start the server:

   [root@server]# openvpn --config example9-5-server.conf

3. Start the client:

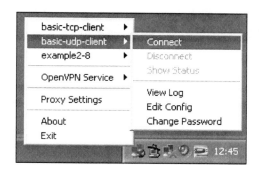

4. Next, we start `iperf` on the server:

   [server]$ iperf -s

5. When we run `iperf` on the Windows PC, the performance is close to 100 KB/s:

```
C:\>iperf -c 192.168.200.1 -fK

Client connecting to 192.168.200.1, TCP port 5001
TCP window size: 8.00 KByte (default)

[1912] local 192.168.200.3 port 1067 connected with 192.168.200.1 port 5001
[ ID] Interval       Transfer     Bandwidth
[1912]  0.0-10.3 sec   872 KBytes  84.9 KBytes/sec

C:\>
```

How it works...

When the OpenVPN client connects to the server, the server pushes out an option to shape outgoing traffic over the VPN tunnel to 100 KB/s. Whenever traffic is sent over the tunnel, the OpenVPN client itself limits the outgoing traffic to a maximum of 100 KB/s. The download speed is not affected by this, and note that the following directive cannot be used on the OpenVPN server itself:

```
shaper 100000
```

To throttle traffic leaving the server, more advanced traffic control tools such as `tc` for Linux should be used.

There's more...

OpenVPN 2.1 on Linux currently does not support traffic shaping very well. If this option is enabled in the Linux client, all network traffic over the tunnel is severely throttled to bytes per second. When OpenVPN 2.0 is used on the exact same Linux client the behaviour is as expected. This has been submitted as a bug but it is not known when it will be fixed.

Tuning UDP-based connections

In this recipe, we focus on some of the basic techniques for optimizing UDP-based VPN tunnels. These techniques need to be applied with care, as there is no fool-proof method for optimizing OpenVPN performance. The actual performance gain varies with each network setup. Therefore, this recipe only shows some of the configuration directives that can be used for this optimization.

Getting ready

We use the following network layout:

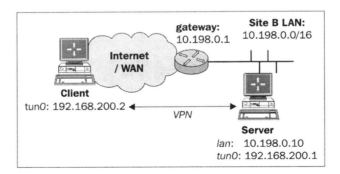

Install OpenVPN 2.0 or higher on two computers. Make sure the computers are connected over a network. Set up the client and server certificates using the first recipe from *Chapter 2, Client-server IP-only Networks*. In this recipe, the server computer was running CentOS 5 Linux and OpenVPN 2.1.1. The client was running Fedora 13 Linux and OpenVPN 2.1.1. Keep the configuration file `basic-udp-server.conf` from the *Chapter 2* recipe *Server-side routing* at hand, as well as the client configuration file `basic-udp-client.conf` from the same recipe.

How to do it...

1. Append the following line to the `basic-udp-server.conf` file:

   `fragment 1400`

   Save it as `example9-6-server.conf`.

2. Start the server:

   `[root@server]# openvpn --config example9-6-server.conf`

3. Similarly, for the client, add a line to the `basic-udp- client.conf` file:

   `fragment 1400`

   Save it as `example9-6-client.conf`.

4. Start the client:

   `[root@client]# openvpn --config example9-6-client.conf`

5. Next, we start `iperf` on the server:

   `[server]$ iperf -s`

6. First, we measure the performance outside the tunnel:

   `[client]$ iperf -c <openvpn-server-ip>`

   `[  3]  0.0-10.1 sec  8.4 MBytes  803 kbits/sec`

   This actually measures the performance of data being sent **TO** the server. The ADSL network used in this recipe has a theoretical upload limit of 1024 kbps, which in practice results in an 800 kbps upload speed. Note that this result is nearly the same as found in the recipe *Optimizing performance using 'iperf'*.

7. Next, we measure the performance inside the tunnel:

   `[client]$ iperf -c 192.168.200.1`

   `[  3]  0.0-10.0 sec  8.2 MBytes  803 kbits/sec`

   With this network setup there is no measurable performance difference between traffic sent outside of the tunnel and traffic sent via the tunnel, even with or without fragmentation.

   Fragmentation does have an effect on the `ping` round-trip times, however.

8. For various values of the `fragment` option, run the `ping` command from client to server:

    `[client]$ ping -c 10 192.168.200.1`

The results are listed in the following table:

Fragmentation size	Ping result
Default (1500)	41 +/- 1 ms
1400	43 +/- 1 ms
400	47 +/- 1 ms

Thus, adding the `fragment` option to the server configuration is not a viable option for this network setup. However, in other network setups, this might improve performance.

How it works...

The OpenVPN configuration directive:

    `fragment 1400`

causes all encrypted packets that are larger than 1400 bytes to be fragmented. If the network latency is low enough, this does not have a noticeable effect on performance, as the `iperf` results. By lowering the fragmentation size, packets are split into more and more packets. This causes the round-trip time for larger packets to increase. If the network latency is already high, this will cause even more latency issues. Hence, the `fragment` option and associated `mssfix` option must be used with care.

There's more...

The `fragment` directive is often used in conjunction with the `mssfix` directive:

    `mssfix [maximum-segment-size]`

This directive announces to TCP sessions running over the tunnel that they should limit their send packet sizes such that after OpenVPN has encapsulated them; the resulting UDP packet size that OpenVPN sends to its peer will not exceed the maximum segment size. It is also used internally by OpenVPN to set the maximum segment size of outbound packets. If no maximum segment size is specified, the value from the `fragment` directive is used.

Ideally, the `mssfix` and `fragment` directives are used together, where `mssfix` will try to keep TCP from needing packet fragmentation in the first place, and if big packets come through anyhow (for example, from protocols other than TCP), the `fragment` directive will internally fragment them.

See also

▸ The next recipe in this chapter, which explains how to tune TCP-based connections in a very similar manner.

Tuning TCP-based connections

In this recipe, we focus on some of the basic techniques for optimizing TCP-based VPN tunnels. In a TCP-based VPN setup, the connection between the VPN endpoints is a regular TCP connection. This has advantages and drawbacks. The main advantage is that it is often easier to set up a TCP connection than a UDP connection, mostly due to firewall restrictions. The main drawback of tunneling TCP traffic over a TCP-based tunnel is that there is chance of severe performance penalties, especially, when the network connection is poor. This performance penalty is caused by the *tcp-over-tcp* syndrome. The TCP protocol guarantees the ordered delivery of packets, thus if a packet is dropped along the way, the packet will be resent. Once the new packet is received, the packet order is restored. Until that time, all packets after the `lost` packet are on hold. The problem with tunnelling TCP traffic over a TCP connection is that **both** layers want to guarantee ordered packet delivery. This can lead to a large amount of retransmits and hence to a large performance penalty.

When tuned correctly, however, an OpenVPN tunnel over a TCP connection can achieve the same performance as an OpenVPN tunnel over a UDP connection. In this recipe, we will show some techniques for tuning such a TCP-based OpenVPN connection.

Getting ready

We use the following network layout:

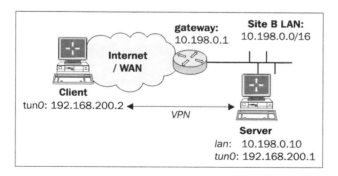

Install OpenVPN 2.0 or higher on two computers. Make sure the computers are connected over a network. Set up the client and server certificates using the first recipe from *Chapter 2, Client-server IP-only Networks*. For this recipe, the server computer was running CentOS 5 Linux and OpenVPN 2.1.1. The client was running Windows XP SP3 and OpenVPN 2.1.1.

How to do it...

1. Create the server configuration file:

```
proto tcp
port 1194
dev tun
server 192.168.200.0 255.255.255.0

ca        /etc/openvpn/cookbook/ca.crt
cert      /etc/openvpn/cookbook/server.crt
key       /etc/openvpn/cookbook/server.key
dh        /etc/openvpn/cookbook/dh1024.pem
tls-auth /etc/openvpn/cookbook/ta.key 0

persist-key
persist-tun
keepalive 10 60

topology subnet

user   nobody
group nobody

daemon
log-append /var/log/openvpn.log

tcp-nodelay
```

Save it as example9-7-server.conf.

2. Start the server:

[root@server]# openvpn --config example9-7-server.conf

3. Next , create the client configuration file:

```
client
proto tcp
remote openvpnserver.example.com
port 1194
```

```
dev tun
nobind

ca        "c:/program files/openvpn/config/ca.crt"
cert      "c:/program files/openvpn/config/client2.crt"
key       "c:/program files/openvpn/config/client2.key"
tls-auth "c:/program files/openvpn/config/ta.key" 1

ns-cert-type server
```

Save it as `example9-7.ovpn`.

4. Start the client:

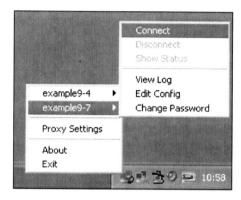

5. Next, start `iperf` on the server:

[server]$ iperf -s

6. Then, measure the performance of the tunnel:

[client]$ iperf -c 192.168.200.1

On this particular network, the following settings were tested:

Protocol	Result
UDP	40 Mbits/se
TCP	32 Mbits/sec
TCP with tcp-nodelay	38 Mbits/sec

As can be seen, the performance of running OpenVPN over TCP is almost identical to the performance of OpenVPN over UDP, when the `--tcp-nodelay` directive is used.

How it works...

When OpenVPN uses TCP as its underlying protocol, all packets are transferred over a regular TCP connection. By default, TCP connections make use of the Nagle algorithm, where smaller packets are held back and collected before they are sent. For an OpenVPN tunnel, this has an adverse effect on performance in most cases, hence it makes sense to disable the Nagle algorithm. By adding the `--tcp-nodelay` directive, we disable the Nagle algorithm and we see an immediate increase in performance.

There's more...

The two important parameters that can be tweaked for TCP-based connections are:

- The `--tcp-nodelay` directive
- The MTU size of the TUN/TAP-Win32 adapter via either the `--tun-mtu` or `--link-mtu` directives

On Linux, the MTU size of the TUN (or TAP) adapter can be adjusted on-the-fly, but on Windows XP, this is not the case. OpenVPN must be configured to match the MTU size as specified on the server. Before the new MTU size is used, however, a registry change must be made and Windows must be rebooted for the new MTU size to take effect. This makes it much harder to find the right MTU size for Window clients.

Starting with Windows Vista, it is now also possible to change the MTU setting on-the-fly, using the `netsh` command:

- First, find the right sub-interface number:

  ```
  [winclient]C:> netsh interface ipv4 show subinterfaces
  ```

- Next, in order to change the MTU size of a sub-interface, use:

  ```
  [winclient]C:> netsh interface ipv4 set subinterface "1" mtu=1400
  ```

Note that these commands must be run with elevated privileges.

If the MTU setting of the Windows TAP-Win32 adapter is larger than the MTU size configured by OpenVPN, the following message can appear in the OpenVPN 2.1 log file:

```
... read from TUN/TAP  [State=AT?c Err=[c:\src\21\tap-win32\tapdrvr.
c/2447] #O=4 Tx=[29510,0] Rx=[15309,0] IrpQ=[0,1,16] PktQ=[0,22,64]
InjQ=[0,1,16]]: More data is available.  (code=234)
```

For this particular network, all changes made to the MTU size (with the appropriate Windows reboot) did not have a positive effect on performance.

Analyzing performance using tcpdump

In this recipe, we will analyze the performance of an OpenVPN setup using the `tcpdump` utility. It is also possible to use the Wireshark utility, which is available for Linux, Windows, and Mac OS X. While this recipe does not cover any new OpenVPN functionality, it is useful to show how such an analysis can be made.

Getting ready

We use the following network layout:

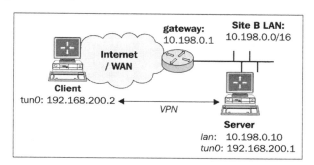

Install OpenVPN 2.0 or higher on two computers. Make sure the computers are connected over a network. Set up the client and server certificates using the first recipe from *Chapter 2, Client-server IP-only Networks*. For this recipe, the server computer was running CentOS 5 Linux and OpenVPN 2.1.1. The client was running Fedora 13 Linux and OpenVPN 2.1.1. Keep the configuration file `example9-6-server.conf` from the recipe *Tuning UDP based connections* at hand, as well as the client configuration, `example9-6-client.conf`, from the same recipe.

How to do it...

1. Start the server:

    `[root@server]# openvpn --config example9-6-server.conf`

2. Next, start the client:

    `[root@client]# openvpn --config example9-6-client.conf`

3. On the server, run `tcpdump` to watch for the incoming packets on the network interface (not the tunnel interface itself):

    `[root@server]# tcpdump -nnl -i eth0 udp port 1194`

    This instructs `tcpdump` to listen on the local network interface for all UDP traffic on port 1194, which is the OpenVPN default.

4. From the client, ping the server's VPN IP address with two different sizes:

```
[client]$ ping -c 2 -s 1300 192.168.200.1
[client]$ ping -c 2 -s 1400 192.168.200.1
```

The following packets are seen in the `tcpdump` screen:

```
Example 9-6
File  Edit  View  Terminal  Help
$ tcpdump -nnl -i eth0 udp port 1194
### ping -s 1300
17:32:06.906635 IP 172.30.0.130.43817 > 172.30.0.1.1194: UDP, length 1373
17:32:06.908359 IP 172.30.0.1.1194 > 172.30.0.130.43817: UDP, length 1373
17:32:07.908039 IP 172.30.0.130.43817 > 172.30.0.1.1194: UDP, length 1373
17:32:07.909785 IP 172.30.0.1.1194 > 172.30.0.130.43817: UDP, length 1373
### ping -s 1400
17:32:11.129258 IP 172.30.0.130.43817 > 172.30.0.1.1194: UDP, length 757
17:32:11.129380 IP 172.30.0.130.43817 > 172.30.0.1.1194: UDP, length 757
17:32:11.131245 IP 172.30.0.1.1194 > 172.30.0.130.43817: UDP, length 757
17:32:11.131368 IP 172.30.0.1.1194 > 172.30.0.130.43817: UDP, length 757
17:32:12.130396 IP 172.30.0.130.43817 > 172.30.0.1.1194: UDP, length 757
17:32:12.130523 IP 172.30.0.130.43817 > 172.30.0.1.1194: UDP, length 757
17:32:12.132641 IP 172.30.0.1.1194 > 172.30.0.130.43817: UDP, length 757
17:32:12.133167 IP 172.30.0.1.1194 > 172.30.0.130.43817: UDP, length 757
```

The first ICMP packets are sent unfragmented, as they are smaller than 1400 bytes. The second set of encrypted ICMP packets is larger than the fragment size (1400) and hence are split into two parts.

How it works...

The OpenVPN configuration directive:

```
fragment 1400
```

causes all the encrypted packets that are larger than 1400 bytes to be fragmented. When watching the encrypted traffic, this can be verified by pinging the OpenVPN server. Note that packets which need to be fragmented are fragmented evenly: all packets have the same size.

Also, note that the following command causes the encrypted packet to be larger than 1400 bytes:

```
[client]$ ping -c 2 -s 1400 192.168.200.1
```

The encryption needed for the secure tunnel adds extra overhead to the packets that are transmitted. This is one of the root causes for a performance penalty when using VPN tunnels (not just OpenVPN) compared to non-encrypted traffic. In most networks, this overhead is not noticed, but it always exists.

See also

▶ Chapter 9's recipe *Tuning UDP-based connections* in this chapter, which explains how to use the `fragment` directive.

10
OS Integration

In this chapter, we will cover:

- ▶ Linux: using `NetworkManager`
- ▶ Linux: using `pull-resolv-conf`
- ▶ Mac OS: using `Tunnelblick`
- ▶ Windows Vista/7: elevated privileges
- ▶ Windows: using the CryptoAPI store
- ▶ Windows: updating the DNS cache
- ▶ Windows: running OpenVPN as a service
- ▶ Windows: public versus private network adapters
- ▶ Windows: routing methods

Introduction

In this chapter, we will focus on how to use OpenVPN on the most-used client operating systems: Linux, Mac OS X, and Windows. For each operating system, an entire chapter could be written to describe the intricacies of running OpenVPN in both the client and server mode, but as space is limited, we will focus only on the interaction of the OpenVPN client with the OS. The purpose of the recipes in this chapter is to outline some of the common pitfalls when running OpenVPN on a particular platform. The recipes focus mainly on the configuration of OpenVPN itself, not on how to integrate a working VPN setup into the rest of the network infrastructure.

Linux: using NetworkManager

When Linux is used as a desktop operating system, the network configuration is configured using the Linux NetworkManager in most of the cases. This package allows a non-root user to start and stop the network connections, connect and disconnect from wireless networks, and also to set up several types of VPN connections, including OpenVPN. In this recipe, we will show how to configure an OpenVPN connection using the GNOME variant of the NetworkManager.

Getting ready

Set up the client and server certificates using the first recipe from *Chapter 2, Client-server IP-only Networks*. For this recipe, the server computer was running CentOS 5 Linux and OpenVPN 2.1.1. The client was running Fedora 13 Linux and OpenVPN 2.1.1. This version of Linux comes with NetworkManager 0.8, including the NetworkManager-openvpn plugin. The NetworkManager-openvpn plugin is not installed by default and needs to be explicitly added to the system. This version is highly recommended when setting up an OpenVPN connection. Versions of the NetworkManager older than 0.7.0 have very limited OpenVPN support and a different configuration file syntax. Keep the configuration file, basic-udp-server.conf, from the *Chapter 2* recipe *Server-side routing* at hand.

How to do it...

1. Start the NetworkManager configuration screen by right-clicking on the NetworkManager icon in the taskbar and selecting **Edit Connections**. A Window will pop up.

2. Choose the tab **VPN** to set up a new VPN connection.

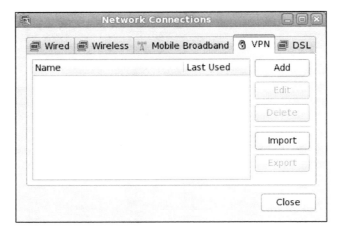

3. Click on the **Add** button to bring up the next screen:

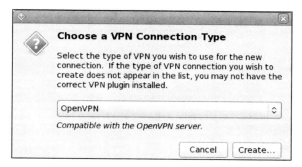

4. Select the VPN type **OpenVPN** and click on the **Create** button. If the VPN connection type **OpenVPN** is not available, then the `NetworkManager-openvpn` plugin is not installed.

5. Fill in the details of the **VPN** tab of the next window:

The **Gateway** is the hostname or IP address of the OpenVPN server. The **Type** of authentication is **Certificates (TLS)**. Then, for the **User Certificate**, **CA Certificate** and **Private Key** browse to the directory where the client files **client1.crt**, **ca.crt**, and **client1.key** are located respectively. Fill in the **Private Key Password**, if required. Do **not** click on the **Apply** button just yet, click on **Advanced** instead.

6. In the next window, go to the tab **TLS Authentication**:

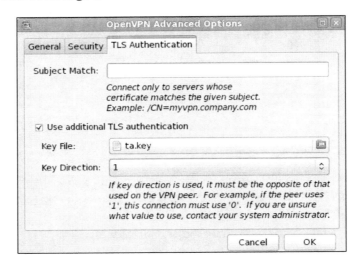

Select **Use additional TLS authentication** and browse to the location of the **ta.key** file. Choose **1** for the key direction.

7. Click on **OK** when done, then click on **Apply** to save the new VPN connection.

8. Next, start the server:

```
[root@server]# openvpn --config basic-udp-server.conf
```

9. And finally, on the client, start the VPN connection by clicking on the `NetworkManager` icon, choosing **VPN Connections**, and selecting **Example10-1**:

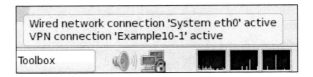

You can verify whether the VPN connection is established correctly by pinging the VPN server IP.

How it works...

The `NetworkManager-openvpn` plugin is a GUI for setting up an OpenVPN client configuration file. All the settings made are the equivalent of setting up the client configuration file as done in the *Chapter 2* recipe *Server-side routing*.

Note that older versions of the `NetworkManager-openvpn` plugin do not support the complete feature set of OpenVPN.

There's more...

The `NetworkManager-openvpn` plugin supports some advanced configuration settings:

Setting up routes using NetworkManager

The `NetworkManager-openvpn` plugin can also be used to set up VPN-specific routes. Open the main VPN configuration screen again, and go to the tab **IPv4 Settings**. Click on the **Routes** button on this screen:

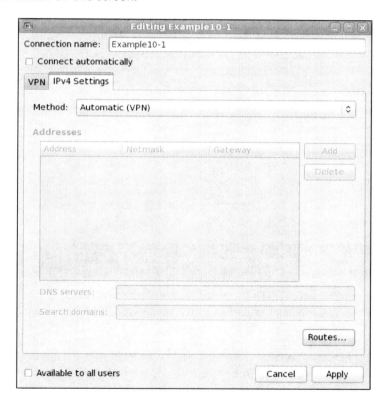

A new window will appear:

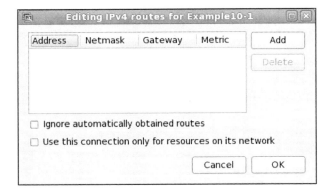

Routes pushed by the server can be overruled using the **Ignore automatically obtained routes**. The behavior of server directive `push "redirect-gateway"` can be overruled by checking the **Use this connection only for resources on its network** checkbox.

DNS settings

The `NetworkManager-openvpn` plugin also updates the `/etc/resolv.conf` file if the OpenVPN server pushes out DNS servers using the following directive:

```
push "dhcp-option DNS a.b.c.d"
```

Scripting

Note that `NetworkManager` does **not** allow scripting or plugins on the client side, as they are a security risk when configured by a non-root user.

Linux: using 'pull-resolv-conf'

One of the most common pitfalls when setting up a VPN connection on Linux is when the OpenVPN server pushes out new DNS settings. In the previous recipe, we saw that the `NetworkManager-openvpn` plugin also updated the system configuration file that contained the DNS setting, `/etc/resolv.conf`. If the command line is used this is not done automatically. By default, OpenVPN comes with two scripts to add and remove DNS servers from the `/etc/resolv.conf` file. This recipe will show how to use these scripts.

Getting ready

We use the following network layout:

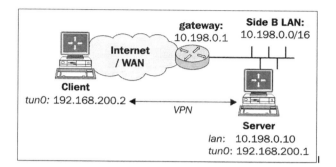

Set up the client and server certificates using the first recipe from *Chapter 2, Client-server IP-only Networks*. For this recipe, the server computer was running CentOS 5 Linux and OpenVPN 2.1.1. The client was running Fedora 13 Linux and OpenVPN 2.1.1. Keep the configuration file `basic-udp-server.conf` from the *Chapter 2* recipe *Server-side routing* at hand, as well as the client configuration file, `basic-udp-client.conf`, from the same recipe.

How to do it...

1. Append the following line to the `basic-udp-server.conf` file:

   push "dhcp-option DNS 10.198.0.1"

   Here, `10.198.0.1` is the address of a DNS server on the VPN server LAN. Save it as `example10-2-server.conf`.

2. Start the server:

   [root@server]# openvpn --config example10-2-server.conf

3. Similarly, for the client, add the following lines to the `basic-udp-client.conf` file:

   script-security 2
   up   "/etc/openvpn/cookbook/client.up"
   down "/etc/openvpn/cookbook/client.down"

   Save it as `example10-2-client.conf`.

4. Copy over the `client.up` and `client.down` files from the OpenVPN `contrib` directory and make them executable. On Fedora 13, these files are located in the directory `/usr/share/doc/openvpn-2.1.1/contrib/pull-resolv-conf`:

    [root@client]# cd /etc/openvpn/cookbook

    [root@client]# cp /usr/share/doc/openvpn-2.1.1/contrib/pull-resolv-conf/client.* .

    [root@client]# chmod 755 client.*

5. And finally, start the client:

    [root@client]# openvpn --config example10-2-client.conf

After the VPN connection comes up, check the contents of the `/etc/resolv.conf` file. The first line should contain the DNS server as specified by the OpenVPN server:

```
nameserver 10.198.0.1
```

When the VPN connection is terminated, the entry is removed again.

How it works...

The scripts supplied with OpenVPN parse the environment variables `foreign_option_*` and look for DOMAIN and DNS settings. These settings are then written out to the beginning of the `/etc/resolv.conf` file. This causes the DNS server and the DOMAIN pushed by the OpenVPN server to take precedence over the system's DNS and DOMAIN settings.

When the VPN connection is dropped, the same settings are removed from the `/etc/resolv.conf` file.

There's more...

Note that when the `NetworkManager-openvpn` plugin is used, these scripts are not necessary, as the `NetworkManager` itself updates the `/etc/resolv.conf` file.

MacOS: using Tunnelblick

This recipe will demonstrate how to set up OpenVPN on a machine running Mac OS X. For Mac OS X, several OpenVPN GUI applications are available. In this recipe, we will show how to use one of them, Tunnelblick (`http://code.google.com/p/tunnelblick/`).

Getting ready

We use the following network layout:

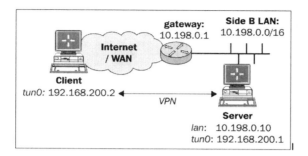

Set up the client and server certificates using the first recipe from *Chapter 2, Client-server IP-only Networks*. For this recipe, the server computer was running CentOS 5 Linux and OpenVPN 2.1.1. The client was running Mac OS X "Leopard", Tunnelblick 3.0, and OpenVPN 2.1.1. Keep the configuration file, `example10-2-server.conf`, from the previous recipe at hand.

How to do it...

1. Launch **Tunnelblick** if it is not running already.
2. Click on the tunnel icon in the task bar, after which the main **Tunnelblick** window will come up:

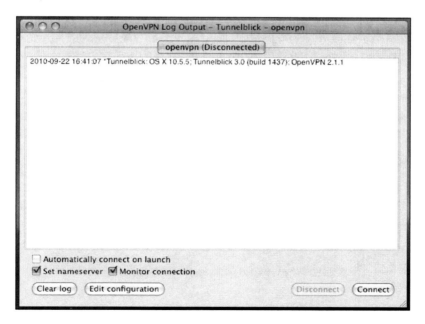

3. Click on **Edit configuration** to launch the **Text Editor** with the default configuration file. Set up the client configuration file as follows:

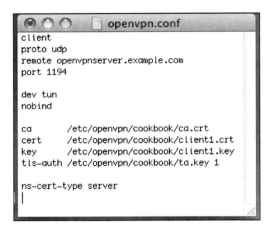

```
client
proto udp
remote openvpnserver.example.com
port 1194

dev tun
nobind

ca       /etc/openvpn/cookbook/ca.crt
cert     /etc/openvpn/cookbook/client1.crt
key      /etc/openvpn/cookbook/client1.key
tls-auth /etc/openvpn/cookbook/ta.key 1

ns-cert-type server
```

Note that this is exactly the same configuration as used in the *Chapter 2* recipe *Server-side routing*. Save the configuration and close the **Text Editor**.

4. When **Tunnelblick** warns that the configuration file is protected, click on **Unprotect and modify** to modify it.

5. Next, start the server:

   ```
   [root@server]# openvpn --config example10-2-server.conf
   ```

6. Then, on the client, click on the **Connect** button in the main **Tunnelblick** screen.

   Before the OpenVPN connection can be established **Tunnelblick** pops up a new window. Because the configuration file was modified, **Tunnelblick** explicitly asks for the **Mac Admin** password in order to repair the permissions:

After the **Mac Admin** password has been entered the OpenVPN connection is established:

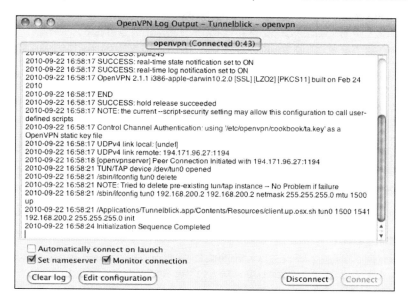

If anything goes wrong during the connection phase, the output messages of **Tunnelblick** and the OpenVPN process can be found in the **All Messages** screen of the **Console** utility. The **Console** utility is normally found in the `Utilities` folder of the system volume:

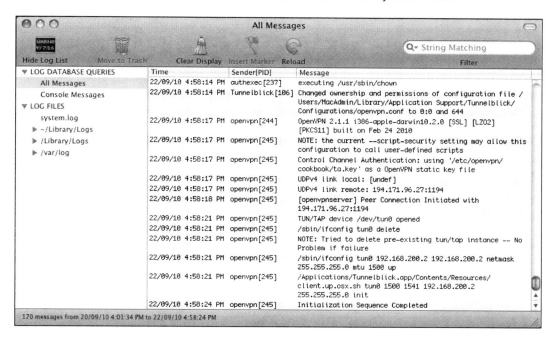

How it works...

The **Tunnelblick** GUI is a wrapper program around the command-line `openvpn` program. It monitors the startup and the shutdown of OpenVPN and it supplies the right input, such as the private key password, if required.

Other than that the Mac OS X version of OpenVPN, it behaves very similar to the Linux and UNIX versions of OpenVPN. Therefore, nearly all scripts that work for Linux and UNIX can be made to work easily for Mac OS X as well.

There's more...

There are a few subtle differences between the UNIX version of OpenVPN and the Mac OS X version. The two major differences are outlined here.

Name resolution

If the checkbox `Set nameserver` is enabled, then Tunnelblick will run an `up` script that interacts with the Mac OS X network layer to use the DNS information pushed out by the OpenVPN server. It will also update the `/etc/resolv.conf` file with this DNS information.

Scripting

Note that Tunnelblick does **not** allow scripting on the client side, as it replaces the `up` and `down` scripts with scripts of its own.

Windows Vista/7: elevated privileges

With the introduction of Windows Vista, Microsoft introduced User Access Control (UAC). UAC is meant to safeguard users from running programs that can modify the operating system itself. Before such a program is run, privilege elevation is required, even if the user has full **Administrator** rights. A dialog box appears that the user must click on before the execution begins. In order to run OpenVPN, elevated privileges are needed, as OpenVPN wants to open a system device and start a VPN connection. Especially, if the routes need to be added to the system, elevated privileges are essential.

This recipe shows how OpenVPN can be set up on Windows Vista/7 with elevated privileges, including how to run `up` and `down` scripts.

Getting ready

Set up the client and server certificates using the first recipe from *Chapter 2, Client-server IP-only Networks*. For this recipe, the server computer was running CentOS 5 Linux and OpenVPN 2.1.1. The client computer was running Windows Vista SP1 and OpenVPN 2.1.3. Keep the configuration file, `basic-udp-server.conf`, from the *Chapter 2* recipe *Server-side routing* at hand. For the client, keep the configuration file, `example6-1.ovpn`, from the *Chapter 6* recipe *Using a client-side up/down script* at hand.

How to do it...

1. First, start the server:

   ```
   [root@server]# openvpn --config basic-udp-server.conf
   ```

2. Next, we modify the client configuration file, `example6-1.ovpn`, by changing the lines:

   ```
   script-security 2
   up    "c:\\program\files\\openvpn\\scripts\\updown.bat"
   down  "c:\\program\files\\openvpn\\scripts\\updown.bat"
   ```

   to:

   ```
   script-security 2 system
   cd  "c:\\program\files\\openvpn\\scripts"
   up    "%windir%\\system32\\cmd.exe /c updown.bat"
   down  "%windir%\\system32\\cmd.exe /c updown.bat"
   ```

   This is required for batch files to work when they are called by the OpenVPN executables on Windows Vista/7. Save this configuration file as `example10-4.ovpn`.

3. Before starting the OpenVPN GUI, right-click on the `OpenVPN GUI` icon that was placed on your desktop after installing the OpenVPN 2.1.3 installer for Windows.

4. In the **Properties** screen that comes up, click on the tab **Compatibility** and enable **Run this program as an administrator**:

Click on **OK**.

5. The next time you start the OpenVPN GUI using this icon, it will prompt for permissions:

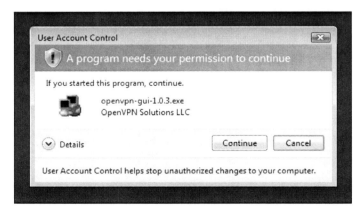

6. Click on **Continue** to start the OpenVPN GUI as usual. At this point, the OpenVPN GUI is running with elevated privileges, which means it has full control over the system.

7. Start the OpenVPN client by launching the `example10-4` configuration file. Verify that the VPN connection is established and that the log file `c:\temp\openvpn.log` has been created.

How it works...

When the OpenVPN GUI application is launched, the user must confirm that it can run with elevated privileges. After that the OpenVPN GUI can launch other executables that will also inherit these privileges. When the GUI launches the `openvpn.exe` process, it can open the VPN adapter, alter the routing tables, and run `up` and `down` programs. One thing it cannot do is directly run batch files, as these are considered too dangerous. By explicitly launching the Windows command shell with the name of the batch file, the OpenVPN process is capable of running an `up` or `down` script.

There's more...

A new OpenVPN GUI application is currently under development, which is capable of running without elevated privileges. It uses a different method for communicating to the `openvpn.exe` process, which still requires such privileges.

Windows: using the CryptoAPI store

OpenVPN has the capability of using the Windows CryptoAPI store to retrieve the public and private key needed for setting up a connection. This improves security somewhat, as the CryptoAPI store is more secure than the plaintext `.crt` and `.key` files that are normally used to set up an OpenVPN connection. In this recipe, we will configure an OpenVPN client to retrieve the required information from the CryptoAPI store when connecting to the server. This recipe was tested on Windows XP and Windows Vista but it will also work on other versions of Windows.

Getting ready

Set up the client and server certificates using the first recipe from *Chapter 2, Client-server IP-only Networks*. For this recipe, the server computer was running CentOS 5 Linux and OpenVPN 2.1.1. The client computer was running Windows XP SP3 and OpenVPN 2.1.1. Keep the configuration file `basic-udp-server.conf` from the *Chapter 2* recipe *Server-side routing* at hand.

How to do it...

1. First, we need to import the client certificate into the CryptoAPI store. In order to do that we must convert the existing `client2.crt` and `client2.key` files to PKCS12 format. Open a Windows command shell and change directory to the location where these files are located:

   ```
   [winclient]C:> cd C:\Program Files\OpenVPN\config
   [winclient]C:\Program Files\OpenVPN\config>..\bin\openssl pkcs12
        -export -in client2.crt -inkey client2.key -out client2.p12
   Loading 'screen' into random state - done
   Enter pass phrase for client2.key: [existing password]
   Enter Export Password: [new export password]
   Verifying - Enter Export Password: [repeat export password]
   ```

2. Next, import the PKCS12 file into the Windows CryptoAPI store:

   ```
   [winclient]C:\Program Files\OpenVPN\config>start client2.p12
   ```

   The certificate import wizard will start.

3. Click **Next** on the first screen, and again **Next** on the second screen. Then, you must supply the **Export password** from the previous step:

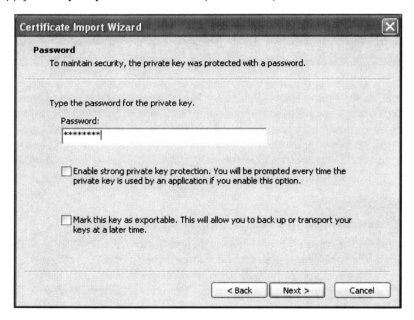

   If you enable **Enable strong private key protection**, the certificate and private key are even better protected, but you will be required to retype the password every time OpenVPN starts.

4. Click **Next**. In the next screen, select the default option **Automatically select the certificate store** and click on **Next** once more. By clicking on **Finish** in the next screen, the certificate import is completed:

5. Create the client configuration file:

```
client
proto udp
remote openvpnserver.example.com
port 1194

dev tun
nobind

ca       "c:/program files/openvpn/config/ca.crt"
tls-auth "c:/program files/openvpn/config/ta.key" 1
cryptoapicert  "SUBJ:OpenVPNClient2"

ns-cert-type server
```

Save the configuration file as example10-5.ovpn.

6. Start the server:

```
[root@server]# openvpn --config basic-udp-server.conf
```

7. Start the VPN connection.

The VPN connection should be established without asking for a private key password. If the CryptoAPI option **Enable strong private key protection** was enabled, a separate dialog will pop up to ask for the CryptoAPI password.

How it works...

The Windows OpenVPN client software is capable of extracting a certificate and public key from the Windows CryptoAPI store if either the certificate subject name is specified using the keyword SUBJ: or if the certificate thumbprint or fingerprint is specified using the keyword THUMB:. After retrieving the certificate and private key from the CryptoAPI store, the VPN connection is established in exactly the same manner as if plaintext certificate and private key files had been used.

There's more...

There are several small yet important details when using the Windows CryptoAPI store:

The CA certificate file

Note that it is still required to specify the CA certificate using the following line:

```
ca c:/program files/openvpn/config/ca.crt
```

In theory, it would be possible to also retrieve the CA certificate from the CryptoAPI store but this is currently not implemented in OpenVPN.

Certificate fingerprint

Instead of supplying:

```
cryptoapicert SUBJ:<subject name>
```

It is also possible to specify:

```
cryptoapicert THUMB:<fingerprint>
```

The fingerprint or thumbprint of an X509 certificate can be both be retrieved by either looking up the Thumb property for the imported certificate in the Windows Certificate store or by typing the OpenSSL command:

```
C:\Program Files\OpenVPN\config>..\bin\openssl x509 \
   -fingerprint -noout -in client2.crt
SHA1 Fingerprint=D7:15:21:1F:11:15:33:58:81:DA:DE:2C:17:1E:36:43:58:4
0:87:07
```

Windows: updating the DNS cache

A frequently recurring question on the openvpn-users mailing lists is related to the DNS name resolution on Windows after the VPN connection is established. If the OpenVPN server pushes out a new DNS server, then this is automatically picked up by the OpenVPN client, yet name resolution does not always work right after establishing the connection. This has little to do with OpenVPN and more to do with the way the Windows DNS caching service works. As this question comes up quite regularly, a new directive `register-dns` was added in OpenVPN 2.1.3. When this directive is specified, OpenVPN updates the Windows DNS cache and registers the VPN IP address in the Windows DNS tables. As this feature appeared only recently, this recipe will also show how the Windows DNS cache can be updated using a script when the VPN connection is established. Some users disable the DNS caching service altogether, which seems to have a little impact on the operating system, except for a small performance penalty when using a slow network.

Getting ready

Set up the client and server certificates using the first recipe from *Chapter 2, Client-server IP-only Networks*. For this recipe, the server computer was running CentOS 5 Linux and OpenVPN 2.1.1. The client computer was running Windows XP SP3 and OpenVPN 2.1.3. Keep the server configuration file, `example10-2-server.conf`, from the recipe *Linux: using pull-resolv-conf* at hand, as well as the client configuration file, `basic-udp-client.ovpn`, from the *Chapter 2* recipe *Using an 'ifconfig-pool' block* at hand.

How to do it...

1. Start the server:

   ```
   [root@server]# openvpn --config example10-2-server.conf
   ```

2. Add a line to the `basic-udp-client.ovpn` configuration file:

   ```
   register-dns
   ```

   Save this configuration file as `example10-6.ovpn`.

3. Start the OpenVPN client.

   The OpenVPN GUI status window will show that the Windows service `dnscache` is restarted:

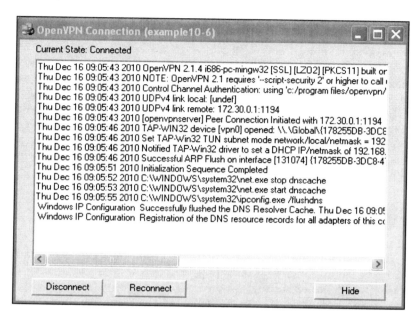

4. After the VPN connection is established, verify that the name resolution is using the VPN-supplied DNS server using, for example, the `nslookup` command.

How it works...

When the VPN connection is established, the OpenVPN client software sends a DHCP packet to the TAP-Win32 adapter with the IP address, default gateway, and the other network-related information, such as a new DNS server. This information is picked up by the operating system but the local DNS caching service is not notified immediately. The newly-introduced `register-dns` directive executes the following commands:

```
net stop dnscache
net start dnscache
ipconfig /flushdns
ipconfig /registerdns
```

By forcing a restart of the DNS caching service, the DNS server supplied by the VPN connection is used immediately.

There's more...

Prior to OpenVPN 2.1.3, it was necessary to update the Windows DNS cache using an `up` script. The client configuration file needed the following directives:

```
script-security 2 system
cd "c:\\program\ files\\openvpn\\config"
up   "%windir%\\system32\\cmd.exe /c example10-6.bat"
```

And a batch file `example10-6.bat` containing:

```
@echo off
net stop dnscache
net start dnscache
```

Windows: running OpenVPN as a service

One of lesser-known features of the Windows version of OpenVPN is its ability to run it as a service. This allows OpenVPN to start and establish a VPN connection without a user logging in on the system. The OpenVPN service is installed by default, but is not started automatically.

In this recipe, we will show how the OpenVPN service can be controlled using the OpenVPN GUI application and how to perform troubleshooting on the service.

Getting ready

In this recipe, the server computer was running CentOS 5 Linux and OpenVPN 2.1.1. The client computer was running Windows XP SP3 and OpenVPN 2.1.3. Keep the configuration file, `basic-udp-server.conf`, from the *Chapter 2* recipe *Server-side routing* at hand, as well as the client configuration file `basic-udp-client.ovpn` from the *Chapter 2* recipe *Using an ifconfig-pool block*.

How to do it...

1. Start the server:

    ```
    [root@server]# openvpn --config basic-udp-server.conf
    ```

2. Before starting the OpenVPN GUI application on the client side, we first launch the Windows registry editor `regedit`. Find the key **HKEY_LOCAL_MACHINE\ SOFTWARE\OpenVPN-GUI**

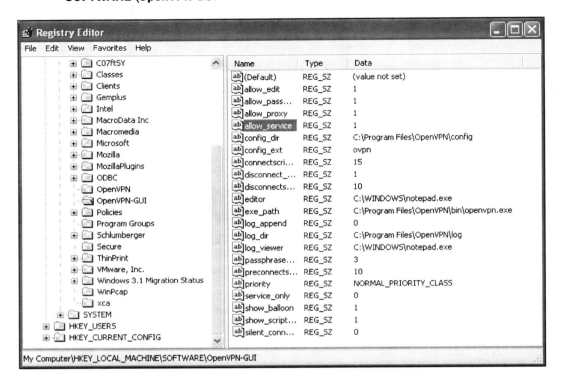

Take note of the `config_dir` registry key, which is normally set to `C:\Program Files\OpenVPN\config`

3. Set the registry key `allow_service` to 1. Also, take note of the registry key `log_dir`, which is normally set to `C:\Program Files\OpenVPN\log`.

4. Now, browse to the registry key **HKEY_LOCAL_MACHINE\SOFTWARE\OpenVPN** and check the `config_dir` and `log_dir` keys again. They should be pointing to the same directories as for the OpenVPN GUI application.

5. Close the registry editor.

6. Launch the OpenVPN GUI. Right click on the icon in the taskbar. A new menu option will have appeared:

    But do not start the service yet.

7. First, modify the client configuration file `basic-udp-client.ovpn` by changing the lines:

    ```
    cert        "c:/program files/openvpn/config/client2.crt"
    key         "c:/program files/openvpn/config/client2.key"
    ```

    to:

    ```
    cert        "c:/program files/openvpn/config/client1.crt"
    key         "c:/program files/openvpn/config/client1.key"
    ```

    The client certificate `client2.key` from *Chapter 2, Client-server IP-only Networks,* is protected by a password, whereas the `client1.key` file is not. Save the configuration file as `example10-7.ovpn`.

8. Move all other `.ovpn` files to another directory to make sure this is the only `.ovpn` in the `config` directory.

9. Now, start the OpenVPN service. After a while, the VPN connection will be established, as can be seen on both the client and the server in the log files.

How it works...

A Windows service is launched at system startup before a user is logged on. The OpenVPN service scans the directory pointed to by the registry key: `HKEY_LOCAL_MACHINE\SOFTWARE\OpenVPN\config_dir`

This starts an OpenVPN process for each file with the extension `.ovpn` in that directory. The output of each of these processes is logged on to the log directory pointed to by the registry key:

`HKEY_LOCAL_MACHINE\SOFTWARE\OpenVPN\log_dir`

Here, the log file name is the same as the configuration name, but now with the extension `.log`. For this recipe, the configuration file was:

`C:\Program Files\OpenVPN\config\example10-7.ovpn`

And the log file was:

`C:\Program Files\OpenVPN\log\example10-7.log`

There is no need to launch the OpenVPN GUI to start these connections, but the GUI application does offer a convenient method of managing the OpenVPN service, if the right registry key is added.

There's more...

There are a few important notes when using the OpenVPN service, which are outlined here.

Automatic service startup

To make the OpenVPN service start at system startup, open the **Services** administrative control panel by going to **Control Panel | Administrative Tools | Services**. Double-click on the **OpenVPN Service** to open the properties and set the **Startup type** to **Automatic**:

Click on **OK** and close the **Services** administrative control panel. Reboot Windows and verify on the server side that the client is connecting at system startup.

OpenVPN User name

When the OpenVPN service is used, the corresponding OpenVPN processes are normally run under the account **SYSTEM**, as can be seen in the following screenshot:

This has some implications regarding the permissions on the configuration files. Special care also needs to be taken when using the `cryptoapicert` directive, as by default those certificates end up in the user certificate store, which is not accessible to the SYSTEM account. It is possible to use the `cryptoapicert` directive, but the imported certificate must be installed as a (local) system certificate and not as a user certificate.

See also

▶   The recipe *Windows: using the CryptoAPI store* earlier in this chapter, which explains how to use the Windows CryptoAPI store, to store the user certificate and private key.

Windows: public versus private network adapters

With Windows Vista and 7, Microsoft introduced the concept of network classes. Network interfaces can be part of a **Private** or **Public** network. When using OpenVPN, one must be careful in which type of network the adapter is placed. By default, OpenVPN's TAP-Win32 adapter is placed in a **Public** network, which has a side-effect that it is not possible to mount file shares. In this recipe, we will show how to change the network type so that the trusted services such as file sharing are possible over a VPN connection. While this has a little to do with configuring the OpenVPN per se, this issue comes up often enough to warrant a recipe.

Getting ready

For this recipe, the server computer was running CentOS 5 Linux and OpenVPN 2.1.1. The client computer was running Windows Vista SP1 and OpenVPN 2.1.3. Keep the configuration file, `basic-udp-server.conf`, from the *Chapter 2* recipe *Server-side routing* at hand, as well as the client configuration file, `basic-udp-client.ovpn`, from the *Chapter 2* recipe *Using an ifconfig-pool block* at hand.

How to do it...

1. Start the server:

    ```
    [root@server]# openvpn --config basic-udp-server.conf
    ```

2. On the Windows client, launch the OpenVPN GUI application with elevated privileges and start the client.

3. After the VPN connection is established, open the **Network and Sharing Center**:

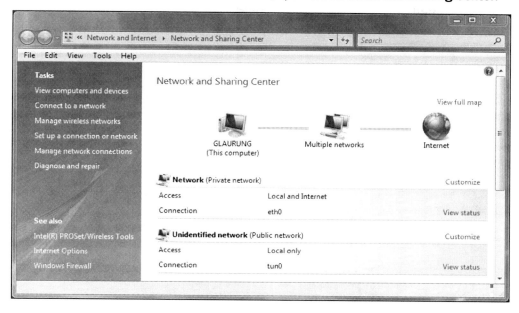

4. Click on **Customize** behind the **Unidentified network**, as the VPN connection (with adapter name **tun0** in this case) has been placed in this network category. A new window will come up:

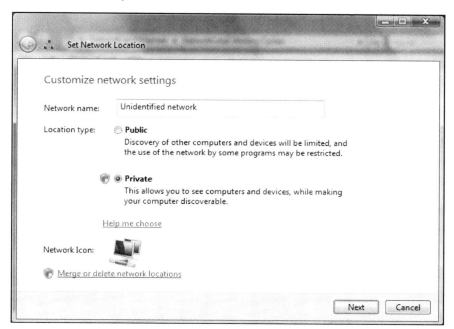

5. Change the network type to **Private** and click on the **Next** button.

6. Click on **Close** to apply the settings.

How it works...

With Windows Vista/7, each network type has different access rights. The network type with the fewest rights is **Public**, which means that the applications can set up TCP/IP connections but they cannot access any of the resources available in the **Private** networks, such as local printers and the local disks. When sharing resources that are on the same network as the OpenVPN client, this can become an issue. By changing the network type of the OpenVPN network adapter to **Private**, the issue can be resolved.

See also

▸ The recipe *Windows Vista/7: elevated privileges* earlier in this chapter, which explains in more detail about how to run the OpenVPN GUI application with elevated privileges.

Windows: routing methods

When routes are pushed to a Windows client, there are two methods for adding these routes to the system routing tables:

▸ Using the IPAPI helper functions (the default)

▸ Using the ROUTE.EXE program

In most cases, the IPAPI method works fine, but sometimes, it is necessary to overrule this behavior. In this recipe, we will show how this is done, and what to look for in the client log file to verify that the right method has been chosen.

Getting ready

Set up the client and server certificates using the first recipe from *Chapter 2, Client-server IP-only Networks*. For this recipe, the server computer was running CentOS 5 Linux and OpenVPN 2.1.1. The client computer was running Windows XP SP3 and OpenVPN 2.1.3. Keep the configuration file, basic-udp-server.conf, from the *Chapter 2* recipe *Server-side routing* at hand, as well as the client configuration file basic-udp-client.ovpn from the *Chapter 2* recipe *Using an ifconfig-pool block* at hand.

How to do it...

1. Start the server:

    [root@server]# openvpn --config basic-udp-server.conf

2. Add the following lines to the `basic-udp-client.ovpn` configuration file:

    verb 5
    route-method ipapi

    Save this configuration file as `example10-9.ovpn`.

3. Start the OpenVPN client.

4. After the connection has been established, bring up the Show Status window again and look at the last lines of the connection log. The log will show lines similar to the following:

    ```
    ...   C:\WINDOWS\system32\route.exe ADD 10.198.0.0 MASK 255.255.0.0
    192.168.200.1
    ... Route addition via IPAPI succeeded [adaptive]
    ... Initialization Sequence Completed
    ```

    Even though the route-method was set to ipapi, the log file prints out the path of the Windows route.exe command. The second line shows that the route was actually added using the IPAPI helper functions.

5. Now, modify the configuration file `example10-9.ovpn` to:

    verb 5
    route-method exe

6. Restart the OpenVPN client.

7. Look at the last lines of the connection log again. This time the message Route addition via IPAPI succeeded [adaptive] will not be present in the log file, which means that the route.exe command was used.

How it works...

The route-method directive has three options:

▶ adaptive: First, try the IPAPI method, fallback to the route.exe method if IPAPI fails. This is the default.

▶ ipapi: Always use the IPAPI helper functions to add routes.

▶ exe: Always use the external program route.exe.

In most cases, the default setting will work fine, although some users report that route-method exe worked better in the original OpenVPN 2.1 release.

Based on this directive, the OpenVPN client will choose how to add routes to the Windows routing tables. Note that if OpenVPN cannot add a route, it will not abort the connection. The current OpenVPN GUI does not detect this and will show a green icon in the taskbar, suggesting a fully successful connection.

There's more...

OpenVPN is preconfigured to look for the `route.exe` program in the directory `C:\WINDOWS\system32`. If Windows is installed in a different directory, the `win-sys` directive can be used. The `win-sys` directive has two options:

- ▶ The directory name where the Windows operating system can be found, for example `D:\WINDOWS`.
- ▶ The special option `env`, which means the OpenVPN client will use the contents of the environment variable `windir` to locate the Windows operating system. This environment variable is always set in a normal Windows setup.

11

Advanced Configuration

In this chapter, we will cover:

- ▶ Including configuration files in config files
- ▶ Multiple remotes & remote-random
- ▶ Details of `ifconfig-pool-persist`
- ▶ Connecting using a SOCKS proxy
- ▶ Connecting via an HTTP proxy
- ▶ Connecting via an HTTP proxy with authentication
- ▶ Using `dyndns`
- ▶ IP-less setups (`ifconfig-noexec`)

Introduction

The recipes in this chapter and the next will cover the advanced configuration of OpenVPN. This chapter will focus on some of the less well-known configuration options that OpenVPN offers, whereas the next chapter will deal mostly with configuration options that are specific to OpenVPN 2.1 and higher. The recipes will cover both advanced server configuration, such as the use of a dynamic DNS provider such as `dyndns`, as well as advanced client configuration, such as using a proxy server to connect to an OpenVPN server.

Including configuration files in config files

One of the lesser-known possibilities when using configuration files is the ability to include other configuration files. This can be especially handy when setting up a complex OpenVPN server, where multiple OpenVPN instances are offered simultaneously. The common configuration directives can be stored in a single file, whereas the connection-specific parts can be stored in a file for each instance. In this recipe, we will set up two OpenVPN instances, one using UDP and the other using TCP as the transport protocol.

Note that this option does not allow for the sharing of VPN IP address ranges between instances.

Getting ready

Set up the client and server certificates using the first recipe from *Chapter 2, Client-server IP-only Networks*. For this recipe, the server computer was running CentOS 5 Linux and OpenVPN 2.1.3.

How to do it...

1. First, create the common configuration file:

```
dev tun

ca        /etc/openvpn/cookbook/ca.crt
cert      /etc/openvpn/cookbook/server.crt
key       /etc/openvpn/cookbook/server.key
dh        /etc/openvpn/cookbook/dh1024.pem
tls-auth /etc/openvpn/cookbook/ta.key 0

persist-key
persist-tun
keepalive 10 60

push "route 10.198.0.0 255.255.0.0"
topology subnet

user   nobody
group nobody

daemon
```

Save it as `example11-1-common.conf`. Note that this configuration file does not include a protocol specification or `server` line. Also, note that we will be using the same server certificate for both OpenVPN instances.

2. Next, create two server configuration files, one for UDP-based connections:

    ```
    config example11-1-common.conf

    proto udp
    port 1194
    server 192.168.100.0 255.255.255.0

    log-append /var/log/openvpn-udp.log
    ```

    Save it as `example11-1-server1.conf`.

3. And one for TCP-based connections:

    ```
    config example11-1-common.conf

    proto tcp
    port 443
    server 192.168.200.0 255.255.255.0

    log-append /var/log/openvpn-tcp.log
    ```

    Save it as `example11-1-server2.conf`. The second instance is listening on the HTTPS port 443, which is an often-used trick to circumvent very strict firewalls, or to work around a badly configured firewall.

4. Start both servers:

    ```
    [root@server]# openvpn --config example11-1-server1.conf
    [root@server]# openvpn --config example11-1-server2.conf
    ```

    Check the log files to see if both the servers have successfully started.

How it works...

OpenVPN configuration files are treated very similarly to command-line options. As the `--config` command-line option is used almost always, it is also possible to use it inside a configuration file again. This allows for a split in the configuration options, where directives that are common to all OpenVPN instances can be stored in a single file for easy maintenance. The instance-specific directives (such as the `server` directive) can then be stored in much smaller configuration files, which are also less likely to change over time. This again eases maintenance of a large-scale OpenVPN server setup.

OpenVPN has a built-in protection mechanism to avoid including the same configuration file recursively.

Multiple remotes and remote-random

OpenVPN has built-in support for automatic failover and load-balancing: if the connection to one OpenVPN server cannot be established, then the next configured server is chosen. The `remote-random` directive can be used to load-balance many OpenVPN clients across multiple OpenVPN servers. In this recipe, we will set up two OpenVPN servers and then use the `remote-random` directive to have a client choose either one of the two servers.

Note that OpenVPN does **not** offer transparent failover, in which case the existing connections are transparently migrated to another server. Transparent failover is much harder to achieve with a VPN setup (not just OpenVPN), as the secure session keys need to be migrated from one server to the other as well. This is currently not possible with OpenVPN.

Getting ready

We use the following network layout:

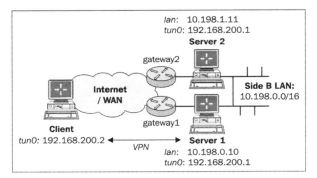

Set up the client and server certificates using the first recipe from *Chapter 2, Client-server IP-only Networks*. For this recipe, the server computers were running CentOS 5 Linux and OpenVPN 2.1.3. The client was running Fedora 13 Linux and OpenVPN 2.1.1. Keep the configuration file `basic-udp-server.conf` from the *Chapter 2* recipe *Server-side routing* at hand.

How to do it...

1. Start both servers:

    ```
    [root@server1]# openvpn --config basic-udp-server.conf
    ```

    ```
    [root@server2]# openvpn --config basic-udp-server.conf
    ```

    Check the log files to see that both the servers have successfully started.

Note that we can use the exact same configuration file on both servers. By using masquerading, the VPN clients will appear to come from either `server1` or `server2`.

2. Set up masquerading on both servers:

```
[root@server1]# iptables -t nat -I POSTROUTING -o eth0 \
    -j MASQUERADE


[root@server2]# iptables -t nat -I POSTROUTING -o eth0 \
    -j MASQUERADE
```

3. Create the client configuration file:

```
client
proto udp
remote openvpnserver1.example.com 1194
remote openvpnserver2.example.com 1194
remote-random
dev tun
nobind


ca        /etc/openvpn/cookbook/ca.crt
cert      /etc/openvpn/cookbook/client1.crt
key       /etc/openvpn/cookbook/client1.key
tls-auth /etc/openvpn/cookbook/ta.key 1


ns-cert-type server
```

Save it as `example11-2-client.conf`.

4. Start the client:

```
[root@client]# openvpn --config example11-2-client.conf
```

The OpenVPN client will randomly choose which server to connect to.

After the connection has been established, stop the first OpenVPN process on the server that the client connected to:

```
[root@server1]# killall openvpn
```

And wait for the client to reconnect. After the default timeout period, the client will reconnect to an alternate server.

How it works...

When the OpenVPN client starts up and `remote-random` is specified, it randomly picks a server from the list of available remote servers. If the VPN connection to this server cannot be established, it will pick the next server from the list, and so on. When the VPN connection is dropped, for example, due to a failing server, the OpenVPN client will try to reconnect after a default timeout period. In the server configuration file used in the *Chapter 2* recipe *Server-side routing*, the timeout period is configured using the `keepalive` option.

There's more...

When setting up a failover OpenVPN solution there are many things to consider, some of which are outlined here.

Mixing TCP and UDP-based setups

It is also possible to mix TCP and UDP-based setups by specifying the protocol type with the `remote` directive:

```
remote openvpnserver1.example.com 1194 udp
remote openvpnserver2.example.com 1194 tcp
```

An OpenVPN 2.1-specific feature known as `connection blocks` is much handier to use in this case. The use of connection blocks is explained in the next chapter.

Advantage of using TCP-based connections

There is one major advantage when using a TCP-based setup in combination with a failover solution. If the OpenVPN server to which a client is connected is unavailable, the TCP connection will fail almost immediately. This leads to a very short timeout period after which the OpenVPN client will try to reconnect. With a UDP-based setup, the client cannot so easily detect whether the server is unavailable and must first wait for the `keepalive` timeout to pass.

Automatically reverting to the first OpenVPN server

A question that is asked from time to time is whether it is possible to configure OpenVPN to also support automatic revert: a second OpenVPN instance is set up to provide a failover solution. When the main OpenVPN server is unavailable, the backup instance takes over. However, when the main OpenVPN server comes back online, the clients are not automatically reconnected to the main server. For this, a client reset (or server reset of the second OpenVPN instance) is required. It is possible to achieve this using scripting but it depends largely on what type of connectivity is considered acceptable: it takes some time for an OpenVPN client to detect when the remote server is not responding and to reconnect. The VPN connectivity will be intermittent in such a setup. Especially when the network connection to the main OpenVPN server is not stable, this can lead to very low availability.

A quick and dirty method to have all clients revert back to the first server is to use the management interface on the second server and disconnect all clients.

See also

▸ *Chapter 2*'s recipe, *Server-side routing*, which explains the basic setup of OpenVPN.

▸ *Chapter 12*'s recipe, *Using connection blocks*, which shows an alternate and more flexible method for supporting multiple servers in a single client configuration file.

Details of ifconfig-pool-persist

One of the options available in OpenVPN that can lead to a lot of confusion is `ifconfig-pool-persist`. This directive tells the OpenVPN server to maintain a persistent list of IP addresses handed out to different clients. When a client reconnects at a later time, the previously-used address is reused. This is only one of three methods for assigning static addresses to an OpenVPN client. The other two methods are:

▸ Using an `ifconfig-push` statement in a `client-connect` script

▸ Using an `ifconfig-push` statement in a `client-configuration` file

both of which take precedence over the entries found in the `ifconfig-pool-persist` file. Experience has shown that it is often a good idea to temporarily disable this option when an OpenVPN setup is not working properly.

In this recipe, we will demonstrate how to use the `ifconfig-pool-persist` and what the pitfalls are.

Getting ready

We use the following network layout:

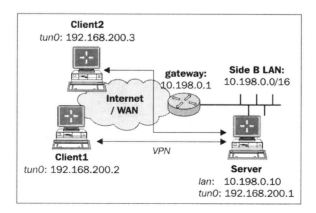

Set up the client and server certificates using the first recipe from *Chapter 2, Client-server IP-only Networks*. For this recipe, the server computer was running CentOS 5 Linux and OpenVPN 2.1.3. The first client was running Fedora 13 Linux and OpenVPN 2.1.1. Keep the configuration file, `basic-udp-server.conf`, from the *Chapter 2* recipe *Server-side routing* at hand, as well as the client configuration file, `basic-udp-client.conf`, from the same recipe. The second client was running Windows XP SP3 and OpenVPN 2.1.3. For this client, keep the client configuration file, `basic-udp-client.ovpn`, from the *Chapter 2* recipe *Using an ifconfig-pool block* at hand.

How to do it...

1. Create the server configuration file by adding the following line to the `basic-udp-server.conf` file:

    `ifconfig-pool-persist /etc/openvpn/cookbook/ipp.txt`

    Save it as `example11-3-server.conf` file.

2. Start the server:

    `[root@server]# openvpn --config example11-3-server.conf`

    An empty file `/etc/openvpn/cookbok/ipp.txt` will be created as the server starts up.

3. Connect the first client:

    `[root@client]# openvpn --config basic-udp-client.conf`

    Normally, this client will be assigned `192.168.200.2`, which is the first available IP address in the `server` IP range.

4. Stop both the client and the server. List the contents of the `ipp.txt` file:

    `[root@server]# cat /etc/openvpn/cookbook/ipp.txt`

    `openvpnclient1,192.168.200.2`

5. Start the server again. Now, connect the second client, which has a different certificate:

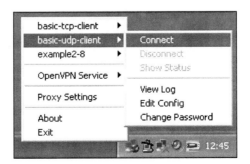

This client will now be assigned the address `192.168.200.3`. Without the `ifconfig-pool-persist` option, it would have been assigned the first available address, which is `192.168.200.2`.

How it works...

When the OpenVPN server starts, it reads the `ipp.txt` file, if it exists, and it tries to re-assign the IP addresses to the client certificates found in the file. Whenever an OpenVPN client with one of the existing client certificates connects, it is assigned the address found in the `ipp.txt` file, unless the server VPN IP address space is too small for the number of already-connected clients. In that case, the client receives the first available address from the server VPN IP address space.

The first client that connected received the first available address, `192.168.200.2`, from the VPN IP server address range. When the OpenVPN server shuts down, this information is recorded in the `ipp.txt` file. The second time the OpenVPN server started, this information was reloaded and the address `192.168.200.2` was held in reserve for the client with client certificate `openvpnclient1`. When the second client connected with client certificate `openvpnclient2`, it received the next available address in the server VPN IP address range, which is `192.168.200.3`. When the server shuts down again, this information is also recorded in the `ipp.txt` file. This means that from now on, the first client will always receive the `.2` address and the second client the `.3` address. However, it is not a guarantee that the listed IP addresses will be assigned to a particular client certificate. The exception occurs when many VPN clients connect to the server. If the VPN IP address range is exhausted and the first client is not connected at that time, its address is recycled for other VPN clients. If the client with the client certificate `openvpnclient1` then tries to connect to the server, it will be assigned the first available address. For a guaranteed assignment, a `client-config-dir` file should be used.

There's more...

When using the `ifconfig-pool-persist` directive, there are a few pitfalls to watch out for:

Specifying the update interval

Because we did not explicitly specify an update interval, the `ipp.txt` file is updated every 600 seconds (10 minutes). This can also be seen by looking at the `ipp.txt` file right after a new client connects: the newly-found client certificate and VPN IP are not listed in the `ipp.txt` file until the first update interval passes or when the OpenVPN server process shuts down.

It is also possible to specify an update interval of 0 seconds, which means that the `ipp.txt` file is never updated. This causes the OpenVPN server to associate IP addresses with the client certificate names found in the `ipp.txt` file at the startup but these associations will never change afterwards.

Caveat: the duplicate-cn option

The `duplicate-cn` option can be used to allow the same client certificate to connect to a number of times. If this option is used, the `ifconfig-pool-persist` option becomes useless, as the same client certificate will be connected twice. This means that the OpenVPN server has to hand out two different IP addresses to each client and the entry in the `ipp.txt` file becomes meaningless.

When 'topology net30' is used

When the server option `topology net30` is used (which is the default for OpenVPN 2.0) the format of the `ipp.txt` file is slightly different. In `net30` topology mode, each client is assigned a `/30` network address consisting of four IP addresses: the network address, the VPN server endpoint address, the actual client VPN IP address, and the broadcast address for the `/30` network. In the `ipp.txt` file, the first of these is recorded:

```
openvpnclient1,192.168.200.4
openvpnclient2,192.168.200.8
```

Connecting using a SOCKS proxy

Under certain circumstances, it is not possible to directly connect to an OpenVPN server. This happens most often when firewalls are restricting UDP-based traffic. In such cases, OpenVPN can connect to an OpenVPN server via an intermediary host known as a proxy. OpenVPN supports two types of proxies: SOCKS and HTTP-based, both of which work only using TCP-based configurations. This recipe will outline how to access an OpenVPN server via a SOCKS proxy, whereas the next two recipes will show how to use an HTTP proxy, both with and without authentication.

SOCKS proxies can very easily be set up using almost any SSH client. On Linux and Mac OS X, it can be done using the `ssh` or `slogin` commands, whereas on Windows, the free SSH client PuTTY can be used.

Getting ready

We use the following network layout:

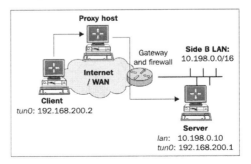

Set up the client and server certificates using the first recipe from *Chapter 2, Client-server IP-only Networks*. For this recipe, the server computer was running CentOS 5 Linux and OpenVPN 2.1.1. The client was running Fedora 13 Linux and OpenVPN 2.1.1. Keep the configuration file, example9-7-server.conf, from the *Chapter 9*'s recipe *Tuning TCP-based connections* at hand. Keep the client configuration file, basic-tcp-client.conf, from the *Chapter 2*'s recipe *Server-side routing* at hand.

How to do it...

1. Start the server:

   [root@server]# openvpn --config example9-7-server.conf

2. Add a line to the client configuration file basic-tcp-client.conf:

   socks-proxy 127.0.0.1 1080

   Save this configuration file as example11-4-client.conf.

3. Set up an SOCKS proxy by setting up an SSH connection to the intermediary host:

   [client]$ ssh -D 1080 proxy-host

4. In another terminal window, start the OpenVPN client:

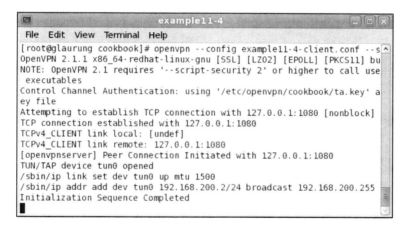

The OpenVPN client first connects to the proxy listening on address 127.0.0.1 and port 1080 and it then sets up a connection to the OpenVPN server address.

How it works...

A SOCKS proxy host acts as an intermediary between the (OpenVPN) client and the server. SOCKS proxies can also be configured in most web browsers and are often used to gain access through a hotel or corporate firewall. The client first connects to the SOCKS proxy host and then requests a new connection to the actual endpoint, which is the OpenVPN server in this case. If the connection is allowed by the SOCKS host, the connection is established and the VPN connection can be set up.

There's more...

Before using a proxy host to set up a VPN connection, there are a few things to consider:

Performance

Proxy hosts tend to have a severe impact on the performance of a VPN setup. Both the bandwidth and the latency are usually affected when proxy hosts are used. This is mostly caused by having to connect to a separate host. There is little that can be done about this drop in performance.

Note #1 on SOCKS proxies via SSH

SSH can be a very handy tool to set up a SOCKS proxy, over which an OpenVPN connection can be set up. Apart from the drawback mentioned above, this introduces another penalty: both the SSH connection and the VPN connection will normally be encrypted. Thus, tunneling traffic over an encrypted VPN link which in itself is tunneled over an encrypted SSH link is double encrypted!

Note #2 on SOCKS proxies via SSH

A question that you should ask yourself if you are tunneling VPN traffic over an SSH tunnel is 'why?'. What type of traffic needs to be tunneled over a VPN link that cannot be tunnelled via a SOCKS-over-SSH tunnel? Most modern web browsers and e-mail clients have built-in support for SOCKS hosts, eliminating the need for a full-blown VPN. File sharing protocols such as Windows File Sharing (CIFS) can also be tunneled over an SSH connection. In those cases, a VPN tunnel adds only extra complexity.

SOCKS proxies using plain-text authentication

In OpenVPN 2.2 and higher, support is added to connect to a SOCKS proxy that required authentication. For OpenVPN 2.2 plain-text authentication support is added. Though the name 'plain text' may suggest otherwise the authentication mechanism is secure, as the connection to the SOCKS proxy host is encrypted first.

See also

▶ The next two recipes in this chapter will deal with connecting via an HTTP proxy.

Connecting via an HTTP proxy

As stated in the previous recipe, it is not possible to directly connect to an OpenVPN server under certain circumstances. In such cases, OpenVPN can connect to an OpenVPN server via an intermediary host known as a proxy. This recipe will outline how to access an OpenVPN server via an HTTP proxy.

The HTTP proxy used in this recipe is a Linux-based Apache `httpd` server with the `mod_proxy` module loaded. This module can be configured to allow `CONNECT` requests. This type of request is needed to connect to secure web servers (HTTPS) as well as to an OpenVPN server. If the `CONNECT` request is not allowed, then the HTTP proxy cannot be used to set up an OpenVPN connection.

Getting ready

We use the following network layout:

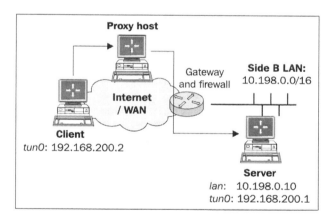

Set up the client and server certificates using the first recipe from *Chapter 2*, Client-server IP-only Networks. For this recipe, the server computer was running CentOS 5 Linux and OpenVPN 2.1.1. The client was running Fedora 13 Linux and OpenVPN 2.1.1. Keep the configuration file `example9-7-server.conf` from the *Chapter 9* recipe *Tuning TCP-based connections* at hand, as well as the client configuration file, `example9-7.ovpn`, from the same recipe.

How to do it...

1. Start the server:

   ```
   [root@server]# openvpn --config example9-7-server.conf
   ```

2. Modify the client configuration file, example9-7.ovpn, by adding the lines:

   ```
   http-proxy http-proxy-host 8888
   verb 4
   ```

   Here, http-proxy-host is either the name or the IP address of the host running the HTTP proxy software. In this recipe, the HTTP proxy was running on port 8888. Save the configuration file as example11-5.ovpn.

3. Start the client:

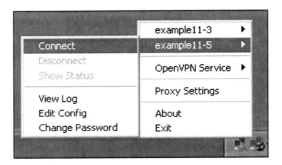

The connection log will show that the OpenVPN client first connects to the HTTP proxy host and then sends an HTTP 'CONNECT' request to connect to the OpenVPN server:

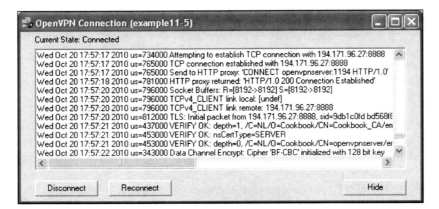

The HTTP proxy host responds with the HTTP code 200 meaning OK, after which the VPN connection is established.

How it works...

An HTTP proxy host acts as an intermediary between the (OpenVPN) client and the server. HTTP proxies can be configured in most web browsers and are often used to gain access through a hotel or a corporate firewall. The client first connects to the HTTP proxy host and then requests a new connection to the actual endpoint using the `HTTP 'CONNECT'` request. If the HTTP proxy host allows the `CONNECT` request, the HTTP code `200` is returned and the connection to the OpenVPN server is granted. From here on, the OpenVPN connection is set up in a similar fashion to a regular TCP-based setup.

There's more...

When using an HTTP proxy host to connect to an OpenVPN server, there are a few caveats:

http-proxy options

There are a few options available in OpenVPN to configure the way in which OpenVPN connects with the HTTP proxy host:

- `http-proxy-timeout [n]`: Sets the timeout when connecting to the HTTP proxy host to `[n]` seconds. The default value is five seconds.
- `http-proxy-option AGENT [string]`: Sets the HTTP agent to `[string]` when connecting to the HTTP proxy host. Some proxies allow connections from "well-known" web browsers only.
- `http-proxy-option VERSION 1.1`: Sets the HTTP protocol version to 1.1. The default is HTTP/1.0. OpenVPN 2.1 is not fully HTTP/1.1 compliant when connecting to an HTTP proxy host, causing some proxies to refuse access. This is fixed in OpenVPN 2.2.

Ducking firewalls

Please note that OpenVPN makes no attempt to hide itself from a firewall. Modern firewalls that perform the so-called deep-packet inspection can easily detect the type of traffic that OpenVPN is using to connect to the OpenVPN server and can block access based on that.

Performance

Similar to SOCKS proxies, HTTP Proxy hosts tend to have an impact on the performance of a VPN setup. Both the bandwidth and the latency are usually affected when proxy hosts are used. This is mostly caused by having to connect to a separate host.

See also

- The previous and next recipe in this chapter deal that with connecting via a SOCKS proxy and connecting via an HTTP proxy with authentication.

Connecting via an HTTP proxy with authentication

As a follow-up to the previous recipe, where a plain HTTP proxy was used to connect to an OpenVPN server, we will show in this recipe how an OpenVPN connection can be set up when the HTTP proxy server requires authentication.

The HTTP proxy used in this recipe is a Linux-based Apache httpd server with the mod_proxy module loaded and configured for Basic authentication.

Getting ready

We use the following network layout:

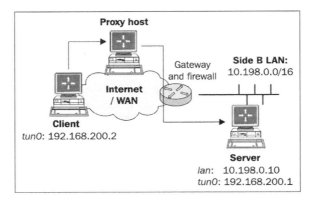

Set up the client and server certificates using the first recipe from *Chapter 2, Client-server IP-only Networks*. For this recipe, the server computer was running CentOS 5 Linux and OpenVPN 2.1.1. The client was running Fedora 13 Linux and OpenVPN 2.1.1. Keep the configuration file example9-7-server.conf from the *Chapter 9's* recipe *Tuning TCP-based connections* at hand, as well as the client configuration file example9-7.ovpn from the same recipe.

How to do it...

1. Start the server:

   ```
   [root@server]# openvpn --config example9-7-server.conf
   ```

2. Set up the HTTP proxy server to support basic authentication. For the Apache httpd server used in this recipe, the following proxy.conf file was used:

   ```
   LoadModule proxy_module modules/mod_proxy.so
   LoadModule proxy_balancer_module modules/mod_proxy_balancer.so
   LoadModule proxy_ftp_module modules/mod_proxy_ftp.so
   ```

```
LoadModule proxy_http_module modules/mod_proxy_http.so
LoadModule proxy_connect_module modules/mod_proxy_connect.so

ProxyRequests On
ProxyVia On
AllowCONNECT 1194
KeepAlive on

<Proxy *>
    Order deny,allow
    Deny from all
    Require user cookbook
    AuthType Basic
    AuthName "Password Required"
    AuthUserFile /etc/httpd/conf/proxy-password
</Proxy>
```

3. Configure the OpenVPN GUI to support HTTP proxies: right click on the OpenVPN
    GUI tray icon and select **Proxy Settings**. Fill in the dialog as follows:

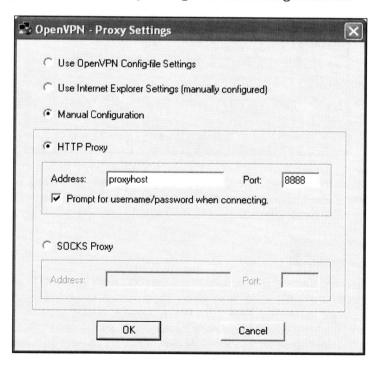

4. Now start the OpenVPN configuration `example9-7`. You will first be prompted for the HTTP proxy username and password:

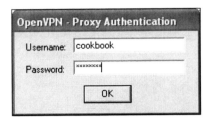

If the right username and password are entered, the HTTP proxy grants access to connect to the OpenVPN server and the VPN connection is established:

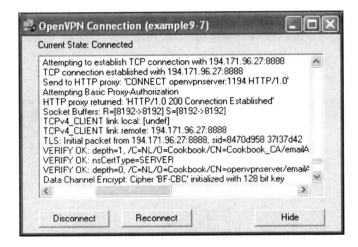

As can be seen from the connection log, the OpenVPN client attempts **Basic Proxy-Authorization** when connecting to the HTTP proxy server. If the authentication is successful, the HTTP proxy grants access to the client to connect to the server.

How it works...

Similar to the previous recipe, the OpenVPN client first connects to the HTTP proxy host. It attempts to authenticate to the HTTP proxy using Basic Authentication, using the username and password supplied in the OpenVPN GUI's **Proxy Settings** dialog. Note that in this case there is no need to modify the client configuration file itself, as the OpenVPN GUI adds the required lines to the configuration files automatically. After successful authentication, the client then sends an `HTTP 'CONNECT'` request to connect to the OpenVPN server. From here on, the OpenVPN connection is set up in a similar fashion to a regular TCP-based setup.

There's more...

OpenVPN supports multiple authentication mechanisms when connecting to an HTTP proxy:

NTLM proxy authorization

OpenVPN also supports HTTP proxies that use NTLM proxy authorization, where NTLM stands for **NT Lan Manager**. Typically, this type of proxy is used in a Microsoft Windows environment. Unfortunately, OpenVPN's implementation of NTLM authorization is rather limited. It does not send out proper NTLMSSP messages and it works only with a very limited set of proxies. To enable support for this type of proxy add:

```
http-proxy proxyhost proxyport stdin ntlm
```

or:

```
http-proxy proxyhost proxyport stdin ntlm2
```

where `stdin` instructs OpenVPN to query the username and password on the command prompt. This type of proxy authorization does not work well with the OpenVPN GUI on Windows.

New features in OpenVPN 2.2

OpenVPN 2.2 adds support for HTTP `digest` authentication, which is more secure than the plain-text authentication outlined in this recipe.

It also adds the option `auto-nct` to the `http-proxy` authentication option to reject weak proxy authentication methods.

See also

▸ The previous recipe in this chapter, where a connection is established using an HTTP proxy without extra authentication.

Using dyndns

Sometimes an OpenVPN server needs to be set up using a dynamic IP address. This means that OpenVPN clients need to connect to a different IP address every time the server's IP address changes. This can happen often when the OpenVPN server is hooked up to the Internet via an ADSL or cable modem connection. In this recipe, we will see how to configure a dynamic DNS name for the OpenVPN server and how the client can be configured to make use of the dynamic DNS name. As a dynamic DNS provider, the free dyndns.org service is used.

Getting ready

For this recipe, the server computer was running CentOS 5 Linux and OpenVPN 2.1.3. The client computer was running Windows XP SP3 and OpenVPN 2.1.1. Keep the configuration file, `basic-udp-server.conf`, from the *Chapter 2* recipe *Server-side routing* at hand, as well as the client configuration file, `basic-udp-client.ovpn`, from the *Chapter 2* recipe *Using an 'ifconfig-pool' block*.

How to do it...

1. Register an account with a dynamic DNS service provider, such as dyndns.org.

2. Register a hostname and assign the current server's IP address to it. For this recipe, the hostname `vpncookbook.dyndns.org` was registered.

3. Check that the DNS name `vpncookbook.dyndns.org` resolves to the right IP address:

   [server1]$ host vpncookbook.dyndns.org

   `vpncookbook.dyndns.org has address 172.30.0.1`

   (the output was modified to hide the actual IP address used).

4. Set up the `ddclient` tool to easily update the dyndns.org's IP address. For this recipe, the following `ddclient.conf` file was used:

   ```
   daemon=0
   syslog=yes
   mail-failure=root
   pid=/var/run/ddclient/ddclient.pid
   ssl=yes
   use=web, web=checkip.dyndns.org/, web-skip='IP Address'
   login=dyndns-username
   password=dyndns-password
   server=members.dyndns.org,   \
   protocol=dyndns2             \
   vpncookbook.dyndns.org
   ```

5. Start the server:

   [root@server1]# openvpn --config basic-udp-server.conf

   Change the client configuration file `basic-udp-client.ovpn` by changing the line:

   `remote openvpnserver.example.com`

   to:

   remote vpncookbook.dyndns.org
   resolv-retry 300

   Save the configuration file as `example11-7.ovpn`.

6. Start the OpenVPN connection:

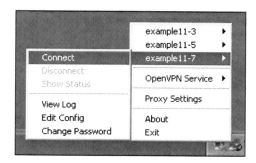

The OpenVPN client will resolve the hostname `vpncookbook.dyndns.org` to the current IP address of the OpenVPN server.

7. Force a new IP address for `vpncookbook.dyndns.org` using either the web interface or the `ddclient` tool.

    ```
    [root@server2]$ ddclient --verbose # output in /var/log/messages
    ```

8. Verify that the hostname `vpncookbook.dyndns.org` now resolves to the new IP address.

9. Start OpenVPN with the exact same configuration on the host with the new IP address:

    ```
    [root@server2]# openvpn --config basic-udp-server.conf
    ```

10. Now, shut down the original OpenVPN server. After a while, the OpenVPN client will reset and it will re-resolve the hostname `vpncookbook.dyndns.org`. This will lead it to connect to the new OpenVPN server.

How it works...

The `dyndns` service allows a user to freely register a hostname. This hostname is resolved to an IP address of choice, but the Time-To-Live flag of the DNS name is very short. This means that DNS servers around the world will cache the resolved IP address for only a very short period of time. The benefit is that if the IP address changes then the DNS resolution is rapidly updated.

By using the `ddclient` tool, we update the DNS-to-IP resolution as soon as a new IP address is assigned to a particular host. Use the `--verbose` flag and check the `/var/log/messages` log to troubleshoot the interaction of the `ddclient` tool and the `dyndns` web service.

On the OpenVPN client side, we use an extra directive:

```
resolv-retry 300
```

to make sure the OpenVPN client tries to resolve the hostname found in the `remote` directive for 300 seconds (= 5 minutes) before giving up. If this directive is not added, then no retries are attempted. This means that there is a chance that the `dyndns` hostname will not resolve, causing the OpenVPN client to abort.

There's more...

Using `dyndns` can be a very powerful and flexible method for setting up a VPN server on a dynamic IP address. However, it does not provide fully automatic failover. On Linux servers, it does integrate quite nicely into the `NetworkManager` tool.

Failover

Note that even with the `dyndns` service, the OpenVPN client still needs to restart in order to reconnect to the server. OpenVPN currently does not support transparent failover, where all existing connections are kept intact during the restart. This was also stated in the recipe *Multiple remotes & remote-random* earlier in this chapter.

NetworkManager and 'ddclient'

Newer versions of the Linux `NetworkManager` tool have a dispatcher plugin for `ddclient`. This plugin is launched whenever an interface receives a new IP address. The plugin can be configured to update the `dyndns` registration when this happens. This causes the hostname-to-IP address resolution to follow the assigned addresses automatically.

Note that this plugin will only be truly effective if the new IP address that the `NetworkManager` receives is the actual public IP address.

See also

> ▸   The recipe *Multiple remotes & remote-random* earlier in this chapter.

IP-less setups (ifconfig-noexec)

The goal of this recipe is to create an OpenVPN tunnel without assigning IP addresses to the endpoints of the tunnel. In a routed network setup, this ensures that the tunnel endpoints can never be reached through themselves, which adds some security and can also make the routing tables a bit shorter. In the OpenVPN configuration files, an IP address needs to be specified, but it is never assigned to the tunnel interface.

This recipe has only been tested on Linux systems, as it requires some network-interface configuration that is not available on other platforms.

Getting ready

We use the following network layout:

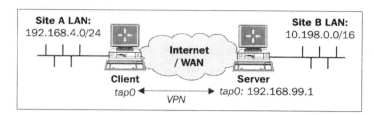

Set up the client and server certificates using the first recipe from *Chapter 2, Client-server IP-only Networks*. In this recipe, the server computer was running CentOS 5 Linux and OpenVPN 2.1.1. The client was running Fedora 12 Linux and OpenVPN 2.1.1. Keep the server config file, `example3-1-server.conf`, from the *Chapter 3* recipe *Simple configuration - non-bridged* at hand.

How to do it...

1. Create the server configuration file by adding a line to the `example3-1-server.conf` file:

   route 192.168.4.0 255.255.255.0 192.168.99.1

   and save it as `example11-8-server.conf`.

2. Start the server:

   [root@server]# openvpn --config example11-8-server.conf

3. Create the client configuration file:

   ```
   client
   proto udp
   remote openvpnserver.example.com
   port 1194

   dev tap
   nobind

   ca       /etc/openvpn/cookbook/ca.crt
   cert     /etc/openvpn/cookbook/client1.crt
   key      /etc/openvpn/cookbook/client1.key
   tls-auth /etc/openvpn/cookbook/ta.key 1

   ns-cert-type server
   ```

```
script-security 2
ifconfig-noexec
up /etc/openvpn/cookbook/example11-8-up.sh

route-noexec
route-up /etc/openvpn/cookbook/example11-8-route-up.sh
```

Save it as `example-11-8-client.conf`.

4. Next, create the `example11-8-up.sh` script:

```
#!/bin/bash

/sbin/ifconfig $1 0.0.0.0 up
# needed for TAP interfaces !!!
echo 1 > /proc/sys/net/ipv4/conf/$1/proxy_arp
```

and save it as `/etc/openvpn/cookbook/example11-8-up.sh`.

5. Similarly, for the `example11-8-route-up.sh` script:

```
#!/bin/bash

# add an explicit route back to the VPN endpoint
/sbin/ip route add $route_vpn_gateway/32 dev $dev

n=1;
while [ $n -le 100 ]
do
  network=`env | sed -n \ "/^route_network_${n}=/s/^route_network_
${n}=//p"`
  netmask=`env | sed -n \
"/^route_netmask_${n}=/s/^route_netmask_${n}=//p"`

  if [ -z "$network" -o -z "$netmask" ]
  then
    break
  fi

  /sbin/ip route add $network/$netmask dev $dev
  let n=n+1
done
```

Save it as `/etc/openvpn/cookbook/example11-8-route-up.sh`.

6. Make sure both scripts are executable and both of them start the client:

[[root@client]# chmod 755 /etc/openvpn/cookbook/example11-8*.sh

[root@client]# openvpn --config example11-8-client.conf

7. After the client successfully connects to the OpenVPN server, check the `tap0` interface and the routing tables, and verify that you can ping the server:

```
[root@client]# ifconfig tap0

tap0        Link encap:Ethernet   HWaddr 66:75:71:0E:57:C4
            UP BROADCAST RUNNING MULTICAST   MTU:1500   Metric:1
[...]
[root@client]# netstat-rn

Kernel IP routing table
Destination Gateway   Genmask         Flags[...]  Iface
192.168.4.0 0.0.0.0   255.255.255.0 U   0  0  0 eth0
10.198.0.0  0.0.0.0   255.255.0.0   U   0  0  0 tap0
[...]
[[root@client]# ping -c 2 192.168.99.1

PING 192.168.99.1 (192.168.99.1) 56(84) bytes of data.
64 bytes from 192.168.99.1: icmp_seq=1 ttl=64 time=25.7 ms
64 bytes from 192.168.99.1: icmp_seq=2 ttl=64 time=26.2 ms
```

How it works...

The OpenVPN server allocates an IP address for the client, but that does not mean that the client interface actually needs to assign these addresses. The `example11-8-up.sh` script does exactly this.

Some older Linux kernels refuse to add a route without an address being assigned to an interface. Hence, we assign the address `0.0.0.0` to the `tun0` interface. To add the routes that are pushed by the server, a special `route-up` script is used, `example11-8-route-up.sh`, which brings up all the routes.

There's more...

Please note the following when considering an IP-less setup:

Point-to-point and TUN-style networks

This recipe can also be used in a point-to-point style environment, where static keys are used to connect two networks. Similarly, it can also be used in a TUN-style setup.

Routing and firewalling

At first, this recipe might seem odd. The advantage of this setup is that the OpenVPN client itself is not reachable by other machines on the VPN. This is handy when connecting many clients to an OpenVPN server, but some clients are used as gateways to the networks behind them (for example, to connect a remote office to the OpenVPN server). By not assigning the remote office gateway an IP address, there is no risk of the gateway itself being attacked from the remote VPN side. Also, server-side firewalling and `iptables` rules can be slightly shorter in this scenario, as there will be no traffic coming from the OpenVPN client with the VPN source address. This is also the reason why the server configuration has an explicit route to the client-side network:

```
route 192.168.4.0 255.255.255.0 192.168.99.1
```

12
New Features of OpenVPN 2.1 and 2.2

In this chapter, we will cover:

- ► Inline certificates
- ► Connection blocks
- ► Port sharing with an HTTPS server
- ► Routing features: `redirect-private`, `allow-pull-fqdn`
- ► Handing out public IPs
- ► OCSP support
- ► New for 2.2: the `x509_user_name` parameter

Introduction

In this chapter, we will focus on some of the new features found in OpenVPN 2.1 and the upcoming 2.2 release. Many recipes from the previous chapters already made use of OpenVPN 2.1-specific features (such as `topology subnet`), but a few other features introduced in OpenVPN 2.1 are less well known. The recipes in this chapter will cover some of these, such as the use of inline certificates, connection blocks, and port-sharing.

The upcoming 2.2 release of OpenVPN is mainly a bug-fix release, though a few new directives were introduced. In the last recipe of this chapter, we will focus on one of them.

Inline certificates

To ease the deployment of OpenVPN configuration, public and private key files, a new feature is available to include all of them in a single file. This is done by integrating the contents of the `ca`, `cert`, `key`, and optionally the `tls-auth` file into the client configuration file itself. So, in this recipe, we will set up such a configuration file and use it to connect to our standard OpenVPN server.

Getting ready

We use the following network layout:

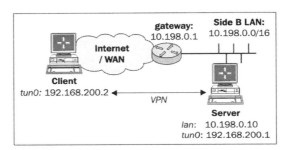

Set up the client and server certificates using the first recipe from *Chapter 2, Client-server IP-only Networks*. For this recipe, the server computers were running CentOS 5 Linux and OpenVPN 2.1.3. The client was running Fedora 13 Linux and OpenVPN 2.1.1. Keep the configuration file `basic-udp-server.conf` from the *Chapter 2* recipe *Server-side routing* at hand.

How to do it...

1. First, start the server:

   ```
   [root@server]# openvpn --config basic-udp-server.conf
   ```

2. Create the client configuration file:

   ```
   client
   proto udp
   remote openvpnserver.example.com
   port 1194
   dev tun
   nobind

   ca        [inline]
   cert      [inline]
   ```

```
key       [inline]
tls-auth [inline] 1

<ca>
-----BEGIN CERTIFICATE-----
# insert base64 blob from ca.crt
-----END CERTIFICATE-----
</ca>

<cert>
-----BEGIN CERTIFICATE-----
# insert base64 blob from client1.crt
-----END CERTIFICATE-----
</cert>

<key>
-----BEGIN PRIVATE KEY-----
# insert base64 blob from client1.key
-----END PRIVATE KEY-----
</key>

<tls-auth>
-----BEGIN OpenVPN Static key V1-----
# insert ta.key
-----END OpenVPN Static key V1-----
</tls-auth>
```

Insert the contents of the `ca.crt`, `client1.crt`, `client1.key` and `ta.key` files in the configuration. Save it as `example12-1-client.conf`.

3. Then, connect the client:

    [root@client]# openvpn --config example12-1-client.conf

How it works...

When OpenVPN parses the configuration directives, `ca`, `cert`, `key`, and `tls-auth` (and `dh` for server configuration files), and it finds the value `[inline]`, then an XML-like block must be present later in the configuration file. The contents of this XML-like block are then read and treated in the same manner as when a file is specified. When all the required configuration files or blocks are present, the connection is established.

Note that it is not required to treat all of the above configuration directives in the same manner. It is also possible to only specify an `[inline]` block for the CA certificate file, as this file tends to be static for all the clients.

Connection blocks

Similar to the inline certificates used in the previous recipe, it is also possible to specify connection blocks. These connection blocks are treated as multiple definitions for remote servers and they are tried in order until a VPN connection is established. The advantage of using a connection block is that for each remote server, server-specific parameters can be specified, such as the protocol (UDP or TCP), the remote port, whether a proxy server should be used , and so on.

In this recipe, we will set up two servers, one listening on a UDP port and the other on a TCP port. We will then configure the OpenVPN client to try the first server using a UDP connection. If the connection cannot be established, the client will attempt to connect to the second server using a TCP connection.

Getting ready

We use the following network layout:

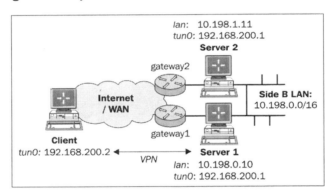

Set up the client and server certificates using the first recipe from *Chapter 2, Client-server IP-only Networks*. For this recipe, the server computers were running CentOS 5 Linux and OpenVPN 2.1.3. The client was running Fedora 13 Linux and OpenVPN 2.1.1. Keep the server configuration file `basic-udp-server.conf` from the *Chapter 2* recipe *Server-side routing* at hand, as well as the server configuration file, `example9-7-server.conf`, from the *Chapter 9* recipe *Tuning TCP-based connections*.

How to do it...

1. Start both the servers:

    ```
    [root@server1]# openvpn --config basic-udp-server.conf

    [root@server2]# openvpn --config example9-7-server.conf
    ```

2. Check the log files to check that both the servers have successfully started.

3. Create the client configuration file:

```
client
dev tun

<connection>
remote openvpnserver1.example.com
proto udp
port 1194
</connection>

<connection>
remote openvpnserver2.example.com
proto tcp
port 1194
</connection>

ca       /etc/openvpn/cookbook/ca.crt
cert     /etc/openvpn/cookbook/client1.crt
key      /etc/openvpn/cookbook/client1.key
tls-auth /etc/openvpn/cookbook/ta.key 1

ns-cert-type server
```

Save it as `example12-2-client.conf`.

4. Start the client:

```
[root@client]# openvpn --config example12-2-client.conf
```

5. After the connection has been established, stop the first OpenVPN process on the server that the client connected to:

```
[root@server1]# killall openvpn
```

And wait for the client to reconnect. After the default timeout period, the client will reconnect to the alternate server using the TCP protocol.

How it works...

When the OpenVPN client starts up, it attempts to connect to the server specified in the first `<connection>` block. If that connection fails, it will try the next `<connection>` block entry and so forth. When an OpenVPN server becomes unavailable or is stopped, the client will automatically restart and try to connect to the first available OpenVPN server again.

The OpenVPN client first parses the global directives, which are specified outside the `<connection>` blocks. For each block, the global directives are then overruled using block-specific directives. This makes it easier to specify in the `<connection>` blocks only those parameters that are different for each connection.

There's more...

Connection blocks, as well as inline certificates, are very handy new features introduced in OpenVPN 2.1. A consequence of these features is that the use of the command line to overrule the directives specified in the `configuration file` becomes harder, if not impossible. There are a few other things to keep in mind when using connection blocks.

Allowed directives inside connection blocks

There are only a few directives allowed inside a connection block:

- `bind`
- `connect-retry, connect-retry-max, connect-timeout`
- `float`
- `http-proxy, http-proxy-option, http-proxy-retry, http-proxy-timeout`
- `local lport`
- `nobind`
- `port`
- `proto`
- `remote, rport`
- `socks-proxy, socks-proxy-retry`

All other directives are considered `global` and can only be specified once.

Pitfalls when mixing TCP and UDP-based setups

Connection blocks make it very easy to mix TCP and UDP-based setups. The downside is that the global parameters specified in the configuration file must be valid for both the TCP and UDP-based setups. This rules out the use of the commonly-used `fragment` directive, as well as a few other tuning parameters. It is expected that this shortcoming of `<connection>` blocks will be addressed in a future version of OpenVPN.

See also

- *Chapter 11*'s recipe, *Multiple remotes & remote-random*, which explains how to achieve the same setup without using connection blocks.

Port sharing with an HTTPS server

A common OpenVPN setup to allow road warriors to reach the home office is to have OpenVPN listen on the secure web server (HTTPS) port 443. The downside is that you can no longer use that port on the OpenVPN server to actually host a secure website. OpenVPN 2.1 introduces a new port-sharing directive, enabling dual use of a TCP port. All traffic that is detected as OpenVPN traffic is processed by the OpenVPN server itself, and all other traffic is forwarded to another (local) machine and/or port.

In this recipe, we will set up an OpenVPN server to share TCP port 443 with a web server and we will show that both OpenVPN and a web browser can successfully connect to this server.

Getting ready

We use the following network layout:

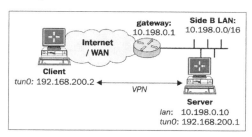

Set up the client and server certificates using the first recipe from *Chapter 2, Client-server IP-only Networks*. For this recipe, the server computer was running CentOS 5 Linux and OpenVPN 2.1.3. The client was running Windows XP SP3 and OpenVPN 2.1.3. Keep the server configuration file, `example9-7-server.conf`, from the *Chapter 9* recipe *Tuning TCP-based connections* at hand, as well as the client configuration file `example9-7.ovpn` from the same recipe.

On the server computer, a secure web server was running on port 8443.

How to do it...

1. Create the server configuration file by modifying the `example9-7-server.conf` file. Change the following line:

   `port 1194`

   Change it to the following:

   `port 443`
   `port-share localhost 8443`
   Save it as `example12-3-server.conf`.

2. Start the server:

    ```
    [root@server]# openvpn --config example12-3-server.conf
    ```

3. Next, modify the client configuration file `example9-7.ovpn` by also changing the port to 443. Save the client configuration file as `example12-3.ovpn`.

4. Start the client:

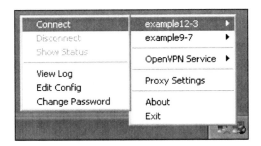

5. Verify that the client can connect to the VPN server. After the client has connected, start a web browser and browse to:

    ```
    https://openvpnserver.example.com
    ```

    The OpenVPN server log file will show lines similar to the following:

    ```
    ... Re-using SSL/TLS context
    ... TCP connection established with <client-ip>:53356
    ... TCPv4_SERVER link local: [undef]
    ... TCPv4_SERVER link remote: <client-ip>:53356
    ... <client-ip>:53356 Non-OpenVPN client protocol detected
    ```

How it works...

When `port-share` is used, OpenVPN will inspect the incoming traffic on port 443. If this traffic is a part of an OpenVPN session or if it is an initial OpenVPN handshake, then the OpenVPN server processes it by itself. If it is not recognizable as OpenVPN traffic, it is forwarded out to the host and port specified in the `port-share` directive.

Hence, it is the OpenVPN server process that is always listening on port 443. The web server must be listening on a different host or different port. With this setup, the same port can be used to offer two different services.

There's more...

The web server that OpenVPN forwards its traffic to must be a secure (HTTPS) web server. This is due to the nature of the inbound SSL traffic on the OpenVPN server itself. It is not possible to forward the traffic to a regular (HTTP) web server. If the traffic is forwarded to port 80, the Apache web server used in this recipe, the following error will appear in the web server error log file:

```
[error] [client 127.0.0.1] Invalid method in request \x16\x03\x01
```

Routing features: redirect-private, allow-pull-fqdn

In OpenVPN 2.1, some of the routing features are expanded. Most notably, there are new options for the directive `redirect-gateway` and several new routing directives are available:

- ▶ `redirect-private`: This option behaves very similar to the `redirect-gateway`, especially when the new parameters are used, but it does **NOT** alter the default gateway.

- ▶ `allow-pull-fqdn`: Allows the client to pull DNS names from the OpenVPN server. Previously, only IP addresses could be pushed or pulled. This option cannot be 'pushed' and needs to be added to the client configuration itself.

- ▶ `route-nopull`: All the options are pulled by a client from the server, except for the routing options. This can be particularly handy when troubleshooting an OpenVPN setup.

- ▶ `max-routes n`: Defines the maximum number of routes that may be defined or pulled from a remote server.

In this recipe, we will focus on the `redirect-private` directive and its parameters, as well as the `allow-pull-fqdn` parameter.

Getting ready

We use the following network layout:

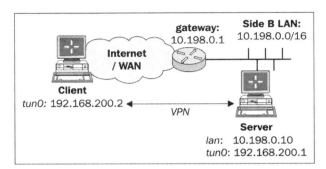

Set up the client and server certificates using the first recipe from *Chapter 2, Client-server IP-only Networks*. For this recipe, the server computer was running CentOS 5 Linux and OpenVPN 2.1.3. The client was running Windows XP SP3 and OpenVPN 2.1.3. Keep the configuration file, `basic-udp-server.conf`, from the *Chapter 2* recipe *Server-side routing* at hand, as well as the client configuration file, `basic-udp-client.ovpn`, from the *Chapter 2* recipe *Using an ifconfig-pool block*.

How to do it...

1. Append the following lines to the `basic-udp-server.conf` file:

   ```
   push "redirect-private bypass-dhcp bypass-dns"
   push "route server.example.com"
   ```

   Save it as `example12-4-server.conf`.

2. Start the server:

   ```
   [root@server]# openvpn --config example12-4-server.conf
   ```

3. Append the following line to the client configuration file, `basic-udp-client.ovpn`, and save it as `example12-4.ovpn`:

   ```
   allow-pull-fqdn
   ```

4. Start the client:

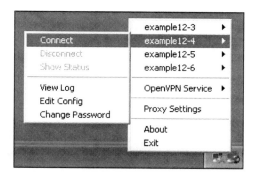

5. Watch the routing table after the connection has been established:

   ❑   If the DHCP or DNS server was on a different subnet than the client itself, then a new route will have been added. This is to ensure that DHCP requests still go to the local DHCP server and are not sent over the VPN tunnel.

   ❑   A route for the host `server.example.com` will have been added.

How it works...

The `bypass-dhcp` and `bypass-dns` options for the directives, `redirect-gateway` and `redirect-private`, cause the OpenVPN client to add an extra route to the DHCP and DNS servers if they are on a different network. In large-scale networks, the DNS server is often not found on the local subnet that the client is connected to. If the route to this DNS server is altered to go through the VPN tunnel after the client has connected, this will cause at the very least a serious performance penalty. More likely, the entire DNS server will become unreachable.

The `allow-pull-fqdn` directive enables the use of a DNS name instead of an IP address when specifying a route. Especially, if a dedicated route to a host with a dynamic IP address needs to be made, this is very useful.

There's more...

Apart from the directives explained in this recipe, there are more routing directives available to control if and how routes are added to the client.

The route-nopull directive

The `route-nopull` directive causes the client to pull all the information from the server but not the routes. This can be very useful for debugging a faulty server setup. It does not mean that no routes are added at all by the OpenVPN client. Only the routes that are specified using `push "route"` will be ignored.

The 'max-routes' directive

The `max-routes` directive is introduced in OpenVPN 2.1, as version 2.1 allows an administrator to push many more routes when compared to OpenVPN 2.0. To prevent a client from being overloaded with routes, the option `max-routes n` is added, where n is the maximum number of routes that can be defined in the client configuration file and/or can pulled from the server.

The default value for this parameter is 100.

Handing out the public IPs

With the `topology subnet` feature that OpenVPN 2.1 offers, it becomes feasible to hand out public IP addresses to connecting clients. For this recipe, we will show how such a setup can be realized. We will re-use a technique from the *Chapter 2* recipe *Proxy-ARP*' to make the VPN clients appear as if they are a part of the remote network. If a dedicated IP address block is available for the VPN clients, then this is not required. The advantage of using the `proxy-arp` method is that it allows us to use only part of an expensive public IP address block.

Getting ready

For this recipe, the server computer was running CentOS 5 Linux and OpenVPN 2.1.3. The client computer was running Windows XP SP3 and OpenVPN 2.1.1. Keep the client configuration file, `basic-udp-client.ovpn`, from the *Chapter 2* recipe *Using an 'ifconfig-pool' block* at hand.

To test this recipe, a public IP address block of 16 addresses was used, but here, we will list a private address block instead (10.0.0.0/255.255.255.240). This block is used as follows:

▸ 10.0.0.18 : This is used for the server's VPN IP address

▸ 10.0.0.19 : Not available

▸ 10.0.0.20 - 10.0.0.25 : Available for VPN clients

▸ 10.0.0.26: Not available

▸ 10.0.0.27: The LAN address of the OpenVPN server itself

▸ 10.0.0.28 - 10.0.0.29 : Not available

▸ 10.0.0.30: The router on the remote LAN

How to do it...

1. Create the server configuration file:

    ```
    mode server
    tls-server
    proto udp
    port 1194
    dev tun

    ifconfig 10.0.0.18 255.255.255.240
    ifconfig-pool 10.0.0.20 10.0.0.25
    push "route 10.0.0.27 255.255.255.255 net_gateway"
    push "route-gateway 10.0.0.30"
    push "redirect-gateway def1"

    ca       /etc/openvpn/cookbook/ca.crt
    cert     /etc/openvpn/cookbook/server.crt
    key      /etc/openvpn/cookbook/server.key
    dh       /etc/openvpn/cookbook/dh1024.pem
    tls-auth /etc/openvpn/cookbook/ta.key 0

    persist-key
    persist-tun
    keepalive 10 60

    topology subnet
    push "topology subnet"

    script-security 2
    client-connect    /etc/openvpn/cookbook/proxyarp-connect.sh
    client-disconnect /etc/openvpn/cookbook/proxyarp-disconnect.sh

    #user   nobody
    #group nobody

    daemon
    log-append /var/log/openvpn.log
    ```

    Note that this server configuration cannot be run as user nobody. Save the configuration file as example12-5-server.conf.

2. Next, create the proxyarp-connect.sh script:

    ```
    #!/bin/bash
    /sbin/arp -i eth0  -Ds $ifconfig_pool_remote_ip eth0 pub
    /sbin/ip route add ${ifconfig_pool_remote_ip}/32 dev tun0
    ```

    Save it as /etc/openvpn/cookbook/proxyarp-connect.sh.

3. Similarly, for the `proxyarp-disconnect.sh` script:

```
#!/bin/bash
/sbin/arp -i eth0  -d $ifconfig_pool_remote_ip
/sbin/ip route del ${ifconfig_pool_remote_ip}/32 dev tun0
```

Save it as `/etc/openvpn/cookbook/proxyarp-disconnect.sh`.

4. Make sure that both the scripts are executable, then start the server:

[root@server]# cd /etc/openvpn/cookbook

[root@server]# chmod 755 proxy-connect.sh proxy-disconnect.sh

[root@server]# openvpn --config example12-5-server.conf

5. Next, start the client. The IP address assigned to the client should be `10.0.0.20`.

6. Use the client to browse the Internet and check its IP address by surfing for example to `http://www.whatismyip.com`.

How it works...

Some notes on the server configuration file, the directives:

```
ifconfig 10.0.0.18 255.255.255.240
ifconfig-pool 10.0.0.20 10.0.0.25
```

Set up a pool of (public) IP address for the clients to use. Because not all of these addresses are available in the `/28` block, we cannot simply use:

```
server 10.0.0.18 255.255.255.240
```

The next statement is to ensure that the VPN server itself is reached via the regular network and not via the VPN tunnel itself:

```
push "route 10.0.0.27 255.255.255.255 net_gateway"
```

In order to redirect all traffic via the VPN tunnel, we need to explicitly state the new default gateway and `redirect-gateway`:

```
push "route-gateway 10.0.0.30"
push "redirect-gateway def1"
```

Normally, the following statement will also cause the topology setting to be pushed to the VPN clients:

```
topology subnet
```

But, as we're not using the `server` directive, this does not happen automatically. By explicitly pushing the topology, we ensure that the clients will also use the correct settings.

The `client-connect` and `client-disconnect` scripts are very similar to the ones used in the *Proxy-ARP* recipe from *Chapter 2, Client-server IP-only Networks*. By using a handy feature of the Linux `arp` command, we can make the remote clients appear to be part of the local network.

There's more...

The `topology subnet` feature was introduced in OpenVPN 2.1. Without this feature, each client would be handed out a miniature `/30` network, which means that each client would use up to four public IP addresses. This made the deployment of handing out public IP addresses to VPN clients very expensive.

See also

▶ *Chapter 2*'s recipe *Proxy-ARP*, which explains in more detail how the Linux/UNIX Proxy-ARP feature works.

OCSP support

A little known fact—the client certificate's serial number is present as an environment variable in scripts—allows OpenVPN to support the **Online Certificate Status Protocol (OCSP)**. This recipe will show how OCSP can be set up and be supported by an OpenVPN server.

Getting ready

We use the following network layout:

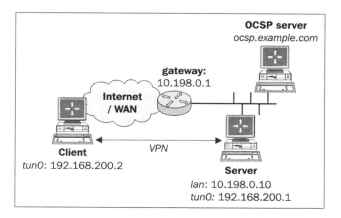

Set up the client and server certificates using the first recipe from *Chapter 2, Client-server IP-only Networks*. For this recipe, the machine on which the CA certificate and private key are stored is `ocsp.example.com`. The server computer was running CentOS 5 Linux and OpenVPN 2.1.3. The client was running Windows XP SP3 and OpenVPN 2.1.3. Keep the configuration file `basic-udp-server.conf` from the *Chapter 2* recipe *Server-side routing* at hand, as well as the client configuration file, `basic-udp-client.ovpn`, from the *Chapter 2* recipe *Using an 'ifconfig-pool' block*.

How to do it...

1. First, start an OCSP server by re-using the PKI created in *Chapter 2, Client-server IP-only Networks*. On the machine `ocsp.example.com` run:

    ```
    [ocsp]$ cd /etc/openvpn/cookbook
    [ocsp]$ openssl ocsp -index keys/index.txt -port 4444 \
        -CA keys/ca.crt -rsigner keys/ca.crt -rkey keys/ca.key \
        -resp_text
    ```

2. Then, create the server configuration file by adding a line to the `basic-udp-server.conf` file:

    ```
    script-security 2
    tls-verify /etc/openvpn/cookbook/example12-6-ocsp.sh
    ```

    Save it as `example12-6-server.conf`.

3. Create the `tls-verify` script:

    ```
    #!/bin/bash

    # if the depth is non-zero , continue processing
    [ "$1" -ne 0 ] && exit 0

    cd /etc/openvpn/cookbook
    oscp_url="http://ocsp.example.com:4444"
    if [ -n "${tls_serial_0}" ]
    then
       status=$(openssl ocsp -issuer ca.crt -CAfile ca.crt \
                    -url "$ocsp_url" \
                    -serial "0x${tls_serial_0}" 2>/dev/null)

       if [ $? -eq 0 ]
       then
         # debug:
         echo "OCSP status: $status"
    ```

```
      if echo "$status" | grep -Fq "0x${tls_serial_0}: good"
      then
        exit 0
      fi
    else
      # debug:
      echo "openssl ocsp command failed!"
    fi
  fi
  exit 1
```

This script is based on the `OCSP_verify.sh` script that is found in the OpenVPN 2.2 `contrib` directory. Save it as `example12-6-ocsp.sh`.

4. Make sure the script is executable, then start the server:

    [root@server]# chmod 755 example12-6-ocsp.sh

    [root@server]# openvpn --config example12-6-server.conf

5. Start the OpenVPN client using the `basic-udp-client.ovpn` configuration file.

6. Check the log file `/var/log/openvpn.log` on the OpenVPN server to see the following output:

    ```
    OCSP status: 0x02: good
    ```

    And the VPN connection will have been established successfully.

How it works...

Because the client's certificate serial number is now present as the environment variable `tls_serial_0`, it becomes possible to support OCSP. By requesting verification with the OCSP server if a certificate is valid (that is, known and neither revoked nor expired) the server can verify that the client has been issued a valid certificate. This could also have been achieved using a Certificate Revocation List (CRL), but in some cases, an OCSP is more convenient to use, as CRLs need to be periodically updated.

See also

▶   *Chapter 4*'s recipe *The use of CRLs*, which explains Certificate Revocation Lists (CRLs). Using CRLs is the most standard method for verifying the validity of certificates.

New for 2.2: the 'x509_user_name' parameter

OpenVPN 2.2 is primarily a bug fix release, but there are a few new features added to version 2.2. In this recipe, we will focus on one of these features. The purpose of the `x509_user_name` parameter is to allow the usage of X509 certificates where the certificate name is not specified by the `/CN=` element. This can be especially useful when using certificates from a third-party source or when integrating certificates into other authorization systems.

Getting ready

We use the following network layout:

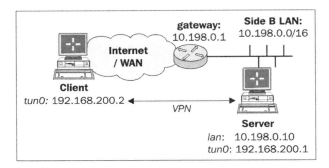

Set up the client and server certificates using the first recipe from *Chapter 2, Client-server IP-only Networks*. In this recipe, the server computer was running CentOS 5 Linux and OpenVPN 2.2-beta3. The client was running Windows XP SP3 and OpenVPN 2.1.3. Keep the configuration file `basic-udp-server.conf` from the *Chapter 2* recipe *Server-side routing* at hand, as well as the client configuration file, `basic-udp-client.ovpn`, from the *Chapter 2* recipe *Using an ifconfig-pool block*.

How to do it...

First, we generate a new certificate using low-level OpenSSL commands. This is because the OpenVPN-supplied `easy-rsa` scripts do not easily allow us to create a script without a `/CN=` part.

1. Generate a new certificate request with a special subject name:

    ```
    [server]$ cd /etc/openvpn/cookbook
    [server]$ openssl req -new -nodes -keyout client6.key \
      -out client6.csr -newkey rsa:2048 \
      -subj    "/C=NL/O=Cookbook/UID=cookbook"
    ```

2. Create an empty OpenSSL extensions file to ensure that the resulting certificate is an X.509 v3 certificate:

   ```
   [server]$ touch openssl-ext.conf
   ```

3. And finally, sign the certificate request using the CA key:

   ```
   [server]$ openssl x509 -req -CA keys/ca.crt -CAkey keys/ca.key \
     -in client6.csr -set_serial 0xAA -sha1 -days 1000 \
     -extfile openssl-ext.conf -out client6.crt
   ```

4. Create the server configuration file by adding the followings line to the `basic-udp-server.conf` file:

   ```
   script-security 2
   client-connect /etc/openvpn/cookbook/example12-7-client-connect.sh

   x509-username-field "UID"
   ```

   Save it as `example12-7-server.conf`.

5. Create the `client-connect` script:

   ```
   #!/bin/bash
   echo "common_name = [$common_name]"
   ```

   And, save it as `example12-7-client-connect.sh`.

6. Make sure the script is executable, then start the server:

   ```
   [root@server]# chmod 755 example12-7-client-connect.sh
   [root@server]# openvpn --config example12-7-server.conf
   ```

7. Copy the `client6.crt` and `client6.key` files to the Windows client using a secure channel; for example, using PuTTY's `pscp` command.

8. Modify the client configuration file `basic-udp-client.ovpn` by changing the lines:

   ```
   cert      /etc/openvpn/cookbook/client2.crt
   key       /etc/openvpn/cookbook/client2.key
   ```

   to:

   ```
   cert      /etc/openvpn/cookbook/client6.crt
   key       /etc/openvpn/cookbook/client6.key
   ```

   Save it as `example12-7.ovpn`.

9. Start the OpenVPN client:

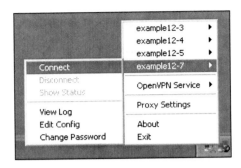

10. Check the log file `/var/log/openvpn.log` on the OpenVPN server to see the following output:

```
common_name = [cookbook]
```

How it works...

With the new `x509_user_name` directive, OpenVPN can extract the connecting client name from a field other than the default `/CN=` field. In this recipe, the section `/UID=` was used. When a client connects with a certificate that has a subject section `/UID=`, the OpenVPN server extracts the client name from this field. This client name is set as the environment variable `common_name` for most server-side scripts and plugins, such as the `client-connect`, `client-disconnect`, and `learn-address` scripts, as well as the `ifconfig-pool-persist` file.

Note that it is not possible to use just any `/<field>=<name>` section as part of an X509 certificate. The `<field>` must be all uppercase and it must be recognized by OpenSSL itself, as otherwise it is not easily possible to generate a certificate.

There's more...

OpenVPN 2.1 behaviour

If the above certificate was used when connecting to an OpenVPN 2.1 server, the client would not have been able to connect. Instead, the following log message would appear in the server log file:

```
VERIFY ERROR: could not extract Common Name from X509 subject string
('/C=NL/O=Cookbook/UID=cookbook') -- note that the Common Name length
is limited to 64 characters
```

Index

easy-rsa scripts
   about 36, 104
   using, on Windows 37
engine_pkcs11 library 143
ethernet adapter 69
expired/revoked certificates
   checking 118, 119
external DHCP server
   /etc/sysconfig/network-scripts, tweaking 94
   configuration 94
   using 90-92
   working 93

F

file basic-udp-server.conf 134
flags, redirect-gateway directive
   bypass-dhcp 54
   bypass-dns 54
   local 54

G

gigabit networks 238

H

hardware token
   initializing 128-130
   key, generating 142-144
   public and private objects 131
   using 133-135
   working 130
hardware token ID
   automatic selection 133
   determining 131-133
   working 132
http-proxy authentication 303
http-proxy options
   http-proxy-option AGENT [string] 299
   http-proxy-option VERSION 1.1 299
   http-proxy-timeout [n] 299
HTTP digest authentication 303
HTTP proxy
   about 297
   caveats 299
   using 297, 298
   working 299

HTTP proxy, with authentication
   NTLM proxy authorization 303
   working 302

I

ICMP protocol 235
ifconfig-pool-persist directive
   about 291
   implementing 291-293
   pitfalls 293
   working 293
ifconfig-pool block
   client-to-client access 59
   configuration files, on Windows 58
   TCP protocol, using 59
   topology subnet 58
   using 54-57
   working 58
inline certificates
   about 312
   implementing 312, 313
   working 313
intermediary CA certificate
   creating 120
   setting up 120, 121
   working 121
IP-less setups
   about 306
   considerations 309
iperf
   about 236, 238
   network layout 236
   working 237, 238
IP fowarding
   setting up permanently 74
iptables command 46, 73

K

key
   generating, on hardware token 142-144
key mismatches 193, 194

L

LARTC (Linux Advanced Routing and Traffic Control) 220

default gateway redirecting 227-231
MULTI: bad source warnings 225, 226
omission, in routing 214-216
return route, missing 208-210
return route, missing using iroute 211-213
routing and permissions on Windows 220, 221
source routing 217-219

routing and permissions on Windows
troubleshooting 220, 221

routing directives
allow-pull-fqdn 319
max-routes n 319
redirect-private 319
route-nopull 319

routing issues
troubleshooting, when connecting client-side LAN 214-216

routing methods
about 282
IPAPI helper functions 282
route.exe program 282
using 282, 283

S

script-security configuration directive 177, 179
script order
determining 174-176
script output
logging 177, 179
security considerations 161
serialized ID 132
server-only CA 122
server-side management interface 65
server-side routing
linear addresses 44
setting up 40-44
setting up, in client/server mode 49-51
TCP protocol, using 45
setenv-safe directive 158, 161
setenv directive 161
shortest setup possible
about 8, 9
non-IP traffic, running over tunnel 10
TCP protocol, using 10

working 9
site-to-site setup
completing 22-25
SOCKS proxy
about 294
performance 296
plain-text authentication, using 296
setting up, SSH used 296
using 294, 295
working 296
source routing
about 217
troubleshooting 217-219
working 219
split tunneling 54
status file
about 59
clients, disconnecting 62
explicit-exit-notify 63
status parameters 62
using 60, 61, 95, 96
using, with TUN-style networks 97
working 62, 97
sub CA 120

T

ta.key file 194
TAP-based connection
setting, in client or server mode 70-72
working 72, 73
TCP-based connections
advantages 290
optimizing 249-251
working 252
TCP and UDP-based setups
mixing 290
tcpdump utility 253
TCP protocol
using 45, 73
Thumb property 272
tinyCA
about 108
URL 108
tls-auth directive 193
tls-auth key 193

Thank you for buying
OpenVPN 2 Cookbook

About Packt Publishing

Packt, pronounced 'packed', published its first book "*Mastering phpMyAdmin for Effective MySQL Management*" in April 2004 and subsequently continued to specialize in publishing highly focused books on specific technologies and solutions.

Our books and publications share the experiences of your fellow IT professionals in adapting and customizing today's systems, applications, and frameworks. Our solution based books give you the knowledge and power to customize the software and technologies you're using to get the job done. Packt books are more specific and less general than the IT books you have seen in the past. Our unique business model allows us to bring you more focused information, giving you more of what you need to know, and less of what you don't.

Packt is a modern, yet unique publishing company, which focuses on producing quality, cutting-edge books for communities of developers, administrators, and newbies alike. For more information, please visit our website: www.packtpub.com.

About Packt Open Source

In 2010, Packt launched two new brands, Packt Open Source and Packt Enterprise, in order to continue its focus on specialization. This book is part of the Packt Open Source brand, home to books published on software built around Open Source licences, and offering information to anybody from advanced developers to budding web designers. The Open Source brand also runs Packt's Open Source Royalty Scheme, by which Packt gives a royalty to each Open Source project about whose software a book is sold.

Writing for Packt

We welcome all inquiries from people who are interested in authoring. Book proposals should be sent to author@packtpub.com. If your book idea is still at an early stage and you would like to discuss it first before writing a formal book proposal, contact us; one of our commissioning editors will get in touch with you.

We're not just looking for published authors; if you have strong technical skills but no writing experience, our experienced editors can help you develop a writing career, or simply get some additional reward for your expertise.

Zabbix 1.8 Network Monitoring

ISBN: 978-1-847197-68-9   Paperback: 428 pages

Monitor your network hardware, servers, and web performance effectively and efficiently

1. Start with the very basics of Zabbix, an enterprise-class open source network monitoring solution, and move up to more advanced tasks later

2. Efficiently manage your hosts, users, and permissions

3. Get alerts and react to changes in monitored parameters by sending out e-mails, SMSs, or even execute commands on remote machines

4. In-depth coverage for both beginners and advanced users with plenty of practical, working examples and clear explanations

Tcl 8.5 Network Programming

ISBN: 978-1-849510-96-7   Paperback: 588 pages

Build network-aware applications using Tcl, a powerful dynamic programming language

1. Develop network-aware applications with Tcl

2. Implement the most important network protocols in Tcl

3. Packed with hands-on-examples, case studies, and clear explanations for better understanding

Please check **www.PacktPub.com** for information on our titles

CPSIA information can be obtained at www.ICGtesting.com
Printed in the USA
BVOW06s2126231013

334404BV00007B/93/P

9 781849 510103